BASIC SPANISH GRAMMAR

Third Edition

Ana C. Jarvis
Chandler-Gilbert Community College

Raquel Lebredo
California Baptist College

Francisco Mena
Crafton Hills College

D. C. Heath and Company
Lexington, Massachusetts   Toronto

Preface

Basic Spanish Grammar, Third Edition, is a guide to the essential points of Spanish grammar for students whose personal goals or professions require a working knowledge of Spanish. It presents concise, simple explanations of the structures that are indispensable for communication and reinforces them with practice exercises.

New to the Third Edition are:

◆ Clarified grammar explanations;

◆ Additional exercises on key grammar points with an emphasis on communication;

◆ *En el laboratorio*, a section at the end of each lesson, which provides taped practice of structure and vocabulary and a listening comprehension exercise;

◆ An audio program including a tapescript to accompany the *En el laboratorio* sections; and

◆ An *Instructor's Manual/Test Guide* providing teaching information and substantial testing materials.

Basic Spanish Grammar, Third Edition, continues to be the nucleus of a complete Spanish program consisting of seven manuals, each accompanied by its own audio program. Five manuals are specifically designed for different professions; *Spanish for Business and Finance*, Third Edition, *Spanish for Law Enforcement*, Third Edition, *Spanish for Medical Personnel*, Third Edition, *Spanish for Social Services*, Third Edition, and *Spanish for Teachers*, Second Edition. Two manuals, *Spanish for Communication*, Third Edition, and *Getting Along in Spanish*, Second Edition, develop practical communication skills.

Each career manual presents specific vocabulary needed for a given profession. Each lesson parallels the same lesson in the *Basic Spanish Grammar*, Third Edition text. This means that students will simultaneously be exposed to the grammatical structure explained in the principal text and to the practical application of that structure in the corresponding manual.

Each lesson in the communication manuals also parallels the same lesson in the grammar text. These manuals have been written at two levels of difficulty with *Spanish for Communication*, Third Edition, being more advanced than *Getting Along in Spanish*, Second Edition. Every effort has been made to develop realistic, practical dialogs and situational exercises that emphasize normal daily communication.

Students studying Spanish for professional reasons have specific needs and limited study time. Aware of the unique situation of these students, we have endeavored to present the material of the entire *Basic Spanish Grammar* program in a way that facilitates its use for individualized instruction.

Basic Spanish Grammar, Third Edition, includes:

1. Two preliminary lessons: The first one presents very basic grammar points, and the second one consists of words and expressions useful to persons in every walk of life (i.e., personal data, greetings and farewells, etc.).

2. Twenty lessons, each containing:
   Grammatical structures
   Conversational exchanges illustrating each grammatical point
   Exercises to practice and reinforce each concept
   New vocabulary introduced in the lesson. Every effort has been made to include high-frequency words and expressions.[1]
   En el laboratorio exercises to be done in conjunction with the audio program.

3. A self-testing section after every five lessons. An answer key is provided in the appendix.

4. The following appendices:
   Rules governing Spanish pronunciation
   Verb paradigms
   Glossary of useful grammatical terms
   List of careers and occupations
   Answer key for self-testing sections
   An end vocabulary including:
   Spanish-English vocabulary
   English-Spanish vocabulary
   Index

---

[1]We suggest that the students familiarize themselves with the vocabulary in each lesson before studying the grammar points.

Manuals

Lesson formats are generally as follows:

1. Dialogs presenting common, practical topics or situations characteristic of each specific profession. For example, "At the doctor's office" and "In the Emergency Room" are two such dialogs in the manual for medical personnel.
2. Pertinent vocabulary
3. Dialog recall practice (in some manuals)
4. Grammatical structure exercises
5. Question-answer exercise
6. Dialog completion
7. Situational exercises
8. Group activities
9. Vocabulary expansion (optional)

Vocabulary reviews are presented after every five lessons. An end vocabulary includes both a Spanish-English vocabulary and an English-Spanish vocabulary. A pronunciation appendix is also included in each manual.

Audio Programs

The new audio program accompanying *Basic Spanish Grammar*, Third Edition, is available on cassettes. A tapescript provides a written version of the vocabulary, structure and listening comprehension exercises to be done with the new *En el laboratorio* sections of the textbook. This addition to *Basic Spanish Grammar*, Third Edition, will be a great help to students who will have more opportunities to hear Spanish outside class.

Each career and communication manual continues to have its cassette program based on the dialogs and vocabulary of each component. This taped material provides important listening comprehension and pronunciation practice.

Instructor's Manual/Test Guide

This new component of *Basic Spanish Grammar*, Third Edition, provides instructors with teaching information and testing materials for the grammar text and its accompanying manuals. The Instructor's Manual contains practical suggestions for organizing the course and for different types of class activities. The Test Guide consists of the following materials:

♦ 20 quizzes, one for each lesson in *Basic Spanish Grammar*, Third Edition

♦ 2 midterm exams covering lessons 1–5 and lessons 11–15 of the grammar text

♦ 2 final exams covering lessons 1–10 and lessons 11–20 of the grammar text

◆ 2 final exams for each of the seven manuals

◆ A sample vocabulary quiz for each of the manuals

◆ Suggestions on grading, point accumulation and scheduling of the tests.

Several textbooks have been written for use in Spanish courses geared to the different professions or to basic communication skills in the language. *Basic Spanish Grammar*, Third Edition, with its manuals, audio programs and Instructor's Manual/Test Guide is the first *complete* program that teaches career-specific and general communication skills through the correct use of pertinent vocabulary and the practice of appropriate grammatical structures.

Acknowledgements

We wish to thank our colleagues who have used the first and second editions of *Basic Spanish Grammar* for their constructive criticism and suggestions.

We are especially grateful to Professor Gerard Wolfe, New York University, for his careful reading of the manuscript, his valuable insights and productive suggestions.

We also want to express our appreciation to the members of the editorial staff at D. C. Heath and Company for their sound observations which have substantially enhanced the quality of the program.

Ana C. Jarvis
Raquel Lebredo
Francisco Mena

Contents

PRELIMINARY LESSON I

PRELIMINARY LESSON II

LESSON 1

LESSON 2

LESSON 3

LESSON 4

LESSON 5

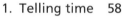

LESSON 6

LESSON 7

LESSON 8

LESSON 9

LESSON 10

LESSON 11

LESSON 12

LESSON 13

LESSON 14

LESSON 15

LESSON 16

LESSON 17

LESSON 18

LESSON 19

LESSON 20

APPENDICES/VOCABULARIES

PRELIMINARY LESSON I

1. Gender
2. Plural forms
3. The definite article
4. The indefinite article
5. Cardinal numbers (0–21)

1. Gender

In Spanish all nouns, including those denoting nonliving things, are either masculine or feminine:

masculine   *feminine*

señor   señora
teléfono   banana

Here are some practical rules to determine the gender of Spanish nouns:

1. Most nouns ending in **-a** or denoting female beings are feminine; most nouns ending in **-o** or referring to male beings are masculine:

    masculine   *feminine*

    teléfono   silla
    dinero   casa
    libro   mesa

    ATENCIÓN: Two important exceptions to this rule are: **día** (*day*), which is masculine, and man**o** (*hand*), which is feminine.

2. There are some words that end in **-a** but are masculine. This is because they are of Greek origin and have kept the gender they had in that language. Some are:

    problema   sistema
    programa   telegrama
    idioma (*language*)   clima (*climate*)

3. Nouns ending in **-sión, -ción, -tad,** and **-dad** are feminine:

    televi**sión**   ciu**dad**
    lec**ción**   liber**tad**

4. The gender of other nouns must be learned: **español** (*Spanish language*) is masculine, while **calle** (*street*) is feminine.

5. Many masculine nouns ending in **-o** have a corresponding form ending in **a**: enfermer**o**, enfermer**a** (*nurse*).

Certain masculine nouns ending in a consonant add **-a** for the corresponding feminine form:

profes**or**   profes**ora**

Exercise

Tell whether the following nouns are feminine or masculine:

1. teléfono   2. día   3. televisión   4. enfermera

5. problema	8. dinero	11. mano	14. señor
6. calle	9. idioma	12. ciudad	15. profesora
7. mesa	10. silla	13. lección	16. programa

2. Plural forms

Nouns are made plural in Spanish by adding an **-s** to those ending in a vowel and an **-es** to those ending in a consonant. Nouns ending in **-z** change the **z** to **c** and add **-es**:

teléfon**o**	teléfon**os**
mes**a**	mes**as**
profesor	profesor**es**
lápi**z**	lápi**ces**
lu**z**	lu**ces**

ATENCIÓN: When an accent mark falls on the *last* syllable of a singular word, it is omitted in the plural form:

lecci**ón**	lecci**ones**

Exercise

Give the plural of the following nouns:

1. silla	5. telegrama	9. clima
2. libro	6. ciudad	10. conversación
3. lápiz	7. lección	11. profesor
4. universidad	8. señor	12. luz

3. The definite article

There are four forms in Spanish equivalent to the English definite article *the:*

	Masculine	*Feminine*
Singular	el	la
Plural	los	las

el profesor	**la** profesora
los profesores	**las** profesoras
el mineral	**la** banana
los minerales	**las** bananas

ATENCIÓN: Try to learn the accompanying definite article when you learn each noun. This will help you to remember its gender.

Exercise

Give the definite articles for the following nouns:

1. universidades	6. señores	11. dinero
2. problema	7. día	12. profesores
3. profesor	8. televisión	13. banana
4. doctor	9. silla	14. telegrama
5. señora	10. profesoras	15. libertad

4. The indefinite article

The indefinite article in Spanish has four forms; they are equivalent to *a*, *an*, and *some*.

	Masculine	Feminine
Singular	un	una
Plural	unos	unas

un profesor   **una** profesora
unos profesores   **unas** profesoras

un lápiz   **una** pluma
unos lápices   **unas** plumas

Exercise

Give the equivalent in Spanish:

1. a pen	4. some chairs	7. a light
2. a professor	5. a problem	8. a program
3. some days	6. a house	9. a pencil

5. Cardinal numbers (0–21)

0	cero	8	ocho
1	uno	9	nueve
2	dos	10	diez
3	tres	11	once
4	cuatro	12	doce
5	cinco	13	trece
6	seis	14	catorce
7	siete	15	quince

16 dieciséis (diez y seis)   19 diecinueve (diez y nueve)
17 diecisiete (diez y siete)   20 veinte
18 dieciocho (diez y ocho)   21 veintiuno (veinte y uno)

Numbers are masculine in Spanish: **el cero, el veinte,** and so on.

Uno becomes **un** in front of a masculine singular noun: *un* **libro** (*one book*). When placed before a feminine noun, **una** is used: *una* **silla** (*one chair*). All other numbers ending in **-uno** or **-una** follow the same pattern: *veintiún* **libros** (*twenty-one books*), *veintiuna* **sillas** (*twenty-one chairs*).

Exercises

A. Read the following numbers aloud:

0	28	7	9	13	11	5	4	20
15	10	14	16	1	8	21	19	12

B. Give the following numbers in Spanish. Name the numbers one by one:

383–5079	254–2675	792–5136	689–0275
985–0746	765–1032	985–7340	872–0695

Vocabulary

COGNATES

la **banana** banana	el, la **profesor**(a) professor
la **ciudad** city	el **programa** program
la **lección** lesson	el **sistema** system
la **libertad** liberty	el **teléfono** telephone
el **mineral** mineral	el **telegrama** telegram
el **problema** problem	la **televisión** television

NOUNS

la **calle** street	la **mano** hand
la **casa** house	el, la **médico**(a), **doctor**(a) M.D., doctor
el **clima** climate	la **mesa** table
el **día** day	la **pluma** pen
el **dinero** money	el **señor** gentleman, sir, Mr.
el, la **enfermero**(a) nurse	la **señora** lady, madam, Mrs.
el **español** Spanish (*language*)	la **silla** chair
el **idioma,** la **lengua** language	
el **lápiz** pencil	
el **libro** book	
la **luz** light	

PRELIMINARY LESSON II

1. Personal data
2. Greetings and farewells
3. Days of the week
4. Cardinal numbers (30–200)
5. Months and seasons of the year

1. Personal data

¿Nombre y apellido?	*Name and surname?*
María Valdés.	*Maria Valdes.*
¿Estado civil?	*Marital status?*
Casada.	*Married.*
¿Apellido de soltera?[1]	*Maiden name?*
Rivas.	*Rivas.*
¿Nacionalidad?	*Nationality? (citizenship)*
Norteamericana.	*North American.*
¿Lugar de nacimiento?	*Place of birth?*
La Habana, Cuba.	*Havana, Cuba.*
¿Edad?	*Age?*
Veintinueve.	*Twenty-nine.*
¿Ocupación?[2]	*Occupation?*
Enfermera.	*Nurse.*
¿Dirección?	*Address?*
Calle Magnolia,[3] número ciento ocho.	*Number one hundred eight Magnolia Street.*
¿Ciudad?	*City?*
Riverside.	*Riverside.*
¿Número de teléfono?[1]	*Phone number?*
682-7530.	*682-7530.*
¿Número de seguro social?	*Social Security number?*
566-14-9023.[4]	*566-14-9023.*

Vocabulary: Personal data

los **años** years
el **apellido** surname
 — **de soltera** maiden name
casado(a) married

la **dirección,** el **domicilio** address
divorciado(a) divorced
la **edad** age
el **estado civil** marital status

---

[1]The preposition **de** + *noun* in Spanish is the equivalent of two nouns used together in English. Notice that the first noun functions as an adjective in English.

[2]See Appendix D for a list of occupations.

[3]In Spanish, the name of the street is placed before the number.

[4]A fictitious number.

la **fecha de nacimiento**   date of birth
femenino   feminine
el **lugar de nacimiento**   place of birth
el **lugar donde trabaja**   place of work
masculino   masculine
la **nacionalidad**   nationality
el **nombre**   name
norteamericano(a)   North American (from the U.S.)
el **número**   number

el **número de la licencia para conducir**   license number
— **de seguro social**   social security number
— **de teléfono**   telephone number
la **ocupación**   occupation
separado(a)   separated
el **sexo**   sex
soltero(a)   single

Exercise

Conduct an interview with another student. Ask the following questions:

1. ¿Nombre y apellido?
2. ¿Estado civil?
3. ¿Apellido de soltera? (*If you are talking to a married woman.*)
4. ¿Nacionalidad?
5. ¿Lugar de nacimiento?
6. ¿Ocupación?
7. ¿Dirección? (¿Domicilio?)
8. ¿Ciudad?
9. ¿Número de teléfono?
10. ¿Número de seguro social?

Now reverse roles; you are the person being interviewed.

2. Greetings and farewells

Buenos días, doctor Rivas.
¿Cómo está usted?
Muy bien, gracias. ¿Y usted?

Good morning, Doctor Rivas.
How are you?
Very well, thank you. And you?

Bien, gracias. Hasta luego.
Adiós.

Fine, thank you. See you later.
Goodbye.

Mucho gusto, profesor Vera.

Pleased to meet you, Professor Vera.

El gusto es mío, señorita Reyes.

The pleasure is mine, Miss Reyes.

Buenas tardes, señora.
Buenas tardes, señor.

Good afternoon, madam.
Good afternoon, sir.

Pase y tome asiento, por favor.	*Come in and sit down, please.*
Gracias.	*Thank you.*
Buenas noches, señorita.	*Good evening, miss.*
¿Cómo está usted?	*How are you?*
No muy bien.	*Not very well.*
Lo siento. Hasta mañana.	*I'm sorry. I'll see you tomorrow.*
Muchas gracias, señor.	*Thank you very much, sir.*
De nada, señora. Adiós.	*You're welcome, madam. Goodbye.*

Vocabulary

GREETINGS AND FAREWELLS

Adiós.	*Goodbye.*
Buenas noches.	*Good evening. (Good night.)*
Buenas tardes.	*Good afternoon.*
Buenos días.	*Good morning. (Good day.)*
¿Cómo está usted?	*How are you?*
El gusto es mío.	*The pleasure is mine.*
Hasta luego.	*I'll see you later. (lit., until later)*
Hasta mañana.	*I'll see you tomorrow.*
Mucho gusto.	*How do you do? (lit., much pleasure)*

FORMAL TITLES

doctor[1] (abbrev. **Dr.**)	*doctor*
profesor	*professor*
señor (abbrev. **Sr.**)	*Mr., sir, gentleman*
señora (abbrev. **Sra.**)	*Mrs., madam, lady*
señorita (abbrev. **Srta.**)	*Miss, young lady*

USEFUL EXPRESSIONS

bien	*well, fine*
De nada.	*You're welcome.*
Lo siento.	*I'm sorry.*
Muchas gracias.	*Thank you very much.*
Muy bien, ¿y usted?	*Very well, and you?*
no	*no, not*
Pase.	*Come in.*
por favor	*please*
Tome asiento.	*Sit down. or Take a seat.*

---

[1]Notice that in Spanish titles are not capitalized except when they are abbreviated.

Exercises

A. First familiarize yourself with each of the above dialogues, and then act them out with another student.

B. What would you say in the following situations?

1. You meet Mr. García in the morning and ask him how he is.
2. You thank Miss Vera for a favor and tell her you will see her tomorrow.
3. You greet Mrs. Nieto (*afternoon*) and ask her to come in and sit down.
4. Professor Maria Rivas says **mucho gusto** to you. You reply.
5. Someone thanks you for a favor. You reply.
6. Mr. Ortiz says he is not feeling well. You reply.

3. Days of the week

¿Qué día es hoy?	*What day is it today?*
Hoy es lunes.	*Today is Monday.*
Hoy es martes, ¿no?	*Today is Tuesday, isn't it?*
No, hoy es miércoles.	*No, today is Wednesday.*
¿Qué día es hoy? ¿Jueves?	*What day is it today? Thursday?*
No, hoy es viernes.	*No, today is Friday.*
Hoy es...sábado...¡no!	*Today is . . . Saturday . . . no!*
domingo...	*Sunday . . .*
Sí, hoy es domingo.	*Yes, today is Sunday.*

Los días de la semana (*The days of the week*)

lunes[1]	Monday	**viernes**	Friday
martes	Tuesday	**sábado**	Saturday
miércoles	Wednesday	**domingo**	Sunday
jueves	Thursday		

ATENCIÓN: In Spanish, the days of the week are masculine: *el* **viernes,** *los* **sábados.** They are not capitalized.

---

[1]In Spanish calendars, the week starts with Monday.

Exercise

The people asking the following questions are always a day ahead. Correct them!

Modelo: —Hoy es lunes, ¿no?
     —**No, hoy es domingo.**

1. Hoy es miércoles, ¿no?
2. Hoy es domingo, ¿no?
3. Hoy es viernes, ¿no?
4. Hoy es martes, ¿no?
5. Hoy es sábado, ¿no?
6. Hoy es jueves, ¿no?

4. Cardinal numbers (30–200)

30 treinta
31 treinta y uno
32 treinta y dos...
40 cuarenta
50 cincuenta
60 sesenta
70 setenta
80 ochenta
90 noventa
100 cien (ciento)
101 ciento uno...
150 ciento cincuenta...
200 doscientos

Exercise

Read the following numbers aloud:

33	48	57	123	30	69	74
80	91	100	65	111	123	200
197	136	115	175	169	185	101

ATENCIÓN: **Ciento** becomes **cien** before a noun:

cien telegramas
cien casas

Remember that **uno** becomes **un** before a masculine noun; **una** before a feminine noun, even in compound numbers:

ciento **un** telegramas
ciento **una** sillas

5. Months and seasons of the year

—¿Qué fecha es hoy?	*What's the date today?*
—Hoy es el quince de enero.	*Today is January the fifteenth.*
—¿Hoy es el primero de mayo?	*Is today May first?*
—No, hoy es el dos de mayo.	*No, today is May second.*

ATENCIÓN: Spanish uses cardinal numbers to refer to dates. The only exception is **primero** (*first*).

Los meses del año (*The months of the year*)

enero	January	**julio**	July
febrero	February	**agosto**	August
marzo	March	**septiembre**	September
abril	April	**octubre**	October
mayo	May	**noviembre**	November
junio	June	**diciembre**	December

ATENCIÓN: The names of the months are not capitalized in Spanish.

Las estaciones del año (*The seasons of the year*)

la **primavera**	spring	el **verano**	summer
el **otoño**	fall	el **invierno**	winter

◆ To ask for the date, say:

¿Qué fecha es hoy?   *What's the date today?*

◆ When telling the date, always begin with the expression **Hoy es el...**:

Hoy es el veinte de mayo.

◆ Start with the number followed by the preposition **de** (*of*), and then the month:

el **quince de mayo**	*May 15th*
el **diez de septiembre**	*September 10th*
el **doce de octubre**	*October 12th*

ATENCIÓN: Notice that the number precedes the month. Thus, **3–6–88** means June 3rd, 1988. In Spanish, the article is usually included when giving the date orally, although it is sometimes omitted in writing.

Exercise

A. The following are important dates to remember. Say them in Spanish:

1. the 4th of July
2. the 31st of October
3. March 21st
4. April 1st

5. the first of January
6. February 14th
7. December 25th

8. June 20th
9. your birthday
10. today's date

B. Do you know in which season the following months fall?

1. febrero
2. agosto
3. mayo
4. enero

5. octubre
6. julio
7. abril
8. noviembre

Personal Information

Provide the information requested.

Apellido y nombres	Fecha de nacimiento		
	DÍA	MES	AÑO

Dirección

....

Teléfono

....

Estado civil   Sexo   Edad

1. _____ soltero(a)   Masculino _____   _____

2. _____ casado(a)   Femenino _____

3. _____ divorciado(a)

4. _____ viudo(a)

5. _____ separado(a)

Nacionalidad ....

Ocupación ....

Lugar donde trabaja ....

Número de seguro social ....

Número de la licencia para conducir ....

1. Subject pronouns
2. The present indicative of **-ar** verbs
3. Interrogative sentences
4. Negative sentences
5. Cardinal numbers (300–1000)

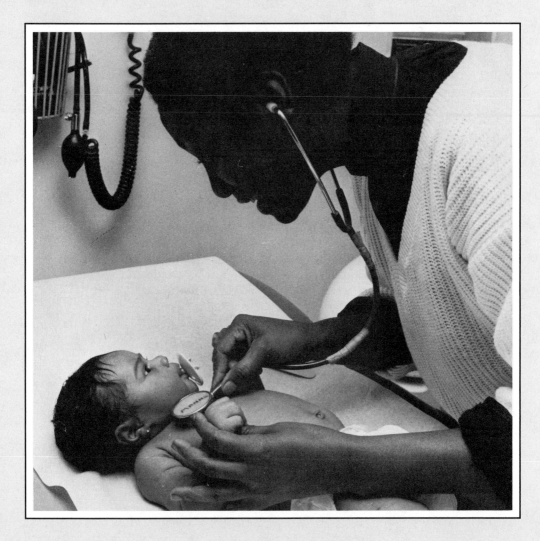

1. Subject pronouns

	Singular		Plural
yo	I	{ nosotros { nosotras	we (*masculine*) we (*feminine*)
tú usted[1]	you (*familiar*) you (*formal*)	ustedes[2]	you
él ella	he she	{ ellos { ellas	they (*masculine*) they (*feminine*)

◆ The masculine plural pronoun may refer to the masculine gender alone or to both genders together:

Juan y Roberto: **ellos**   *John and Robert:* **they**
Juan y María: **ellos**   *John and Mary:* **they**

ATENCIÓN: Use the **tú** form as the equivalent of *you* when addressing a close friend, a relative, or a child. Use the **usted** form in *all* other instances. Notice that **ustedes** is used for both familiar and polite plural.

Exercise

Which subject pronoun would be used for each of the following?

Modelo: You refer to *Mr. Smith* as . . .
          él

1. You point to yourself and say . . .
2. You refer to Mrs. Smith as . . .
3. You are talking to a little boy and you call him . . .
4. You are talking to a woman you've just met and you call her . . .
5. Your mother refers to herself and her sister as . . .
6. Your father refers to himself and his sister as . . .
7. You are talking to a few people and you call them . . .
8. You refer to Mr. Smith and his daughter as . . .
9. You refer to Mrs. Smith and her daughter as . . .
10. You refer to Mr. and Mrs. Smith as . . .

2. The present indicative of regular -ar verbs

The infinitive of all Spanish verbs consists of a stem (such as **habl-**) and an ending (such as **-ar**). When looking up a verb in the dictionary, you will always find it listed under the infinitive (e.g., **hablar:** *to speak*). Spanish

[1]Abbreviated **Ud.**
[2]Abbreviated **Uds.**

verbs are classified according to their endings. There are three conjugations: **-ar**, **-er**, and **-ir**. The stem does not change; the endings change with the subjects. Regular verbs ending in **-ar** are conjugated like **hablar**.

hablar (to speak)		
Singular		
	Stem Ending	
yo	habl- **o**	Yo **hablo** español.[1]
tú	habl- **as**	Tú **hablas** español.
Ud.	habl- **a**	Ud. **habla** español.
él	habl- **a**	Juan **habla** español. Él **habla** español.
ella	habl- **a**	Ana **habla** español. Ella **habla** español.
Plural		
nosotros	habl- **amos**	Nosotros **hablamos** español.
Uds.	habl- **an**	Uds. **hablan** español.
ellos	habl- **an**	Ellos **hablan** español.
ellas	habl- **an**	Ellas **hablan** español.

◆ The present tense in Spanish is equivalent to three forms in English:

Yo **hablo** italiano.
$$\begin{cases} \textit{I speak Italian.} \\ \textit{I do speak Italian.} \\ \textit{I am speaking Italian.} \end{cases}$$

◆ Since the verb endings indicate who the speaker is, the subject pronouns are frequently omitted:

—**Hablas** inglés, ¿no?   *You (familiar) speak English, don't you?*

—Sí, **hablo** inglés.   *Yes, I speak English.*

◆ However, subject pronouns may be used for emphasis or clarification:

—**Ellos hablan** inglés, ¿no?   *They speak English, don't they?*

—**Ella habla** inglés.   *She speaks English.*
Él habla español.   *He speaks Spanish.*

Some common verbs that follow the same pattern are:
trabajar (*to work*), **necesitar** (*to need*), and **estudiar** (*to study*).

—El señor Paz **trabaja** en un hospital, ¿no?   *Mr. Paz works at a hospital, doesn't he?*

—No, él **trabaja** en un restaurante.   *No, he works at a restaurant.*

[1]Names of languages and nationalities are not capitalized in Spanish.

—Ud. **necesita** una solicitud,   *You need an application, don't*
   ¿no?   *you?*
—Sí, **necesito** una, por favor.   *Yes, I need one, please.*
—Uds. **estudian** francés en la   *You study French at the*
   universidad, ¿no?   *university, don't you?*
—No, pero **estudiamos** inglés.   *No, but we study English.*

ATENCIÓN: When speaking about a third person (indirect address) and using a title with the last name, the definite article is placed before the title (**El señor Paz habla español.**). It is not used when speaking directly to someone (**Buenos días, *señor* Paz.**).

Exercises

A. Say where these people work, what they study and what they need:

trabajar: yo / un restaurante
                 Anita / el hospital
                 tú / Los Ángeles
                 nosotros / la universidad

estudiar: Uds. / francés
                 Carlos / italiano
                 Ud. / la lección dos
                 él y yo / español

necesitar: Ana y Rosa / dinero
                 nosotras / una mesa
                 yo / los lápices
                 tú / una solicitud

B. Provide the missing information about yourself and other people:

1. Ella trabaja en Los Ángeles y yo...
2. Carlos estudia italiano y nosotros...
3. Yo necesito una pluma y tú...
4. Nosotros hablamos inglés y el profesor...
5. Tú y yo trabajamos en la cafetería y ellos...
6. Tú estudias la lección dos y yo...
7. María necesita sillas y nosotros...
8. Ellos hablan francés y yo...

3. Interrogative sentences

There are three ways of asking a question in Spanish to elicit a *yes / no* answer:

1. ¿**Ustedes** necesitan dinero?⎫
2. ¿Necesitan **ustedes** dinero?⎬   Sí, nosotros necesitamos dinero.
3. ¿Necesitan dinero **ustedes?**⎭

These three questions ask for the same information and have the same meaning. Example 1 is a declarative sentence that is made interrogative by a change in intonation:

Ustedes necesitan dinero.   ¿Ustedes necesitan dinero?

Example 2 is an interrogative sentence formed by placing the subject (**ustedes**) after the verb. In example 3, the subject (**ustedes**) has been placed at the end of the sentence. Notice that two question marks are used in Spanish, an inverted one at the beginning of the sentence as well as one at the end.

ATENCIÓN: An auxiliary verb such as *do* or *does* is not used in Spanish to form an interrogative sentence.

Exercise

Use two other ways of asking the following questions:

Modelo: —¿**Elena** trabaja en Buenos Aires?
     —¿Trabaja **Elena** en Buenos Aires?
     —¿Trabaja en Buenos Aires **Elena?**

1. ¿Ud. necesita dinero?
2. ¿Ella estudia inglés?
3. ¿Uds. hablan español?
4. ¿Pedro necesita la solicitud?
5. ¿Tú trabajas en California?

4. Negative sentences

To make a sentence negative, simply place the word **no** in front of the verb:

Ella   habla inglés.   *She   speaks English.*
Ella **no** habla inglés.   *She **doesn't** speak English.*

ATENCIÓN: Spanish does not use an auxiliary verb such as the English *do* or *does* in a negative sentence.

If the answer to a question is negative, the word **no** appears twice: at the beginning of the sentence, as in English, and also in front of the verb:

¿Necesitas las carpetas?   *Do you need the folders?*
No, (yo) **no** necesito las   *No, I don't need the folders; I*
  carpetas; necesito los sobres.   *need the envelopes.*

ATENCIÓN: The subject pronoun need not appear in the answer.

Exercise

Using the information provided in parentheses, answer the following questions in the negative:

Modelo: —¿Ud. trabaja en un restaurante?   (oficina)
          —No, (yo) no trabajo en un restaurante; trabajo en una oficina.

1. ¿Uds. necesitan los sobres?   (carpetas)
2. ¿Tú estudias francés?   (español)
3. ¿Hablan italiano en París?   (francés)
4. ¿Trabaja en la cafetería el profesor?   (la universidad)
5. ¿Estudian la lección dos?   (lección tres)

5. Cardinal numbers (300–1000)

300 trescientos	700 setecientos
400 cuatrocientos	800 ochocientos
500 quinientos	900 novecientos
600 seiscientos	1,000 mil[1]

When counting in Spanish beyond a thousand, do not count in hundreds. After a thousand, the numbers are represented thus: **dos mil, tres mil, catorce mil**, etc. Notice that a period is used instead of a comma:

1.987   **mil novecientos ochenta y siete**

Exercise

Read the following numbers aloud:

896	380	519	937	722
1.305	451	978	643	504
1.000	15.893	11.906	27.567	565.736

Vocabulary

COGNATES

el **hospital**	hospital	el **restaurante**	restaurant
el **italiano**	Italian (*language*)	la **universidad**	university

NOUNS

la **carpeta**	the folder	la **oficina**	office
el **francés**	French (*language*)	el **sobre**	envelope
el **inglés**	English (*language*)	la **solicitud**	application

[1]Notice that the indefinite article is not used before the word **mil**.

VERBS

estudiar   to study
hablar   to speak, to talk
necesitar   to need
trabajar   to work

OTHER WORDS
AND EXPRESSIONS

en   in, at
pero   but
sí   yes

EN EL LABORATORIO

The following material is to be used with the tape in the language laboratory.

I. Vocabulary

Repeat each word after the speaker. When repeating words that are cognates, notice the difference in pronunciation between English and Spanish.

Cognates:	el hospital el italiano el restaurante la universidad
Nouns:	la carpeta el inglés el francés la oficina el sobre la solicitud
Verbs:	estudiar hablar necesitar trabajar
Other words *and expressions:*	en pero sí

Read the following numbers in Spanish. Repeat the correct answer after the speaker's confirmation. Listen to the model:

Modelo: 1581
       Mil quinientos ochenta y uno.

1. 322
2. 430
3. 547
4. 659
5. 761
6. 878
7. 985
8. 1.000
9. 1.543
10. 12.715

II. Structure Practice

A. Repeat each sentence, then substitute the new subject given by the speaker.

Be sure the verbs agree with the new subject. Repeat the correct answer after the speaker's confirmation.

Modelo: Yo estudio español.
       Nosotros estudiamos español.

1. Yo estudio español.
   (nosotros / Ud. / ellos)
2. Ella trabaja en el hospital.
   (Yo / Uds. / tú)
3. Tú necesitas dinero.
   (Él / nosotros / ellas)

B. Change each sentence to the interrogative form by placing the subject at the end of the sentence. Repeat the correct answer after the speaker's confirmation. Listen to the model:

Modelo: —Teresa necesita dinero.
　　　　—¿Necesita dinero Teresa?

1. La señora López estudia inglés.
2. El señor Vega habla francés.
3. La señorita Díaz necesita los sobres.
4. Uds. trabajan en la oficina.

C. Change each of the following sentences to the negative. Repeat the correct answer after the speaker's confirmation. Listen to the model:

Modelo: —Yo hablo inglés.
　　　　—Yo no hablo inglés.

1. Eva y Luis hablan español.
2. Nosotros estudiamos en la universidad.
3. Ella trabaja en un restaurante.
4. Yo necesito una solicitud.

III.   Listening and Comprehension

Listen carefully to the dialogue. It will be repeated twice.

(*Dialogue*)

Now the speaker will make statements concerning the conversation you just heard. After each statement, say whether it is true (**verdadero**) or false (**falso**). The speaker will confirm the correct answer.

LESSON 2

1. Position of adjectives

A. Descriptive adjectives (such as adjectives of color, size, etc.) generally follow the noun in Spanish:

> el libro **rojo**   *the **red** book*
> la casa **grande**   *the **big** house*
> la carpeta **azul**   *the **blue** folder*

B. Adjectives denoting nationality always follow the noun:

> el profesor **norteamericano**   *the **North American** professor*

C. Other kinds of adjectives (possessive, demonstrative, numerals, etc.) precede the noun, as in English:

> **cinco** lápices   ***five** pencils*

Exercise

Give the Spanish equivalent:

1. the blue pencil
2. the big city
3. the American doctor
4. fifteen chairs
5. the big table
6. the red book

2. Forms of adjectives

Adjectives whose masculine singular form ends in **-o** have four forms, ending in **-o, -a, -os, -as.** Most other adjectives have only two forms, a singular and a plural. Like nouns, adjectives are made plural by adding **-s, -es,** or by changing **z** to **c** and adding **-es.**

Singular		Plural	
Masculine	*Feminine*	*Masculine*	*Feminine*
negro (*black*)	negra	negros	negras
inteligente	inteligente	inteligentes	inteligentes
feliz (*happy*)	feliz	felices	felices
verde (*green*)	verde	verdes	verdes

Adjectives of nationality that end in a consonant are made feminine by adding **-a** to the masculine singular form:

> español   española
> alemán   alemana

Exercise

Match the items in column A with those in column B.

A	B
1. señor _____	a. rojos
2. mesa _____	b. inteligentes
3. señoritas _____	c. español
4. libros _____	d. negra

3. Agreement of articles, adjectives, and nouns

The article, the noun, and the adjective agree in number and gender in Spanish:

> **la** silla blanca   *the white chair*
> **el** libro blanco   *the white book*
> **las** sillas blancas   *the white chairs*
> **los** libros blancos   *the white books*

Exercise

Make the adjectives agree with the nouns in the list, and add the corresponding definite article:

1. _____ mesa   negra   3. _____ profesor   inteligente
   _____ libro   _____   _____ profesores   _____
   _____ sillas   _____   _____ profesora   _____
   _____ lápices _____   _____ profesoras   _____
2. _____ señor   español   4. _____ señorita   feliz
   _____ señores _____   _____ señor   _____
   _____ señoras _____   _____ señoritas   _____
   _____ señora   _____   _____ señores   _____

4. The present indicative of -er and -ir verbs

Regular verbs ending in **-er** are conjugated like **comer**.
Regular verbs ending in **-ir** are conjugated like **vivir**.

comer *(to eat)*		vivir *(to live)*	
yo	com- **o**	yo	viv- **o**
tú	com- **es**	tú	viv- **es**
Ud.		Ud.	
él	com- **e**	él	viv- **e**
ella		ella	

comer (to eat)		vivir (to live)	
nosotros	com- **emos**	nosotros	viv- **imos**
Uds. ⎫		Uds. ⎫	
ellos ⎬	com- **en**	ellos ⎬	viv- **en**
ellas ⎭		ellas ⎭	

Some other common verbs that follow the same patterns are: **beber** (*to drink*), **aprender** (*to learn*), **leer** (*to read*), **comprender** (*to understand*), **escribir** (*to write*), **abrir** (*to open*), **recibir** (*to receive*), and **decidir** (*to decide*).

—¿Tú **bebes** café o té?   *Do you drink coffee or tea?*
—**Bebo** café.   *I drink coffee.*

—¿**Comen** Uds. temprano?   *Do you eat early?*
—No, **comemos** tarde.   *No, we eat late.*

—¿Dónde **vive** Ud.?   *Where do you live?*
—**Vivo** en la calle Unión.   *I live on Union Street.*

—¿**Escribe** el profesor en   *Does the professor write in*
  español?   *Spanish?*
—Sí, **escribe** en español.   *Yes, he writes in Spanish.*

Exercises

A. Conjugate the verbs according to the new subject:

1. Yo no como temprano.   (nosotros, Uds., Ana, tú, Ud.)
2. Eva escribe en español.   (Ud., ellos, yo, nosotros, tú)

B. I will tell you what *I* do, and you will tell me what everyone else does:

Modelo: Yo bebo café.   (Elsa)
       Elsa bebe té.

1. Yo no comprendo la lección dos.   (nosotros)
2. Yo vivo en la calle Magnolia.   (Alberto)
3. Yo como temprano.   (Adela)
4. Yo escribo con una pluma verde.   (Marta y Rosa)
5. Yo necesito un libro.   (nosotras)
6. Yo leo en español.   (Alina)
7. Yo recibo veinte pesos.   (ellos)
8. Yo decido estudiar inglés.   (Ana y yo)
9. Yo abro la carpeta.   (él)
10. Yo aprendo inglés.   (los estudiantes)

5. The personal a

In Spanish, as in English, a verb has a subject and may have one or more objects. The function of the object is to complete the idea expressed by the verb.

In English, the direct object cannot be separated from the verb by a preposition: *She killed* **the burglar.** *He sees* **the nurse.** In the preceding sentences, *the burglar* and *the nurse* are direct objects.

In Spanish, the preposition a must be used before a direct object that refers to a definite person. This preposition is called "the personal a" and has no equivalent in English:

> Yo visito a Carmen.
> I visit   Carmen.

The personal a is not used when the direct object is not a person.

—¿A quién espera Ud.?	*Whom are you waiting for?*
—Espero a la profesora.	*I'm waiting for the professor.*
—¿Qué esperas?	*What are you waiting for?*
—Espero el ómnibus.	*I'm waiting for the bus.*
—¿Visitan Uds. a Rafael?	*Do you visit Rafael?*
—No, visitamos a Pedro.	*No, we visit Pedro.*
—¿Visitan los estudiantes el museo o el teatro?	*Are the students visiting the museum or the theater?*
—Visitan el museo.	*They are visiting the museum.*

Exercise

A Spanish-speaking friend needs you as an interpreter.

1. We are waiting for the professor. (*fem.*)
2. What are the students visiting? The theater?
3. They are waiting for the bus.
4. Who visits Mary?
5. We are waiting for Carmen.

Vocabulary

COGNATES

el, la **estudiante**   student
inteligente   intelligent
el **museo**   museum
el **teatro**   theater

NOUNS

el **café**   coffee
el **ómnibus, autobús**   bus
el **té**   tea

VERBS

abrir   to open
aprender   to learn
beber   to drink
comer   to eat
comprender   to understand
decidir   to decide
escribir   to write
esperar   to wait for
leer   to read
recibir   to receive
visitar   to visit
vivir   to live

ADJECTIVES

alemán (alemana)   German
azul   blue
blanco(a)   white
español(a)   Spanish
feliz   happy
grande   big
negro(a)   black
rojo(a)   red
verde   green

OTHER WORDS
AND EXPRESSIONS

¿dónde?   where?
o   or
¿qué?   what?
¿quién?   who?, whom?
tarde   late
temprano   early

EN EL LABORATORIO

The following material is to be used with the tape in the language laboratory.

I. Vocabulary

Repeat each word after the speaker. When repeating words that are cognates, notice the difference in pronunciation between English and Spanish.

Cognates:	el estudiante inteligente el museo el teatro
Nouns:	el café el ómnibus, el autobús el té
Verbs:	abrir aprender beber comer comprender decidir escribir esperar leer recibir visitar vivir
Adjectives:	alemán alemana azul blanco español feliz grande negro rojo verde
Other words *and expressions:*	¿dónde? o ¿qué? ¿quién? tarde temprano

II. Structure Practice

A. Change each of the following phrases according to the new clue. Repeat the correct answer after the speaker's confirmation. Listen to the model:

Modelo: un señor español   (señorita)
          una señorita española

1. (libros)
2. (sillas)
3. (señora)
4. (lápiz)

5. (libro)
6. (estudiantes)
7. (profesora)
8. (ciudad)

B. Answer the questions, always using the second choice. Omit the subject. Repeat the correct answer after the speaker's confirmation. Listen to the model:

Modelo: —¿Ana vive en la calle Cinco o en la calle Siete?
          —Vive en la calle Siete.

31

C. Answer the questions, using the cues provided. Remember to use the personal **a,** when needed. Repeat the correct answer after the speaker's confirmation. Listen to the model:

Modelo: —¿A quién esperas?   (Carlos)
        —Espero **a** Carlos.

1. (el museo)
2. (la señora Vega)
3. (el ómnibus)
4. (dinero)
5. (la profesora)

III. *Listening and Comprehension*

1. Listen carefully to the dialogue. It will be read twice.

   (*Dialogue 1*)

   Now the speaker will make statements concerning the conversation you just heard. After each statement, say whether it is true (**verdadero**) or false (**falso**). The speaker will confirm the correct answer.

2. Listen carefully to the dialogue. It will be read twice.

   (*Dialogue 2*)

   Now the speaker will make statements concerning the conversation you just heard. After each statement, say whether it is true (**verdadero**) or false (**falso**). The speaker will confirm the correct answer.

LESSON 3

1. Possession with **de**
2. Possessive adjectives
3. The present indicative of **ser**
4. The irregular verbs **ir, dar,** and **estar**
5. The verbs **ser** and **estar** (summary of uses)

1. Possession with de

De + *noun* is used to express possession or relationship in Spanish; the apostrophe is not used:

EXAMPLES:

El hijo **de Raúl**   *Raul's son (lit., the son of Raul)*
El libro **de María**   *Mary's book*
las preguntas **de la recepcionista**   *the receptionist's questions*
la profesión **de los señores**   *the gentlemen's profession*

ATENCIÓN: Notice the use of the definite article before the words **hijo,**
  preguntas and **profesión.**

Exercise

Give the Spanish equivalent:

1. Isabel's son
2. Mary's house
3. Carmen's profession
4. The students' book
5. The receptionist's phone number

2. Possessive adjectives

Forms of the Possessive Adjectives		
Singular	*Plural*	
mi	mis	my
tu	tus	your (*familiar*)
su	sus	his her its your their
nuestro(a)	**nuestro(as)**	our

A.   Possessive adjectives agree in number with the nouns they modify:

—¿Necesita Ud. **mi** cuaderno?   *Do you need **my** notebook?*
—No, no necesito **su** cuaderno.   *No, I don't need **your**
                                        notebook.*

—¿Necesita Ud. **mis**
cuadernos?

*Do you need **my** notebooks?*

—No, no necesito **sus**
cuadernos.

*No, I don't need **your**
notebooks.*

B. Since both **su** and **sus** may have different meanings, the form **de él** (**de
ella, de ellos, de ellas, de Ud., de Uds.**) may be substituted to avoid
confusion:

—¿Con quién hablan Uds.?

With whom are you talking?

—Hablamos con **su** amigo.

*We are talking with **his** (or:
her, your, their) friend.*

—Hablamos con el amigo **de
Ud.**

*We are talking with **your**
friend.*

—¿Estudia con **mi** libro?

*Are you studying with **my**
book?*

—No, estudio con el libro **de
ella.**

*No, I'm studying with **her**
book.*

ATENCIÓN: These forms of the possessive adjectives always precede the
nouns they introduce and are never stressed.

C. **Nuestro** is the only possessive adjective that has the feminine endings **-a,
-as.** The others use the same endings for both the masculine and feminine genders:

¿Con quién debemos hablar?

With whom should we speak?

Debemos hablar con **nuestras**
profesoras.

*We should speak with our
professors.*

Exercise

Tell us to whom these things belong by giving the possessive adjectives in
Spanish. Whenever **su** (**sus**) is required, give the alternate form with **de:**

Modelo: (*his*) _____ silla
su silla / la silla de él

1. (*my*) _____ amigos
2. (*his*) _____ libro / _____ libro _____ _____.
3. (*our*) _____ casa
4. (*her*) _____ idioma / _____ idioma _____ _____.
5. (*your* —**Ud.**) _____ dinero / _____ dinero _____ _____.
6. (*my*) _____ cuaderno
7. (*our*) _____ recepcionista

8. (*your*—**tú**) _____ profesión
9. (*your*—**Uds.**) _____ lápices / _____ lápices _____ _____ .
10. (*their*—fem.) _____ lección / _____ lecciones _____ _____ .

3. The present indicative of **ser**

The verb **ser** is an irregular verb. Its forms are not like the forms of regular -**er** verbs.

yo	**soy**	I am
tú	**eres**	you are (*familiar*)
Ud.		you are (*formal*)
él	**es**	he is
ella		she is
nosotros	**somos**	we are
Uds.		you are
ellos	**son**	they are (*masculine*)
ellas		they are (*feminine*)

¿Son altos los hijos de Juan?	*Are Juan's sons tall?*
Sí, ellos **son altos.**	*Yes, they are tall.*
¿Es difícil tu lección de español?	*Is your Spanish lesson difficult?*
No, mi lección **es fácil.**	*No, my lesson is easy.*
¿De dónde **es** Ud.?	*Where are you from?*
Yo **soy de** Buenos Aires.	*I am from Buenos Aires.*
¿Son Uds. **norteamericanos?**	*Are your North American?*
Sí, **somos** norteamericanos.	*Yes, we are North American.*

Exercise

Using the verb **ser**, complete the following conversations:

1. —¿De dónde _____ tú, Anita?
   —_____ de Buenos Aires. ¿De dónde _____ Ud., señora?
   —Yo _____ de Montevideo.
2. —¿Uds. _____ norteamericanos?
   —Sí, _____ de California.
3. —¿_____ muy difíciles tus lecciones?
   —La lección dos _____ fácil...

4. The irregular verbs **ir, dar,** and **estar**

	ir (*to go*)	**dar** (*to give*)	**estar** (*to be*)
yo	voy	doy	estoy
tú	vas	das	estás
Ud. él } ella	va	da	está
nosotros	vamos	damos	estamos
Uds. ellos } ellas	van	dan	están

—¿A dónde **va** Ud.?   *Where are you going?*
—**Voy** a la biblioteca.   *I'm going to the library.*

—¿**Dan** Uds. dinero para las   *Do you give money for the*
  fiestas?   *parties?*
—Sí, **damos** dinero.   *Yes, we give money.*

—¿Dónde **está** Elena?   *Where is Elena?*
—Ella **está** en el hotel.   *She is at the hotel.*

Exercise

A. Using the present indicative of **ir, dar,** and **estar,** tell us what these people give, where they are, and where they are going:

1. Él _____ su nombre y dirección.
2. Yo _____ a la biblioteca. Debo estudiar.
3. ¿Dónde _____ mis libros?
4. Ud. _____ a Los Ángeles con los hijos de él.
5. Ellos _____ dinero.
6. Uds. _____ en México.
7. Yo no _____ mi número de teléfono.
8. Nosotras _____ a la casa de María.
9. ¿_____ Ud. en el hotel?
10. Yo _____ en el hospital.

B. Tell us something about yourself by answering the following:

1. ¿Ud. da su número de teléfono?
2. ¿Van Uds. a la universidad los domingos?
3. ¿Dónde están sus libros?
4. ¿Ud. va a la biblioteca los sábados?
5. ¿Ud. está en la universidad?

5. The verbs **ser** and **estar** (summary of uses)

Although both **ser** and **estar** are equivalent to the English verb *to be*, they are not interchangeable. They are used to indicate the following:

ser	estar
1. Possession	1. Current condition (usually the product of a change)
2. Profession	2. Location
3. Nationality	
4. Origin	
5. Basic characteristics (color, shape, size, etc.)	
6. Marital status	
7. Expressions of time and dates	
8. Material that things are made of	

—El auto **es** de Pedro, ¿no?　　　*The car is Pedro's, isn't it?*
—No, **es** de Juan.　　　*No, it's Juan's.*

—¿Cuál **es** la profesión de José?　　　*What is José's profession?*
—José **es** ingeniero.　　　*José is an engineer.*

—Elena **es** muy inteligente.　　　*Elena is very intelligent.*
—Ella **es** de la Argentina, ¿no?　　　*She's from Argentina, isn't she?*
—Sí, **es** argentina, pero ahora **está** en los Estados Unidos.　　　*Yes, she's an Argentinian, but now she's in the United States.*

—¿Cómo **es** Angel?　　　*What is Angel like?*
—**Es** alto y muy guapo.　　　*He is tall and very handsome.*

—¿**Es** Ud. casada?　　　*Are you married?*
—No, **soy** soltera.　　　*No, I am single.*

—¿Qué día **es** hoy?　　　*What day is today?*
—Hoy **es** martes.　　　*Today is Tuesday.*

—¿**Es** la mesa de madera?　　　*Is the table (made) of wood?*
—No, **es** de metal.　　　*No, it is made of metal.*

—¿Cómo **está** Ud.?　　　*How are you?*
—**Estoy** bien, gracias.　　　*I am fine, thanks.*

—¿Dónde **está** su hijo?   *Where is your son?*
—**Está** en el hospital. **Está**   *He is in the hospital. He is*
enfermo.   *sick.*

Exercise

A. ¿**Ser** or **estar?** Which will it be?

1. —¿Cómo _____ Amelia?
   —_____ muy inteligente.
   —¿De dónde _____ ella?
   —_____ española, pero ahora _____ en los Estados Unidos.
   —¿_____ soltera?
   —No, _____ casada.
   —¿Hoy no trabaja?
   —No..., _____ enferma.
2. —¿Las sillas _____ de metal?
   —No, _____ de madera.
   —¿_____ de Ernesto?
   —No, _____ de Raquel.
3. —¿Cuál _____ su profesión, señor Paz?
   —_____ ingeniero.
4. —¿Cómo _____ sus hijos?
   —_____ altos y guapos.

B. Using **ser** or **estar,** give us the following information about yourself:

1. your nationality and origin
2. your profession (student)
3. your marital status
4. some basic characteristics
5. how you are (healthwise)
6. where you are

Vocabulary

COGNATES

argentino(a) Argentinian
el **auto, automóvil** car, automobile
el **hotel** hotel

el, la **ingeniero(a)** engineer
el **metal** metal
la **profesión** profession
el, la **recepcionista**[1] receptionist

---

[1]For nouns ending in **-ista,** change only the article to indicate gender.

NOUNS

el, la **amigo(a)**   friend
la **biblioteca**   library
el **cuaderno**   notebook
los **Estados Unidos**   United
      States
la **hija**   daughter
el **hijo**   son
la **madera**   wood

VERBS

dar   to give
deber   must, should
estar   to be
ir   to go
ser   to be

ADJECTIVES

alto(a)   tall
difícil   difficult
enfermo(a)   sick, ill
fácil   easy
guapo(a)   handsome

OTHER WORDS
AND EXPRESSIONS

a   to
¿a dónde?   where to?
ahora   now
¿cómo?   how
¿cómo es?   what is he (she) like?
¿con quién?   with whom?
¿cuál?   what? which one?
de   of, from
¿de dónde?   where from?
muy   very

EN EL LABORATORIO

The following material is to be used with the tape in the language laboratory.

I. *Vocabulary*

Repeat each word after the speaker. When repeating words that are cognates, notice the difference in pronunciation between English and Spanish.

Cognates:	argentino el auto, el automóvil el hotel
	el ingeniero el metal la profesión
	el recepcionista
Nouns:	el amigo la biblioteca el cuaderno
	los Estados Unidos la hija el hijo la madera
Verbs:	dar deber estar ir ser
Adjectives:	alto difícil enfermo fácil guapo
Other words and expressions:	a ¿a dónde? ahora cómo ¿cómo es?
	¿con quién? ¿cuál? de ¿de dónde? muy

II. *Structure Practice*

A. Following the model, say to whom the following belong, using the cues provided. Repeat the correct answer after the speaker's confirmation.

Modelo: —el libro   (Susana)
   —Es el libro de Susana.

1. (Antonio)
2. (los estudiantes)
3. (Juan)
4. (la profesora)
5. (Estela)

B. Answer the questions, always selecting the second choice. Repeat the correct answer after the speaker. Listen to the model:

Modelo: —¿Tú eres de la Argentina o de los Estados Unidos?
   —Soy de los Estados Unidos.

III. Listening and Comprehension

1. Listen carefully to the narration. It will be read twice.

   (*Narration 1*)

   Now the speaker will make statements concerning the narration you just heard. After each statement, say whether it is true (**verdadero**) or false (**falso**). The speaker will confirm the correct answer.

2. Listen carefully to the narration. It will be read twice.

   (*Narration 2*)

   Now the speaker will make statements concerning the narration you just heard. After each statement, say whether it is true (**verdadero**) or false (**falso**). The speaker will confirm the correct answer.

LESSON 4

1. Contractions

There are only two contractions in Spanish:

♦ The preposition **de** (*of, from*) plus the article **el** are contracted to form **del**:

> Leen los libros **de + el** profesor.   Leen los libros **del** profesor.

♦ The preposition **a** (*to, toward*) or the personal **a** plus the article **el** are contracted to form **al**:

> Esperamos **a + el** profesor.   Esperamos **al** profesor.

ATENCIÓN: None of the other combinations of preposition and definite article (**de la, de los, de las, a la, a los, a las**) are contracted.

—¿Llaman Uds. **al** gerente **del** hotel?	*Are you calling the hotel manager?*
—No, llamamos **a la** supervisora.	*No, we're calling the supervisor.*
—¿Vas **a la** tienda?	*Are you going to the store?*
—No, voy **al** mercado.	*No, I'm going to the market.*
—El diccionario es **del** profesor, ¿no?	*The dictionary is the teacher's, isn't it?*
—No, el diccionario es **de los** estudiantes.	*No, the dictionary belongs to the students.*

Exercise

Complete the sentences using one of the following: **de la, de las, del, de los, a la, a las, al, a los**:

1. Necesito los cuadernos _____ estudiantes.
2. El diccionario es _____ profesor.
3. La casa es _____ señora Pérez.
4. Esperamos _____ gerente y _____ supervisora.
5. ¿Cuándo vamos _____ mercado?
6. Recibimos dinero _____ universidad.
7. ¿Llamas _____ profesoras _____ hijos _____ señor Soto?
8. El gerente llama _____ profesores.

2. Comparison of adjectives and adverbs

A. In Spanish, the comparative of most adjectives and adverbs is formed by placing **más** (*more*) or **menos** (*less*) before the adjective or the adverb and **que** after:

más			adjective		
	+		*or*	+	**que**
menos			adverb		

In the above construction, **que** is equivalent to *than*.

—Jorge es muy alto, ¿no?   *Jorge is very tall, isn't he?*

—Sí, pero yo soy **más** alta **que**   *Yes, but I am taller than he.*
él.

—¿Quién llega **más** tarde? ¿Tú   *Who arrives later? You or she?*
o ella?

—Ella llega **más** tarde **que** yo.   *She arrives later than I.*

B. In an equal comparison **tan...como** is used:

			adjective		
tan	+		*or*	+	**como**
			adverb		

Tan...como is equivalent to *as . . . as:*

—¿Está Ud. **tan** cansada **como**   *Are you as tired as they?*
ellos?

—No, yo estoy menos cansada   *No, I am less tired than they.*
que ellos.

C. The superlative construction is similar to the comparative. It is formed by placing the definite article before the person or thing being compared:

definite article	+	[noun]	+	**más**	+	adjective

—¿Quién es **la** muchacha **más**   *Who is the prettiest girl in the*
bonita **de** la clase?   *class?*

—Elena es **la** muchacha **más**   *Elena is the prettiest girl in the*
bonita **de** la clase.   *class.*

ATENCIÓN: 1. After a superlative construction, *in* is expressed by **de** in Spanish.
2. In many instances, the noun may not be expressed in a superlative.

Elena es **la más** bonita **de** la   *Elena is the prettiest (one) in*
clase.   *the class.*

Exercises

A. Complete the following sentences with the Spanish equivalent of the words in parentheses:

1. Rosa es _____ Marcia.   (*prettier than*)
2. El supervisor llega _____ ellos.   (*as early as*)
3. Mis estudiantes son _____ Uds.   (*less intelligent than*)
4. Mi hijo es _____ yo.   (*as tall as*)
5. El gerente llega _____ Uds.   (*later than*)
6. Es _____ libro.   (*the most difficult lesson in the*)
7. Elena es _____ la clase.   (*the least intelligent girl in*)
8. Ud. está _____ Rafael.   (*less tired than*)

B. Compare these people, places or things to each other:

Modelo: Vermont / California   (pequeño)
        Vermont es más pequeño que California.

1. Texas / Rhode Island   (grande)
2. tu amigo / tú   (alto)
3. tú (trabajas mucho) / tu profesor (trabaja mucho)
4. Tom Selleck (Jaclyn Smith) yo   (guapo / bonita)
5. Cuba / Brasil   (pequeño)

3. Irregular comparison of adjectives and adverbs

Adjectives		Adverbs		Comparative		Superlative	
bueno	*good*	bien	*well*	mejor	*better*	el mejor	*the best*
malo	*bad*	mal	*badly*	peor	*worse*	el peor	*the worst*
mucho	*much*	mucho	*much*	más	*most*	el más	*the most*
poco	*little*	poco	*little*	menos	*less*	el menos	*the least*
grande	*big*			mayor	*bigger, older*	el mayor	*the biggest, oldest*
pequeño	*small*			menor	*smaller, younger*	el menor	*the smallest, youngest*

ATENCIÓN: When the adjectives **grande** and **pequeño** refer to size, the regular forms are generally used: **más grande** (*bigger*) and **más pequeño** (*smaller*). When referring to age, the irregular forms are used: **mayor** (*older*) and **menor** (*younger*).

—¿Quién estudia **más?** ¿Ud. o Marta?	*Who studies more? You or Marta?*
—Yo estudio **mucho,** pero Marta estudia **más.**	*I study a great deal, but Marta studies more.*
—¿Quién es **mayor?** ¿Ud. o Elsa?	*Who is older? You or Elsa?*
—Elsa. Ella es **la mayor** de la clase.	*Elsa. She is the oldest in the class.*
—¿Su esposo habla español tan **bien** como Ud.?	*Does your husband speak Spanish as well as you do?*
—No, él habla español mucho **mejor** que yo.	*No, he speaks Spanish much better than I.*
—La casa de Ana es **más grande** que la casa de Eva, ¿no?	*Ana's house is bigger than Eva's house, isn't it?*
—No, la casa de Ana es **más pequeña** que la casa de Eva.	*No, Ana's house is smaller than Eva's house.*

Exercises

A. Compare these people to each other using comparative adjectives.

Modelo: Olga es _____ Anita.
Olga es **más alta que** Anita.

1. Marisa es _____ Olga.
2. José es _____ Antonio.
3. Olga es _____ Antonio.
4. Antonio es _____ todos.
5. José es _____ todos.
6. Anita es _____ Marisa.
7. Olga es _____ Marisa.
8. Anita es _____ todos.

B.   Be an interpreter. Tell us how to say the following in Spanish.

1. I read many books, but he reads more.
2. Cuba is bigger than Puerto Rico.
3. My son is older than your daughter.
4. My professors are better than Robert's professors.
5. He speaks English worse than I.
6. Are you the youngest in the class, Ann?
7. The store is smaller than the market.
8. I write well, but you write better, Miss Soto.
9. You drink little coffee, but I drink less.
10. Our books are bad, but your book is the worst.

4. The irregular verbs **tener** and **venir**

tener (*to have*)		venir (*to come*)	
yo	**tengo**	yo	**vengo**
tú	**tienes**	tú	**vienes**
Ud.		Ud.	
él }	**tiene**	él }	**viene**
ella		ella	
nosotros	**tenemos**	nosotros	**venimos**
Uds.		Uds.	
ellos }	**tienen**	ellos }	**vienen**
ellas		ellas	

—¿Con quién **viene** Ud.? ¿Con   *With whom are you coming?*
su hijo?   *With your son?*
—No, **vengo** sola.   *No, I am coming alone.*

—¿Cuántas hijas **tiene** Ud.?   *How many daughters do you have?*

—**Tengo** tres hijas.   *I have three daughters.*

ATENCIÓN: The personal **a** is not used with the verb **tener.**

—Ana, ¿**tienes** novio?   *Ana, do you have a boyfriend?*

—No, no **tengo** novio.   *No, I don't have a boyfriend.*

ATENCIÓN: With the verb **tener,** the indefinite article is not used in Spanish when the numerical concept is not emphasized: **No, no** *tengo* **novio.**

Exercise

¿**Tener** or **venir?** Which one would you use?

1. Yo no _____ novia.
2. ¿Con quién _____ Uds. a la clase?
3. ¿David _____ tarde o temprano?
4. Ellos no _____ la dirección de Pedro, pero nosotros _____ su número de teléfono.
5. ¿Cuándo _____ ellos? Yo _____ temprano.
6. Yo _____ seis sillas. ¿Cuántas sillas _____ tú?
7. Yo _____ sola, pero Marisa _____ con Oscar.
8. ¿Cuántos muchachos _____ Uds. en la clase?
9. ¿Cuál es el mejor profesor que Uds. _____?
10. Él _____ una casa muy grande.

5. Expressions with **tener**

Many useful idiomatic expressions are formed with the verb **tener:**

tener calor   to be hot
tener frío   to be cold
tener hambre   to be hungry
tener sed   to be thirsty
tener cuidado   to be careful
tener sueño   to be sleepy
tener prisa   to be in a hurry
tener miedo   to be scared, afraid
tener razón   to be right
tener...años (de edad)   to be . . . years old

ATENCIÓN: The equivalent of *I am very hungry,* for example, is **Tengo mucha hambre** (literally, *I have much hunger*).

—¿**Tienes hambre,** Carlos?   *Are you hungry, Carlos?*

—No, pero **tengo** mucha **sed.**   *No, but I am very thirsty.*

—¿Cuántos **años tiene** su hija?   *How old is your daughter?*
—Mi hija **tiene** seis **años.**   *My daughter is six years old.*

—Deseo hablar con el   *I wish to speak with the*
  instructor, por favor.   *instructor, please.*
—Ahora no. Lo siento. Él   *Not now. I'm sorry. He's in a*
  tiene mucha **prisa.**   *big hurry.*
—**Tiene razón.** Es tarde.   *You're right. It's late.*

Exercises

A. Tell what is happening in each of the pictures. Follow the model:

Modelo:

Ella....
Ella tiene hambre.

1. Carlos....

2. Él....

3. Yo....

4. Ellas....

5. ¿Ud....?

6. Tú....

7. Nélida....

B. Answer the following questions, first in the affirmative and then in the negative:

1. ¿Tiene Ud. hambre?
2. ¿Tienen Uds. miedo?
3. ¿Tienes sueño?
4. ¿Tiene mucha sed el profesor (la profesora)?
5. ¿Tú tienes diez años?
6. ¿Tengo yo razón?
7. ¿Tienen Uds. prisa?
8. ¿Tiene Ud. calor?
9. ¿Tienen Uds. frío?

Vocabulary

COGNATES

la **clase** class	el, la **instructor**(a) instructor
el **diccionario** dictionary	el, la **supervisor**(a) supervisor

NOUNS

el, la **gerente**   manager
el **mercado**   market
la **muchacha**, la **chica**   girl, young woman
el **muchacho**, el **chico**   boy, young man
la **novia**   girlfriend
el **novio**   boyfriend
la **tienda**   store

ADJECTIVES

bonito(a)   pretty
bueno(a)   good
cansado(a)   tired
malo(a)   bad
mayor   older, bigger
menor   younger, smaller
pequeño(a)   small, little (*size*)
poco(a)   little (*quantity*)

VERBS

llamar to call
llegar to arrive
tener to have
venir to come

OTHER WORDS
AND EXPRESSIONS

¿a quién? to whom?
con with
¿cuándo? when?
¿cuántos(as)? how many?
muy very
pero but

EN EL LABORATORIO ━━━━━━

LESSON 4

The following material is to be used with the tape in the language laboratory.

I. Vocabulary

Repeat each word after the speaker. When repeating words that are cognates, notice the difference in pronunciation between English and Spanish.

Cognates:	la clase el diccionario el instructor el supervisor
Nouns:	la chica, la muchacha el chico, el muchacho el gerente el mercado la novia el novio la tienda
Verbs:	llamar llegar tener venir
Adjectives:	bonito bueno cansado malo mayor menor pequeño poco
Other words and expressions:	¿a quién? con ¿cuándo? ¿cuántos? muy pero

II. Structure Practice

A. Answer the questions, using the cues provided. Repeat the correct answer after the speaker's confirmation. Listen to the model:

Modelo: —¿A dónde vas?   (hotel)
—Voy al hotel.

1. (hospital)
2. (biblioteca)
3. (profesor)
4. (médico)
5. (señor Díaz)
6. (cafetería)
7. (señorita Vera)

B. Answer the questions, always selecting the second choice. Repeat the correct answer after the speaker's confirmation. Listen to the model:

Modelo: —¿Quién es más alto, Alberto o Mario?
—Mario es más alto que Alberto.

C. Answer the questions in the affirmative, always using *mucho* or *mucha*, as needed. Repeat the correct answer after the speaker's confirmation. Listen to the model:

Modelo: —¿Tienes hambre?
—Sí, tengo mucha hambre.

III. Listening and Comprehension

1. Listen carefully to the dialogue. It will be read twice.

   (*Dialogue 1*)

   Now the speaker will make statements concerning the conversation you just heard. After each statement, say whether it is true (**verdadero**) or false (**falso**). The speaker will confirm the correct answer.

2. Listen carefully to the dialogue. It will be read twice.

   (*Dialogue 2*)

   Now the speaker will make statements concerning the conversation you just heard. After each statement, say whether it is true (**verdadero**) or false (**falso**). The speaker will confirm the correct answer.

LESSON 5

1. Telling time
2. Stem-changing verbs (**e:ie**)
3. **Ir a** + infinitive
4. Uses of **hay**
5. Ordinal numbers and their uses

1. Telling time

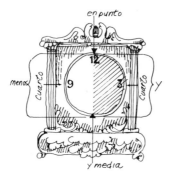

A. Remember the following points when telling time in Spanish:

1. **Es** is used with **una:**

> **Es** la una y cuarto.   *It is a quarter after one.*

    Son is used with all the other hours:

> **Son** las dos y cuarto   *It is a quarter after two.*
> **Son** las cinco y diez.   *It is ten after five.*

2. The definite article is always used before the hour:

> Es **la** una y veinte.   *It is twenty after one.*
> Son **las** cuatro y media.   *It is four thirty.*

3. The hour is given first, then the minutes:

> Son las **cuatro** y **diez.**   *It is ten after four* (literally: *"four and ten"*).

4. The equivalent of *past* or *after* is **y:**

> Son las doce **y** cinco.   *It is five after twelve.*

5. The equivalent of *to* or *till* is **menos.** It is used with fractions of time up to a half hour:

> Son las ocho **menos** veinte.   *It is twenty to eight.*

When telling time, the order is the following:

> 1. **Es** or **Son**
> 2. **la** or **las**
> 3. the hour
> 4. **y** or **menos**
> 5. the minutes

Es	Son
la	las
una	cinco
y	menos
veinte.	diez.

ATENCIÓN: The equivalent of *at + time* is **a** + **la(s)** + *time:*

A la una.   *At one o'clock.*
A las cinco y media.   *At five thirty.*

B. There is a difference between **de la** and **por la** when used with time.

1. When a specific time is mentioned, **de la (mañana, tarde, noche)** should be used:

Mi clase de inglés es a las seis **de** la tarde.   *My English class is at six in the evening.*

2. When a specific time is *not* mentioned, **por la (mañana, tarde, noche)** should be used:

Nosotros trabajamos **por la** mañana.   *We work in the morning.*
Juan estudia **por la** tarde.   *Juan studies in the afternoon.*

Exercises

A. ¿Qué hora es?

B. Be an interpreter. Tell us how to say the following in Spanish.

1. We are coming at two-thirty in the afternoon.
2. He is going to the library in the morning.

3. They don't work in the evening.
4. It's three (o'clock) in the morning!
5. I am arriving at nine o'clock in the evening.
6. They are hungry at four in the afternoon.
7. Pedro studies in the morning.
8. We go to our Spanish class at eight (o'clock) in the morning.
9. He reads in the evening.
10. They go to the hospital at six (o'clock).
11. I visit the museum at three-thirty.
12. She calls the supervisor at nine (o'clock).

2. Stem-changing verbs (e:ie)

Certain verbs undergo a change in the stem in the present indicative. When the last stem vowel is a stressed **e**, it changes to **ie**.

preferir *(to prefer)*	
prefiero	preferimos
prefieres	
prefiere	prefieren

◆ Notice that the stem vowel is not stressed in the verb form corresponding to **nosotros**, and therefore the **e** does not change to **ie**.

◆ Stem-changing verbs have regular endings like other -ar, -er, and -ir verbs.

ATENCIÓN: Some other verbs that undergo the same change are: **cerrar** *(to close)*, **perder** *(to lose)*, **comenzar**[1] *(to begin)*, **querer** *(to want)*, **entender** *(to understand)*, and **empezar**[1] *(to begin)*.

—¿**Quieres** ir al cine?
Do you want to go to the movies?

—No, no **quiero** ir al cine.
No, I don't want to go to the movies.

—¿Por qué no?
Why not?

—Porque **prefiero** ir al concierto.
Because I prefer to go to the concert.

—¿A qué hora **cierran** Uds.?
What time do you close?

—**Cerramos** a las nueve.
We close at nine.

—¿Cuándo **comienzan** las clases?
When do classes start?

—**Comienzan** en septiembre.
They start in September.

[1]When **comenzar** and **empezar** are followed by an infinitive, the preposition **a** is used: **Yo comienzo** *(empiezo)* **a trabajar a las seis.** Notice that these two verbs are synonymous.

—Pedro **entiende** el francés y | *Pedro understands French and*
el alemán, ¿no? | *German, doesn't he?*
—**Entiende** el francés, pero no | *He understands French, but he*
entiende el alemán. | *doesn't understand German.*

Exercises

A. Complete the following sentences with the present indicative of **pre-ferir, cerrar, empezar, comenzar, querer, perder,** and **entender,** as needed. Use each verb once:

1. Nosotros no _____ estudiar alemán; _____ estudiar francés.
2. El concierto _____ a las ocho de la noche.
3. Yo no _____ la lección.
4. ¿Por qué _____ (tú) el libro?
5. Las clases _____ en marzo.
6. Roberto _____ su dinero en Las Vegas.

B. Finish the following in an original manner:

1. Luis comienza a trabajar a las siete y nosotros...
2. Tú prefieres ir al cine y yo...
3. Nosotros cerramos a las nueve y ellos...
4. Yo empiezo a estudiar el lunes y Uds....
5. Rafael quiere aprender francés y nosotros...
6. Yo no entiendo inglés y ustedes...

3. Ir a + infinitive

The construction **ir a** + *infinitive* is used to express future time. It is equivalent to the English expression *to be going to*. The formula is:

ir	+	a	+	infinitive	
Yo voy		a		**viajar**	**solo.**
I'm going				*to travel*	*alone.*

—¿Qué **vas a comprar?** | *What are you going to buy?*
—**Voy a comprar** una camisa y | *I'm going to buy a shirt and a*
una blusa. | *blouse.*

—¿Cuánto dinero tienes? | *How much money do you have?*
—Cincuenta dólares. | *Fifty dollars.*

—¿Con quién **van a ir** Uds. a | *With whom are you going (to*
la reunión? | *go) to the meeting?*

—**Vamos a ir** con la hermana de Enrique y el hermano de Juan.	*We are going (to go) with Enrique's sister and Juan's brother.*
—¿A qué hora **va a empezar** la clase?	*What time is the class going to start?*
—**Va a empezar** a las siete.	*It's going to start at seven.*

Exercise

A. Item substitution:

1. Tú **vas** a viajar.   (Nosotros, Mi hermana, Yo, Ud., Ellos)
2. El gerente **va** a hablar con ella.   (Yo, Uds., Nosotras, Tú)

B. Change the following, to tell us what these people are going to do instead of what they do:

1. Yo voy al cine solo.
2. ¿Tú compras camisas blancas?
3. La junta comienza a las siete.
4. Mis hermanos hablan español.
5. Ella da su nombre y apellido.
6. Nosotros viajamos a Lima.

4. Uses of hay

The form **hay** means *there is* or *there are*. It has no subject and must not be confused with **es** (*it is*) and **son** (they are).

¿**Hay** reunión hoy? No, no **hay** reunión.	*Is there (any) meeting today? No, there isn't (any) meeting.*
¿**Hay** vuelos para Lima hoy? Sí, **hay** un vuelo a las ocho de la noche.	*Are there flights to Lima today? Yes, there is one flight at eight P.M.*

Exercise

Answer the following questions:

1. ¿Cuántos estudiantes hay en la clase?
2. ¿Hay reunión de estudiantes hoy?
3. ¿Hay un vuelo para Bogotá esta noche?
4. Hoy es domingo. ¿Hay clase?
5. ¿Cuántos teatros hay en su ciudad?
6. ¿Hay niños en la clase?

5. Ordinal numbers and their uses

primero(a)	*first*	sexto(a)	*sixth*
segundo(a)	*second*	séptimo(a)	*seventh*
tercero(a)	*third*	octavo(a)	*eighth*
cuarto(a)	*fourth*	noveno(a)	*ninth*
quinto(a)	*fifth*	décimo(a)	*tenth*

◆ The ordinal numbers **primero** and **tercero** drop the final **-o** before masculine singular nouns:

¿Qué día llegan Uds.?	*What day are you arriving?*
Llegamos el **primer** día del mes.	*We are arriving the first day of the month.*

◆ Ordinal numbers agree in gender and number with the nouns they modify:

¿Qué oficina prefiere?	*Which office do you prefer?*
Prefiero **la** quinta oficina.	*I prefer the fifth (one).*

◆ Ordinal numbers are seldom used after *the tenth*:

¿En qué piso viven Uds.?	*On which floor do you live?*
Vivimos en el piso **doce**.	*We live on the twelfth floor.*

◆ Remember that cardinal numbers are used in Spanish for dates except for *the first*:

¿Qué día es hoy?	*What day is it today?*
Hoy es el **treinta** de abril. Mañana es el **primero** de mayo.	*Today is April 30th. Tomorrow is the first day of May.*

Exercises

Complete the following sentences with the correct ordinal number:

1. Él es el _____ estudiante. (*first*)
2. Yo vivo en el _____ piso. (*fifth*)
3. Ella prefiere la _____ mesa. (*second*)
4. La oficina de mi esposo está en el _____ piso. (*third*)
5. Llegamos el _____ de mayo. (*first*)
6. Los chicos llegan en los _____ días del mes. (*first*)
7. Yo quiero la _____, la _____, y la _____ sillas. (*fourth / sixth / seventh*)
8. No tenemos clases la _____ semana. Tenemos clases la _____ semana. (*ninth / tenth*)

Vocabulary

COGNATES

la **blusa**   blouse
el **concierto**   concert
el **dólar**   dollar

NOUNS

el **alemán**   German (*language*)
la **camisa**   shirt
el **cine**   movie (*theater*)
la **hermana**   sister
el **hermano**   brother
la **mañana**   morning
la **noche**   (*late*) evening, night
el **piso**   floor (*story*)
la **reunión, junta**   meeting
la **tarde**   afternoon
el **vuelo**   flight

VERBS

cerrar (e:ie)   to close
comenzar (e:ie)   to begin, to start
comprar   to buy
desear   to wish
empezar (e:ie)   to begin, to start
entender (e:ie)   to understand
perder (e:ie)   to lose
preferir (e:ie)   to prefer
querer (e:ie)   to want
viajar   to travel

OTHER WORDS
AND EXPRESSIONS

¿cuánto(a)?   how much?
para   to, in order to
¿por qué?   why?
porque   because

Summary of interrogative words

¿a dónde?   where to?
¿a quién?   to whom?
¿cuál(es)   which?
¿cuándo?   when?
¿cuánto(a)?   how much?
¿cuántos(as)?   how many?
¿de dónde?   from where?
¿dónde?   where?
¿por qué?   why?
¿qué?   what?
¿quién(es)   who?

¿A dónde vas?
¿A quién llamas?
¿Cuál prefieres?
¿Cuándo vienen ellos?
¿Cuánto dinero necesitas?
¿Cuántas camisas quieres?
¿De dónde es Ud.?
¿Dónde está el cine Rex?
¿Por qué no van al concierto?
¿Qué desea comprar, señora?
¿Quiénes van a venir a la reunión?

EN EL LABORATORIO

The following material is to be used with the tape in the language laboratory.

I. Vocabulary

Repeat each word after the speaker. When repeating words that are cognates, notice the difference in pronunciation between English and Spanish.

Cognates: la blusa   el concierto   el dólar

Nouns: el alemán   la camisa   el cine   la hermana
el hermano   la mañana   la noche   el piso
la reunión, la junta   la tarde   el vuelo

Verbs: cerrar   comenzar   comprar   desear   empezar
entender   perder   preferir   querer   viajar

*Other words
and expressions:*   ¿cuánto?   para   ¿por qué?   porque

II. Structure Practice

A.   Change the verb in each sentence according to the new subject. Repeat
the correct answer after the speaker's confirmation.

1. (Uds.)   5. (ellos)
2. (tú)   6. (Ud.)
3. (ella)   7. (él)
4. (yo)

B.   Answer the questions, using the cues provided. Repeat the correct
answer after the speaker's confirmation. Listen to the model:

Modelo: —¿Cuándo vas a venir tú?   (el viernes)
—Voy a venir el viernes.

1. (al cine)   4. (el quinto)
2. (una blusa)   5. (con mi hermano)
3. (a las nueve)   6. (el gerente)

C. Give the ordinal number that corresponds to each cardinal number. Repeat the correct answer after the speaker's confirmation. Listen to the model:

Modelo: cuatro: cuarto

1. nueve   6. seis
2. tres   7. diez
3. cinco   8. dos
4. uno   9. siete
5. ocho

III. Listening and Comprehension

1. Listen carefully to the dialogue. It will be read twice.

   (Dialogue)

   Now the speaker will make statements concerning the conversation you just heard. After each statement, say whether it is true (**verdadero**) or false (**falso**). The speaker will confirm the correct answer.

2. Listen carefully to the narration. It will be read twice.

   (Narration)

   Now the speaker will make statements concerning the narration you just heard. After each statement, say whether it is true (**verdadero**) or false (**falso**). The speaker will confirm the correct answer.

TEST YOURSELF

Lesson 1

A. Subject pronouns

Give the plural of the following:

1. yo (*masc.*)
2. él
3. usted
4. ella
5. yo (*fem.*)

B. Present indicative of **-ar** verbs

Complete the following sentences with the Spanish equivalent of the verbs in parentheses:

1. Yo _____ español.   (*speak*)
2. Nosotros _____ en la oficina.   (*work*)
3. Alberto _____ francés.   (*studies*)
4. ¿_____ tú la solicitud?   (*need*)
5. Ana y Raúl _____ en el hospital.   (*work*)
6. ¿Ud. _____ italiano?   (*speak*)

C. Interrogative sentences / Negative sentences

Make the following sentences interrogative, then negative:

1. Elena trabaja en Buenos Aires.
2. Uds. hablan inglés.
3. Tú necesitas dinero.
4. Juan y Amalia estudian español.
5. Ud. trabaja en Los Ángeles.

D. Cardinal numbers (300–1000)

Give the answers to the following problems: (+: **más**; −: **menos**) (e.g., doscientos **más** doscientos **son** cuatrocientos)

1. setecientos − doscientos =
2. cien + novecientos =
3. trescientos + doscientos cincuenta =
4. mil − ochocientos =
5. cuatrocientos + quinientos =
6. seiscientos − ciento cincuenta =

Lesson 2

A. Position of adjectives

Give the Spanish equivalent:

1. five blue books
2. two North American ladies
3. a big restaurant
4. the German students
5. an intelligent professor

B. Agreement of adjectives, articles, and nouns

Make the following plural:

1. la casa verde
2. el lápiz negro
3. el profesor inteligente
4. la silla grande
5. el libro blanco
6. la señorita feliz

C. Present indicative of **-er** and **-ir** verbs

Give the Spanish equivalent:

1. Where do you live, Mrs. Vera?
2. They drink coffee. I drink tea.
3. We read the lessons.
4. He decides to study English.
5. Do you (**tú**) understand?
6. You (**Uds.**) eat early.
7. She writes in Spanish.
8. We open the books.
9. I'm learning Spanish.
10. They don't receive the money.

D. The personal **a**

Read the following sentences. Use the personal **a** when needed:

1. ¿Esperan Uds. _____ el ómnibus?
2. Nosotros no visitamos _____ la señora Pérez.
3. Ellos visitan _____ los museos.
4. Rosa espera _____ Carlos.
5. Los estudiantes visitan _____ los profesores.

Lesson 3

A. Possession with **de**

Arrange the following in complete sentences according to the model.

Modelo: Yo / necesitar / señorita Peña / libro
Yo necesito el libro de la señorita Peña.

1. Nosotros / recibir / Carlos / dinero
2. Ella / leer / la recepcionista / solicitud
3. Los estudiantes / visitar / Enrique / esposa
4. ¿Tú / esperar / Teresa / amiga?
5. Ud. / no necesitar / María / auto

B. Possessive adjectives

Use the possessive adjective that corresponds to each subject. Follow the model.

Modelo: **Yo** necesito _____ libro.
Yo necesito mi libro.

1. **¿Tú** necesitas _____ mesa?
2. **Ella** necesita _____ lápices. (los lápices _____ _____)
3. **Nosotros** necesitamos _____ cuaderno.
4. **Ud.** necesita _____ pluma. (la pluma _____ _____)
5. **Yo** necesito _____ sillas de metal.
6. **Tú** necesitas a _____ amigos.
7. **Nosotros** necesitamos _____ plumas.
8. **Él** necesita _____ teléfono. (el teléfono _____ _____)

C. Present indicative of **ser**

Answer the following questions in the affirmative:

1. ¿Es Ud. alto(a)?
2. ¿Eres de California?
3. ¿Son Uds. felices?
4. ¿Soy yo el (la) profesor(a)?
5. ¿Es difícil tu lección de español?
6. ¿Son ellos ingenieros?

D. The irregular verbs **ir, dar,** and **estar**

Change the verbs according to each new subject. Make all other necessary changes:

1. **Yo doy mi** número de teléfono.   (Ellos, Nosotros, Tú, Uds., Ella)
2. **Ud. está** en **su** casa.   (Yo, Ellos, Nosotros, Ella, Tú, Uds.)
3. **Ella va** a **sus** clases.   (Nosotros, Ud., Tú, Yo, Ellos)

E. The verbs **ser** and **estar**

Write sentences using the following pairs of items and **ser** or **estar**, as needed. Follow the model.

Modelo: Mi esposo / profesor
     Mi esposo es profesor.

1. La mesa / de madera
2. La señorita López / enferma hoy
3. Las casas / de mi hija
4. Los estudiantes / argentinos
5. El profesor / en el hospital
6. Yo / de Puerto Rico
7. Nosotros / bien
8. María / alta
9. Gustavo y yo / casados
10. Mañana / sábado
11. ¿Cuál / su profesión?
12. El hijo de la señora Nieto / ingeniero

Lesson 4

A. Contractions

Give the Spanish equivalents:

1. We are waiting for the supervisor.
2. She visits Mr. Linares and Mrs. Viera.
3. The money is Mr. Peña's.
4. He doesn't go to the store. He goes to the market.
5. We need to call the instructor.

B. The comparative of adjectives and adverbs

Answer the following questions in the negative:

1. ¿Es Ud. tan alto(a) como el profesor (la profesora)?
2. ¿Llega el profesor (la profesora) más tarde que los estudiantes?
3. ¿Es Ud. el (la) estudiante menos inteligente de la clase?
4. ¿Es Ud. la persona más feliz de la clase?
5. ¿Es Ud. el (la) peor estudiante?

6. ¿Es Ud. mayor que sus amigos?
7. ¿Soy yo el (la) mejor de la clase?
8. ¿La casa de tu amigo es más grande que tu casa?

C. The irregular verbs **tener** and **venir**

Change the verb according to each new subject. Make all other necessary changes:

1. **Yo vengo** con **mi** hijo.   (Nosotros, Tú, Ellos, Ud., Él, Uds.)
2. **Nosotros tenemos nuestros** diccionarios.   (Yo, Ella, Tú, Uds.)

D. Expressions with **tener**

Give the Spanish equivalent:

1. Charles is not hungry, but he is very thirsty.
2. They are very careful.
3. My daughter is not afraid.
4. You are right, Miss Vera. The instructor is in a hurry.
5. I am twenty-seven years old. How old are you, Anita?
6. I'm not hot; I'm cold.

Lesson 5

A. Telling time

Answer the following questions:

1. ¿A qué hora es su clase de español?
2. ¿A qué hora comen Uds.?
3. ¿A qué hora va Ud. a la universidad?
4. ¿Estudia Ud. por la mañana, por la tarde o por la noche?
5. ¿A qué hora llega el profesor a clase?
6. ¿Qué hora es?

B. Stem-changing verbs (**e:ie**)

Answer the following questions:

1. ¿Prefieren Uds. estudiar francés o alemán?
2. ¿Quieres ir al cine hoy?
3. ¿A qué hora empieza la clase de español?
4. ¿Entienden Uds. las lecciones?
5. ¿Pierden Uds. mucho dinero en Las Vegas?
6. ¿A qué hora cierran la biblioteca?

7. ¿A qué hora comienza su programa de televisión favorito?
8. ¿Prefieren Uds. viajar en el verano o en el invierno?

C. **Ir a** plus *infinitive*

Complete the following sentences using **ir a** plus the infinitive of the verb given in parentheses. Follow the model.

Modelo: Yo _____ por la tarde. *(study)*
Yo voy a estudiar por la tarde.

1. Nosotros _____ a las dos. *(eat)*
2. Él _____ una camisa. *(buy)*
3. ¿A qué hora _____ la reunión? *(start)*
4. Tú no _____ a tu hermano. *(visit)*
5. Mi hija _____ en el vuelo de las ocho de la noche. *(arrive)*
6. Yo _____ sola. *(come)*
7. Nosotros _____ mucho dinero. *(need)*
8. ¿_____ Uds. a casa de Roberto? *(go)*

D. Uses of **hay**

Give the Spanish equivalent:

1. How many students are there?
2. There is not (any) money.
3. There are two flights to Lima.
4. There is a meeting today.
5. How many chairs are there?

E. Ordinal numbers

Give the corresponding ordinal number for each of the following cardinal numbers:

1. cinco / día
2. ocho / mes
3. diez / piso
4. uno / estudiantes
5. tres / libro
6. nueve / casa
7. dos / semana
8. seis / reunión
9. cuatro / clase
10. siete / auto

LESSON 6

1. Some uses of the definite article
2. Stem-changing verbs (**o:ue**)
3. Affirmative and negative expressions
4. Uses of **tener que** and **hay que**
5. Pronouns as object of a preposition

1. Some uses of the definite article

A. The definite article is used in Spanish with expressions of time, the seasons, and the days of the week:

—¿Cuándo es su clase de español?   *When is your Spanish class?*

—Tengo clase de español **los**[1] lunes, miércoles y viernes, a las nueve.   *I have Spanish class on Mondays, Wednesdays, and Fridays at nine.*

ATENCIÓN: The definite article is omitted with the seasons and days of the week when used after the verb **ser:**

—¿Es primavera ahora en Chile?   *Is it spring in Chile now?*

—Sí, es primavera.   *Yes, it is spring.*

—¿Qué día es hoy?   *What day is today?*

—Hoy es domingo.   *Today is Sunday.*

B. The definite article precedes nouns used in a general sense:

—¿Qué quieren **las** mujeres y **los** hombres de hoy?   *What do today's women and men want?*

—Quieren **la** igualdad.   *They want equality.*

C. The definite article is used with abstract nouns:

—¿Es importante **la** libertad?   *Is freedom important?*

—Sí, **la** libertad es importante.   *Yes, freedom is important.*

D. The definite article is used before **próximo** (*next*) and **pasado** (*last*) with expressions of time:

—¿Las clases comienzan **la** semana **próxima?**   *Do classes start next week?*

—Sí, comienzan **la** semana que viene.   *Yes, they start next week.*

E. The definite article is used with the nouns **cárcel, iglesia,** and **escuela** when they are preceded by a preposition:

—¿Vas **a la iglesia** los viernes?   *Do you go to church on Fridays?*

—No, voy **a la escuela.**   *No, I go to school.*

---

[1]Notice that the definite article is used here as the equivalent of *on.*

Exercises

A. Is the definite article needed or not? Decide as you complete the dialogues:

1. —¿Tú vas a _____ iglesia hoy?
   —No, hoy es _____ sábado, y yo voy a _____ iglesia _____ domingos.
   —¿Vas a _____ escuela _____ lunes?
   —No, _____ lunes no tengo clases.
2. —¿Uds. van a viajar a la Argentina en julio?
   —No, porque cuando en los Estados Unidos es _____ verano, en la Argentina es _____ invierno y nosotros preferimos _____ verano.
3. —_____ hombres son más inteligentes que _____ mujeres.
   —¡No! _____ mujeres somos tan inteligentes como _____ hombres.
4. —¿A dónde vas a ir _____ domingo próximo?
   —Voy a ir a visitar a Julio, que está en _____ cárcel.

B. Be an interpreter. Tell us how to say the following in Spanish:

1. Are you going to school or to church, Miss Vera?
2. Freedom is very important.
3. Do you prefer fall or spring?
4. I don't have classes on Wednesdays.
5. Is today Sunday?
6. The class starts next week.

2. Stem-changing verbs (o:ue)

As you learned in Lesson 5, certain verbs undergo a change in the stem in the present indicative. When the last stem vowel is a stressed **o**, it changes to **ue**.

volver (*to return*)	
vuelvo	volvemos
vuelves	
vuelve	vuelven

◆ Notice that the stem vowel is not stressed in the verb form corresponding to **nosotros**; therefore, the **o** does not change to **ue**.

—¿Cuándo **vuelven** Uds.?   *When are you coming back?*
—**Volvemos** a las siete.   *We are coming back at seven.*

◆ Some other common verbs that undergo the same change in the stem are: the -ar verbs **recordar** (*to remember*) and **volar** (*to fly*); the -er verb **poder** (*to be able*); and the -ir verb **dormir** (*to sleep*).

—¿**Puede** Ud. trabajar mañana?	*Are you able to work tomorrow?*
—Sí. ¡Ah! No, porque ahora **recuerdo** que voy a estudiar.	*Yes. Oh! No, because now I remember that I'm going to study.*
—¿Cuándo **vuela** Ud.?	*When are you flying?*
—**Vuelo** la semana que viene.	*I'm flying next week.*
—¿Cuándo **pueden** Uds. ir al hospital?	*When can you go to the hospital?*
—**Podemos** ir mañana.	*We can go tomorrow.*
—¿Cuántas horas **duerme** él?	*How many hours does he sleep?*
—Él **duerme** diez horas.	*He sleeps ten hours.*

Exercise

Complete the following sentences with the correct form of the verb given in parentheses:

1. ¿Cuándo _____ (volver) Ud. de México?
2. Yo no _____ (recordar) su número de teléfono.
3. Nosotras _____ (volar) la semana que viene.
4. Ellos no _____ (poder) ir con sus hijos ahora.
5. Tú no _____ (volver) en el verano porque no _____ (poder).
6. Uds. _____ (volar) en mayo.
7. Yo _____ (poder) venir mañana.
8. ¿_____ (recordar) Ud. a la hija de Juan?
9. Nosotros _____ (dormir) mucho pero él _____ (dormir) más.
10. Nosotras no _____ (poder) estudiar hoy.

3. Affirmative and negative expressions

A. Study the expressions in the following tables:

Affirmative		Negative	
algo	*something, anything*	nada	*nothing*
alguien	*someone, anyone*	nadie	*nobody, no one*
alguno(a)		ninguno(a)	
algún	*any, some*	ningún	*none, not any*
algunos(as)			

Affirmative		Negative	
siempre	*always*	nunca	} *never*
alguna vez	*ever*	jamás	
algunas veces	*sometimes*		
también	*also, too*	tampoco	*neither*
o...o	*either . . . or*	ni...ni	*neither . . . nor*

—¿Hay **algo** en la mesa?   *Is there anything on the table?*
—No, no hay **nada**.   *No, there is nothing.*

—¿Hay **alguien** con el director?   *Is there anyone with the director?*
—No, no hay **nadie**.   *No, there is nobody.*

—¿Van Uds. **siempre** a Los Ángeles?   *Do you always go to Los Angeles?*
—No, no vamos **nunca**.   *No, we never go.*

—¿Quieren venir Uds. **también**?   *Do you want to come too?*
—No, Juan no quiere ir, **ni** yo tampoco.   *No, Juan doesn't want to go and neither do I.*

—¿Qué quiere Ud.? ¿El piano **o** la radio?   *What do you want? The piano or the radio?*
—No quiero **ni** el piano **ni** la radio.   *I want neither the piano nor the radio.*

◆ **Alguno** and **ninguno** drop the **-o** before a masculine singular noun, but **alguna** and **ninguna** keep the final **-a**.

—¿Hay **algún** libro o **alguna** pluma en la mesa?   *Is there any book or pen on the table?*
—No, no hay **ningún** libro ni **ninguna** pluma.   *No, there isn't any book or pen.*

◆ **Alguno(a)** may be used in the plural form, but **ninguno(a)** is used in the singular form.

—¿Desea comprar **algunos** regalos?   *Do you want to buy any presents?*
—No, no deseo comprar **ningún** regalo.   *No, I don't want to buy any presents.*

—¿Vienen **algunas** chicas a la reunión?   *Are some girls coming to the meeting?*
—No, no viene **ninguna** chica.   *No, no girls are coming.*

B. A double negative is frequently used in Spanish. In this construction, the adverb **no** is placed before the verb. The second negative word either follows the verb or appears at the end of the sentence. However, if the negative word precedes the verb, **no** is never used:

—¿Habla Ud. alemán **siempre?**   *Do you always speak German?*
—No, yo **no** hablo alemán **nunca.**   *No, I never speak German.*
(**Yo nunca** hablo alemán.)

—¿Compra Ud. **algo** aquí?   *Do you buy anything here?*
—No, aquí **no** compro **nada nunca.**   *No, I never buy anything here.*
(**Nunca** compro **nada** aquí.)

Exercise

Answer the following questions in the negative:

1. ¿Necesita Ud. algo?
2. ¿Hay alguien aquí?
3. ¿Estudia Ud. siempre por la noche?
4. ¿Quieres el piano o la radio?
5. ¿Va a comprar Ud. algunos regalos?
6. Juan no va a la reunión. ¿Vas tú?
7. ¿Va Ud. a Los Ángeles algunas veces?

4. Uses of **tener que** and **hay que**

A. The Spanish equivalent of *to have to* is **tener que:**

—¿Qué **tiene que** hacer hoy?   *What do you have to do today?*
—**Tengo que** trabajar.   *I have to work.*

B. The Spanish equivalent of *one must* is **hay que:**

—¿Qué **hay que** hacer para tener éxito?   *What must one do to succeed?*
—**Hay que** trabajar.   *One must work.*

ATENCIÓN: Note that **tener que** and **hay que** are followed by the *infinitive.*

Exercise

Complete the following sentences with **hay que** or the correct form **tener que,** as needed:

1. Para tener éxito, _____ trabajar.

2. Yo _____ estudiar mucho.
3. Nosotros _____ volar a Chicago la semana que viene.
4. _____ dormir ocho horas.
5. Ud. _____ volver a las diez de la noche.
6. _____ comenzar más tarde.
7. Uds. no _____ venir hoy.
8. Para aprender, _____ estudiar.

5. Pronouns as object of a preposition

mí	me	**nosotros**	us
ti	you (*familiar*)		
Ud.	you (*formal*)	**Uds.**	you (*formal, plural*)
él	him	**ellos**	them (*masc.*)
ella	her	**ellas**	them (*fem.*)

◆ Notice that only the first and second persons singular (**mí, ti**) have special forms. The other persons use the forms of the subject pronouns.

◆ When used with the preposition **con**, the first and second person singular forms become **conmigo** and **contigo**:

—¿Vas a casa **conmigo?**	*Are you going home with me?*
—No, no voy **contigo.** Voy **con ellos.**	*No, I'm not going with you.* *I'm going with them.*
—¿Es **para nosotros** el regalo?	*Is the present for us?*
—Sí, es **para Uds.**	*Yes, it's for you.*
—¿Hablan **de ti?**	*Are they talking about you?*
—No, no hablan **de mí.**	*No, they're not talking about me.*

Exercise

Complete the following sentences with the correct forms of the pronouns:

1. Ella va a la tienda con _____. (*us*)
2. El regalo es para _____. (*him*)
3. Ellos siempre hablan de _____, no de _____. (*you*, fam. sing. / *me*)
4. La blusa es para _____. (*her*)
5. Nosotros venimos con _____. (*you*, fam. sing.)
6. Pedro viene a clase con _____. (*me*)

Vocabulary

COGNATES

el, la **director**(a)   director   el **piano**   piano
la **igualdad**   equality   la **radio**   radio
importante   important

NOUNS

la **cárcel**   jail, prison
la **escuela**   school
el **hombre**   man
la **hora**   hour
la **iglesia**   church
el **mes**   month
la **mujer**   woman
el **regalo**   present, gift

VERBS

dormir (o:ue)   to sleep
hacer[1]   to do, to make
poder (o:ue)   to be able
recordar (o:ue)   to remember
volar (o:ue)   to fly
volver (o:ue)   to return, to come
  (go) back

ADJECTIVES

pasado(a)   last
próximo(a)   next

OTHER WORDS
AND EXPRESSIONS

a casa   home
aquí   here
de   about
en   on
mañana   tomorrow
para   in order to, for
porque   because
que viene   next, coming
tener éxito   to succeed

[1]Conjugated in Lesson 7.

EN EL LABORATORIO

LESSON 6

The following material is to be used with the tape in the language laboratory.

I. Vocabulary

Repeat each word after the speaker. When repeating words that are cognates, notice the difference in pronunciation between English and Spanish.

Cognates:	el director la igualdad importante el piano la radio
Nouns:	la cárcel la escuela el hombre la hora la iglesia el mes la mujer el regalo
Verbs:	dormir hacer poder recordar volar volver
Adjectives:	pasado próximo
Other words and expressions:	a casa aquí de en mañana para porque que viene tener éxito

II. Structure Practice

A. Answer the questions, always selecting the first choice. Repeat the correct answer after the speaker's confirmation. Listen to the model:

Modelo: —¿Tú vas a la iglesia los sábados o los domingos?
　　　　　—Yo voy a la iglesia los sábados.

B. Answer the questions, using the cues provided. Repeat the correct answer after the speaker's confirmation. Listen to the model:

Modelo: —¿Cuándo puede volver usted?   (mañana)
　　　　　—Puedo volver mañana.

1. (a las dos y cuarto)
2. (el lunes)
3. (ocho horas)
4. (los sábados)
5. (con el señor Álvarez)

C. Change the following negative statements to the affirmative. Repeat the correct answer after the speaker's confirmation. Listen to the model.

Modelo: Ellos nunca van.
Ellos siempre van.

D. Say what these people *have to do,* instead of what they do. Repeat the correct answer after the speaker's confirmation. Listen to the model:

Modelo: Ellos van conmigo.
Ellos tienen que ir conmigo.

III.   Listening and Comprehension

Listen carefully to the narration. It will be read twice.

(*Narration*)

Now the speaker will make statements concerning the narration you just heard. After each statement, say whether it is true (**verdadero**) or false (**falso**). The speaker will confirm the correct answer.

LESSON 7

1. Stem-changing verbs (**e:i**)
2. Irregular first persons
3. **Saber** contrasted with **conocer**
4. The impersonal **se**
5. Direct object pronouns

1. Stem-changing verbs (e:i)

Certain -**ir** verbs undergo a special change in the stem. When the last stem
vowel is a stressed **e**, the **e** changes to **i** in the present indicative:

servir (to serve)	
sirvo	servimos
sirves	
sirve	sirven

◆ Notice that the stem vowel is not stressed in the verb form corresponding to
nosotros; therefore, the **e** does not change to **i.**

—¿Qué **sirven** Uds.?   *What do you serve?*
—**Servimos** café.   *We serve coffee.*

◆ Some other common verbs that undergo the same changes in the stem are:
pedir (*to ask for*), **seguir** (*to follow, to continue*), and **repetir** (*to repeat*).
Verbs like **seguir** drop the **u** before an **a** or an **o: yo sigo.** For example,
conseguir (*to obtain*): **yo consigo.**

◆ The verb **decir** (*to say, to tell*) undergoes the same change, but in addition
it is irregular in the first person singular: **yo digo.**

—¿Qué **sirven** en la cafetería   *What do they serve in the*
de la universidad?   *college cafeteria?*
—**Sirven** sopa, ensalada, carne   *They serve soup, salad, meat,*
y postre.   *and dessert.*

—¿Qué **pide** Enrique?   *What is Enrique ordering?*
—**Pide** un refresco.   *He's ordering a soda.*

—¿A quién **siguen** Uds.?   *Whom are you following?*
—**Seguimos** a nuestra maestra.   *We are following our teacher.*

—¿**Dice** Ud. la verdad   *Do you always tell the truth?*
siempre?
—Sí, yo siempre **digo** la   *Yes, I always tell the truth.*
verdad.

Exercise

Complete these dialogues, using the verbs provided:

servir/pedir/   1. —En este restaurante mexicano _____ una sopa muy
decir   buena.
                     —Cuando yo vengo aquí siempre _____ tamales.
                     —Yo siempre _____ que los tamales de aquí son los
                     mejores.

conseguir/   2. —Carlos, ¿dónde _____ tú libros en español?
conseguir/   —Yo _____ algunos en Los Ángeles y algunos en México.
seguir/decir   —¿Tú _____ en la clase de la Dra. Peña?
                  —Sí, y ella siempre _____ que yo soy su estudiante
                  favorito.
decir/servir/ 3. —Los chicos _____ que tú siempre _____ carne y
servir   ensalada.
                  —No es verdad; algunas veces _____ sopa.

The three types of stem-changing verbs

Here is a list of stem-changing verbs studied up to now. Every time you learn
a new one, add it to the list.

e:ie	*o:ue*	*e:i*
preferir	volver	conseguir
cerrar	recordar	pedir
perder	volar	decir
comenzar	poder	repetir
querer	dormir	seguir
entender		servir
empezar		

2. Irregular first persons

Some common verbs are irregular in the present indicative only in the first
person singular. The other persons are regular:

Verb	*yo form*	*Regular forms*
salir (*to go out*)	**salgo**	sales, sale, salimos, salen
hacer (*to do, make*)	**hago**	haces, hace, hacemos, hacen
poner (*to put, place*)	**pongo**	pones, pone, ponemos, ponen
traer (*to bring*)	**traigo**	traes, trae, traemos, traen
conducir (*to drive; to conduct*)	**conduzco**	conduces, conduce, conducimos, conducen
traducir (*to translate*)	**traduzco**	traduces, traduce, traducimos, traducen
conocer (*to know*)	**conozco**	conoces, conoce, conocemos, conocen
ver (*to see*)	**veo**	ves, ve, vemos, ven
saber (*to know*)	**sé**	sabes, sabe, sabemos, saben

—¿**Sale** Ud. a menudo?   *Do you go out often?*
—Sí, yo **salgo** a menudo.   *Yes, I go out often.*

—¿Dónde **pone** Ud. la información?	*Where do you put the information?*
—Yo **pongo** la información en el fichero.	*I put the information in the file.*
—¿**Sabe** Ud. conducir?	*Do you know how to drive?*
—Sí, yo **sé** conducir. **Conduzco** el coche de mi hermano.	*Yes, I know how to drive. I drive my brother's car.*
—¿**Conoce** Ud. a mi hermano?	*Do you know my brother?*
—Sí, yo **conozco** a su hermano.	*Yes, I know your brother.*

Exercise

Tell us something about you by answering these questions:

1. ¿Sale Ud. a menudo?
2. ¿Ve Ud. a sus amigos los sábados?
3. ¿Hace Ud. algo los domingos?
4. ¿Conoce Ud. la ciudad de Nueva York?
5. ¿Conduce Ud. bien?
6. ¿Sabe Ud. francés?
7. ¿Traduce Ud. del español al inglés?
8. ¿Trae Ud. sus libros a clase?
9. ¿Dónde pone Ud. sus libros?

3. **Saber** contrasted with **conocer**

There are two verbs in Spanish that mean *to know:* **saber** and **conocer.**

A.   **Saber** means to know something by heart, to know how to do something, or to know a fact:

—¿**Sabe** Ud. alemán?	*Do you know German?*
—Sí, yo **sé** alemán.	*Yes, I know German.*
—¿**Saben** ellos nadar?	*Do they know how to swim?*
—Sí, ellos **saben** nadar.	*Yes, they know how to swim.*
—¿**Sabes** qué hora es?	*Do you know what time it is?*
—Sí, son las ocho.	*Yes, it's eight o'clock.*

B.   **Conocer** means to be familiar or acquainted with a person, a thing, or a place:

—¿**Conoce** a la hija del vecino?	*Do you know the neighbor's daughter?*
—¿A Marta? Sí.	*Marta? Yes.*

—**Conocen** Uds. las novelas de Cervantes?	*Do you know Cervantes' novels?*
—Sí, **conocemos** algunas.	*Yes, we know some (of them).*
—¿**Conoces** Puerto Rico?	*Do you know Puerto Rico?*
—No, yo no **conozco** Puerto Rico.	*No, I don't know Puerto Rico.*

Exercise

Tell us what these people know or don't know, using **saber** or **conocer**:

1. Ellos / California
2. Ud. / a mi vecino
3. ¿Tú / la lección de hoy?
4. Él ya / al supervisor
5. Yo no / nadar
6. Uds. / las novelas de Cervantes
7. Yo no / qué día es hoy
8. Yo no / la ciudad de México
9. Nosotras no / francés ni alemán
10. Ellas / al hijo del profesor

4. The impersonal se

A. In Spanish, the reflexive pronoun **se** is used before the third person of the verb (either singular or plural, depending on the subject) as the equivalent of the passive voice in English:

*The library **is opened** at eight.*
La biblioteca **se abre** a las ocho.

*The offices **are closed** at five.*
Las oficinas **se cierran** a las cinco.

Notice the use of **se** in the following impersonal constructions, announcements, and general directions:

—¿A qué hora **se abre** la biblioteca?	*What time does the library open?*
—Se **abre** a las ocho.	*It opens at eight.*
—¿A qué hora **se cierran** los bancos?	*What time do banks close?*
—Los bancos **se cierran** a las tres de la tarde.	*Banks close at 3 P.M.*
—¿Aquí **se habla** inglés?	*Is English spoken here?*
—No, **se habla** sólo español.	*No, only Spanish is spoken (here).*

B. **Se** is also used with the third person singular of the verb as the equivalent of *one, they,* or *people,* when the subject of the verb is not definite:

—¿Cómo **se dice** *always* en español?

How does one say "always" in Spanish?

—**Se dice** "siempre".

One says "siempre".

Exercise

Luis Otero, a student from Chile, is visiting your home town and needs some information. Can you answer his questions?

1. ¿A qué hora se abre la biblioteca?
2. ¿Se habla español aquí?
3. ¿Cómo se dice *dirección* en inglés?
4. ¿A qué hora se cierran las tiendas aquí?
5. ¿Se abren las oficinas de la universidad los domingos?
6. ¿A qué hora se cierra el museo?
7. ¿Se abren los bancos los sábados?
8. ¿Cómo se escribe su apellido?

5. Direct object pronouns

The forms of the direct object pronouns are as follows:

Subject	Direct Object	
yo	**me** (me)	Ella **me** visita.
tú	**te** (you, *familiar*)	Yo **te** sigo.
Ud.	**lo** (you, *masc., formal*)	Yo **lo** conozco. (a Ud.)[1]
	la (you, *fem., formal*)	Yo **la** conozco. (a Ud.)[1]
él	**lo** (him, it)	Él **lo** ve.
ella	**la** (her, it)	Él **la** ve.
nosotros nosotras	**nos** (us, *masc. and fem.*)	Tú **nos** comprendes.
Uds.	**los** (you, *masc., pl., formal*)	Nosotros **los** visitamos. (a Uds.)[1]
	las (you, *fem., pl., formal*)	Nosotros **las** visitamos. (a Uds.)[1]
ellos	**los** (them, *masc.*)	Él **los** ve.
ellas	**las** (them, *fem.*)	Él **las** ve.

[1]**A Ud./a Uds.** Use for clarification.

A. The direct object pronoun replaces the direct object noun and is placed *before* the conjugated verb:

Yo conozco al señor Lima.
Yo   **lo**   conozco.

Ella escribe la carta.
Ella   **la**   escribe.

Nosotros vemos a nuestros amigos.
Nosotros   **los**   vemos.

B. In a negative sentence the **no** must precede the object pronoun:

Yo traduzco las lecciones.
Yo   **las**   traduzco.
Yo   **no**   **las**   traduzco.

C. If a conjugated verb and an infinitive appear together, the direct object pronoun may be placed before the conjugated verb or attached to the infinitive:

Te quiero ver. ⎫
    Quiero ver**te.** ⎬   *I want to see you.*

—¿**Me** ves ahora?   *Do you see me now?*
—Sí, ahora **te** veo.   *Yes, now I see you.*

—¿Conduce Ud. el coche?   *Do you drive the car?*
—Sí, yo **lo** conduzco.   *Yes, I drive it.*

—¿Pone Ud. la información en   *Do you put the information in*
  el fichero?   *the file?*
—Sí, yo **la** pongo en el fichero. *Yes, I put it in the file.*

—¿Pides los pasaportes?   *Are you asking for the*
                                     passports?
—Sí, **los** pido.   *Yes, I am asking for them.*

—¿Vas a traer las cartas?   *Are you going to bring the*
                                     letters?
—Sí, **las** voy a traer *or*   *Yes, I am going to bring them.*
—Sí,   voy a traer**las.**

Exercises

A. Your Mexican friend is asking you who does things. You tell him you have to do everything.

Modelo: —¿Quién sirve el café?
—Yo **lo** sirvo.

1. ¿Quién trae los refrescos?
2. ¿Quién hace la ensalada?
3. ¿Quién conduce el coche?
4. ¿Quién abre la oficina?
5. ¿Quién traduce las lecciones?
6. ¿Quién lee los libros?
7. ¿Quién pone la información en el fichero?
8. ¿Quién escribe las cartas?
9. ¿Quién compra la carne?
10. ¿Quién llama a las chicas?

B. You are planning a trip to Spain. How are you getting ready for it? What is going to happen there? Answer, always using direct object pronouns.

1. ¿Tiene Ud. su pasaporte?
2. ¿Sabe Ud. hablar bien el español?
3. ¿Van a esperarlo(a) sus amigos?
4. ¿Va a ver a sus profesores allí?
5. ¿Va a visitar los museos?
6. ¿Va a conducir su coche?
7. ¿Ud. va a llamarnos?
8. ¿Va a llevarme a España con Ud.?

C. Be an interpreter. Tell us how to say the following in Spanish:

1. Do you call him?
2. Does he want to see her?
3. The books? I am going to bring them. (*both ways*)
4. She doesn't visit us.
5. Now I see you, Ana.
6. You don't know me, Mr. Lima.

Vocabulary

COGNATES

el **banco**   bank
la **cafetería**   cafeteria
la **información**   information
la **novela**   novel
el **pasaporte**   passport

NOUNS

la **carne**   meat
la **carta**   letter
el **coche, carro**   car
la **ensalada**   salad
el **fichero, archivo**   file
el, la **maestro(a)**   teacher
      (*elementary school*)
el **postre**   dessert
el **refresco**   soda, beverage
la **sopa**   soup
el, la **vecino(a)**   neighbor
la **verdad**   truth

VERBS

conducir   to conduct, to drive
conocer   to know, to be
   acquainted with
conseguir (e:i)   to obtain, to get
decir (e:i)   to say, to tell

nadar   to swim
pedir (e:i)   to request, to ask for,
   to order
poner   to put, to place
repetir (e:i)   to repeat
saber   to know how, to know a
   fact
salir   to go out, to leave
seguir (e:i)   to follow, to continue
servir (e:i)   to serve
traducir   to translate
traer   to bring
ver   to see

OTHER WORDS
AND EXPRESSIONS

a menudo, muchas veces   often
ya   already, now

EN EL LABORATORIO

The following material is to be used with the tape in the language laboratory.

I. Vocabulary

Repeat each word after the speaker. When repeating words that are cognates, notice the difference in pronunciation between English and Spanish.

Cognates:	el banco la cafetería la información la novela el pasaporte
Nouns:	la carne la carta el coche el carro la ensalada el fichero, el archivo el maestro el postre el refresco la sopa el vecino la verdad
Verbs:	conducir conocer conseguir decir nadar pedir poner repetir saber salir seguir servir traducir traer ver
Other words and expressions:	a menudo muchas veces ya

II. Structure Practice

A. Change each sentence, using the verb provided. Repeat the correct answer after the speaker's confirmation. Follow the model:

Modelo: Yo quiero carne.   (pedir)
　　　　Yo pido carne.

B. Answer the questions, always selecting the first choice. Repeat the correct answer after the speaker's confirmation. Follow the model:

Modelo: —¿Conduces un Ford o un Chevrolet?
　　　　—Conduzco un Ford.

C. Answer the questions using the cue provided. Repeat the correct answer after the speaker's confirmation. Follow the model:

Modelo: ¿A qué hora se abre el banco?   (a las diez)
   El banco se abre a las diez.

1. (a las nueve)
2. (español)
3. (archivo)
4. (no)
5. (a las doce)

D. Answer in the negative. Replace the direct objects with the appropriate pronouns. Repeat the correct answer after the speaker's confirmation. Follow the model:

Modelo: —¿Ud. conoce a **Carlos?**
   —No, no **lo** conozco.

1. ¿Tú **me** llamas mañana?
2. ¿Yo **los** visito **a Uds.?**
3. ¿Uds. ponen **el dinero** en el banco?
4. ¿**Te** esperan tus amigos?
5. ¿Quieres ver **a tu amiga?**

III.   Listening and Comprehension

Listen carefully to the dialogue. It will be read twice.

(*Dialogue*)

Now the speaker will make statements concerning the conversation you just heard. After each statement, say whether it is true (**verdadero**) or false (**falso**). The speaker will confirm the correct answer.

1. Demonstrative adjectives and pronouns
2. The present progressive
3. Indirect object pronouns
4. Direct and indirect object pronouns used together
5. **Pedir** contrasted with **preguntar**

1. Demonstrative adjectives and pronouns

A. Demonstrative adjectives

Demonstrative adjectives point out persons or things. They agree in gender and number with the nouns they modify or point out.

The forms of the demonstrative adjectives are as follows:

Masculine		Feminine		Neuter	
Singular	*Plural*	*Singular*	*Plural*		
éste	éstos	ésta	éstas	esto	this (*one*), these
ése	ésos	ésa	ésas	eso	that (*one*), those
aquél	aquéllos	aquélla	aquéllas	aquello	that (*one*), those (*at a distance*)

—¿Para quién son **estas** revistas?

—**Estas** revistas son para Marta y **esos** cuadernos son para Jorge.

Who are these magazines for?

These magazines are for Marta, and those notebooks are for Jorge.

—¿Podemos comer hoy en **este** restaurante?

—No, vamos a comer en **aquella** cafetería que está allá.

Can we eat at this restaurant today?

No, we are going to eat at that cafeteria (which is) over there.

Exercise

Change the demonstrative adjectives according to the new nouns:

1. Este cuaderno, _____ casa, _____ revistas, _____ programas.
2. Esas ciudades, _____ biblioteca, _____ lápices, _____ idioma.
3. Aquella cafetería, _____ sillas, _____ museo, _____ números.

B. Demonstrative pronouns

The demonstrative pronouns are the same as the demonstrative adjectives, except that the pronouns have a written accent mark.

The forms of the demonstrative pronouns are as follows:

Masculine		Feminine		
Singular	Plural	Singular	Plural	
este	estos	esta	estas	this, these
ese	esos	esa	esas	that, those
aquel	aquellos	aquella	aquellas	that, those (*at a distance*)

◆ Each demonstrative pronoun has a neuter form. The neuter pronoun has no accent, because there are no corresponding demonstrative adjectives.

◆ The neuter forms are used to refer to situations, ideas or things, and are equivalent to the English *this, that matter, this, that business,* and *this, that stuff.*

—¿Qué corbata quiere Ud.? **¿Ésta** o **aquélla?**

—Quiero **aquélla.**

Which tie do you want? This one or that one (over there)?

I want that one (over there).

—¿Necesitan Uds. estos periódicos o **ésos?**

—No, necesitamos **aquél** que está en la mesa.

Do you need these newspapers or those (ones)?

No, we need that one (which is) on the table.

—¿Qué crees de **eso?**   *What do you think about that?*
—Creo que **eso** es un   *I think that is a problem for*
   problema para el presidente.   *the president.*

—¿Qué es **esto?**   *What is this?*
—No lo sé.   *I don't know.*

Exercise

Complete the following sentences with the Spanish equivalent of the pronouns in parentheses:

1. Quiero este libro y _____ (*that one*).
2. Necesitamos esa pluma y _____ (*that one [over there]*).
3. Compramos esos lápices y _____ (*these*).
4. Recibimos este periódico y _____ (*those*).
5. ¿Estudia Ud. esta lección o _____ (*that one*)?
6. ¿Comienza Ud. con este programa o con _____ (*that one [over there]*)?
7. ¿Prefieren ellos estas mesas de madera o _____ (*those [over there]*)?
8. ¿Va Ud. a leer este libro o _____ (*those*)?
9. Deseo aquellas revistas y _____ (*these*).
10. ¿Van Uds. a comprar esa corbata o _____ (*this one*)?
11. Ellas no saben qué es _____ (*this*).
12. ¿Quién dice _____ (*that*)?

2. The present progressive

A. The present progressive describes an action that is in progress at the moment we are talking. In Spanish, it is formed with the present tense of **estar** and the Spanish equivalent of the -*ing* form[1] of the conjugated verb.

-ing Form Endings		
hablar	**comer**	**vivir**
habl- **ando**	com- **iendo**	viv- **iendo**

B. Some irregular -*ing* forms:

   pedir **pidiendo**   servir **sirviendo**

[1]The equivalent of the -*ing* form of the verb is called **el gerundio** in Spanish.

decir **diciendo**   leer **leyendo**[2]
dormir **durmiendo**   traer **trayendo**[2]

—¿Qué **estás haciendo** en este   *What are you doing right now*
momento?   *(at this moment)?*
—**Estoy tomando** leche.   *I'm drinking milk.*

—¿Qué **estás comiendo?**   *What are you eating?*
—**Estoy comiendo** el postre.   *I'm eating dessert.*

—¿Qué lección **está leyendo**   *What lesson are you reading?*
Ud.?
—**Estoy leyendo** la lección de   *I'm reading the chemistry*
química.   *lesson.*

ATENCIÓN: The present progressive is *never* used in Spanish to refer to a
future action: **Salgo mañana.** *I'm leaving tomorrow.* The present indicative is used for actions that will occur in the near future.

Verbs such as **ser, estar, ir** (**yendo**), and **venir** (**viniendo**), are rarely used
in the progressive construction.

Exercise

Tell us what these people are doing right now:

Modelo: Yo (tomar café)
Yo estoy tomando café.

1. Julia (leer su lección de química)
2. Ellos (pedir dinero)
3. Nosotros (decir la verdad)
4. Ud. (comer en este restaurante)
5. José (servir la sopa)
6. Ella (dormir en el hotel)
7. Tú (hablar con el presidente)
8. Yo (esperar a Rosa)

3. Indirect object pronouns

An indirect object tells *to whom* or *for whom* something is done. An indirect
object pronoun can be used in place of the indirect object. In Spanish the
indirect object pronoun includes the meaning *to* or *for*. Yo **les** mando los
libros. (*a los estudiantes*)

---

[2]Notice that the **-i** of **-iendo** becomes **y** between vowels.

The forms of the indirect object pronouns are as follows:

Subject	Indirect Object	
yo	me (to)(me)	Él me da las revistas.
tú	te (to)(you, *familiar*)	Yo te doy el cuaderno.
Ud.	le (to)(you, *formal, masc. and fem.*)	Ella le compra una corbata.
él ella	le (to)(him, her)	Yo le hablo en inglés.
nosotros nosotras	nos (to)(us, *masc. and fem.*)	Ella nos da la lección.
Uds.	les (to)(you, *formal pl., masc. and fem.*)	Yo les digo la verdad.
ellos ellas	les (to)(them, *masc. and fem.*)	El presidente les da el dinero.

A. The forms of the indirect object pronouns are the same as the forms of the direct object pronouns, except in the third person. Indirect object pronouns are usually placed *in front* of the verb.

> —¿Quién **les** compra a Uds. los pasajes?
>
> *Who buys you the tickets?*
>
> —Mi padre **nos** compra los pasajes.
>
> *My father buys us the tickets.*
>
> —¿En qué idioma **le** hablas?
>
> *In which language do you speak to him?*
>
> —**Le** hablo en español.
>
> *I speak to him in Spanish.*

EXCEPTIONS:

1. When an infinitive follows the conjugated verb, the indirect object pronoun may be placed in front of the conjugated verb or attached to the infinitive:

> **Te** voy a comprar   un abrigo.
> Voy a comprar**te** un abrigo.

2. With the present progressive forms, the indirect object pronouns can be placed in front of the conjugated verb or after the "gerundio".

> **Le** estoy escribiendo   a mi esposo.
> Estoy escribiéndo**le** a mi esposo.

ATENCIÓN: The indirect object pronouns **le** and **les** require clarification when the person to whom they refer is not specified. Spanish provides clarification by using the preposition **a** + *personal (subject) pronoun.*

Le doy la información.	*I give the information . . .* (to whom? to him? to her? to you?)
but: **Le** doy la información **a ella.**	*I give the information **to her.***

This form is also used to express emphasis.

Le doy el pasaje **a él.**	*I give the ticket **to him*** (and to nobody else).

The prepositional form provides clarification; it is not, however, a substitute for the indirect object pronoun. The prepositional form may be omitted, but the indirect object pronoun must always be used.

—¿Qué **le** vas a traer (a Roberto)?
—**Le** voy a traer un libro.

3. With affirmative commands, the indirect object pronouns are always attached to the end of the verb. The affirmative formal commands (**Ud.** and **Uds.**) are discussed in Lesson 9.

Exercises

A. Express the following, using indirect object pronouns:

Modelo: Ella trae el abrigo *para él.*
Ella *le* trae el abrigo.

1. Yo compro los cuadernos *para ti.*
2. Nosotros vamos a traer los refrescos *para Uds.*   (*both ways*)
3. Ada hace la sopa *para mí.*
4. Ellos están escribiendo una carta *para ella.*   (*both ways*)
5. Yo voy a traer los pasajes para Ud.   (*both ways*)
6. Fernando compra los libros *para nosotros.*

B. Answer the following questions, using the information in parentheses:

1. ¿Qué vas a comprarle a tu hijo?   (un automóvil)
2. ¿Qué les da a Uds. el profesor?   (unos cuadernos)
3. ¿Quién te escribe?   (mi novio / mi novia)
4. ¿Qué vas a traerme?   (un abrigo)
5. ¿Qué les vas a mandar a tus hijas?   (unas blusas)
6. ¿Cuándo nos va a escribir Ud.?   (mañana)

C. Be an interpreter. Tell us how to say the following in Spanish:

1. I always give you the tickets, Mr. Smith.
2. Are you writing to him at this moment?   (*two forms*)
3. My husband always tells me the truth.

4. Are you going to buy us a magazine?   (*two forms*)
5. I speak to them (*fem.*) in English.
6. I'm going to bring the milk to my dad.   (*two forms*)

4. Direct and indirect object pronouns used together

A. When both an indirect object pronoun and a direct object pronoun are used in the same sentence, the indirect object pronoun always appears first:

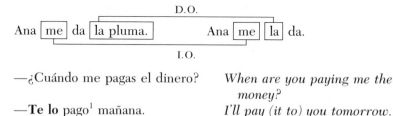

—¿Cuándo me pagas el dinero?   *When are you paying me the money?*

—**Te lo** pago[1] mañana.   *I'll pay (it to) you tomorrow.*

B. With an infinitive, the pronouns may be placed either before the main verb or attached to the infinitive:

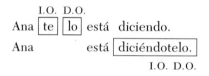

—Necesito el diccionario.   *I need the dictionary. Can you*
¿Puedes prestár**melo**?   *lend it to me?*
—Sí, **te lo** puedo prestar.   *Yes, I can lend it to you.*

C. With a gerund, the pronouns can be placed either before the conjugated verb or after the gerund.

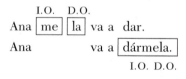

D. If both pronouns begin with **l**, the indirect object pronoun (**le** or **les**) is changed to **se**.

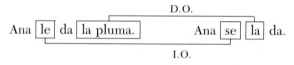

---

[1]The present indicative is frequently used in Spanish to express future time.

For clarification, it is sometimes necessary to add: **a él, a ella, a Ud., a Uds., a ellos, a ellas, a José,** etc.

—¿**Le** sirves la comida **a él** o **a ella?**	*Do you serve dinner to him or to her?*
—**Se** la sirvo **a él.**	*I serve it to him.*
—¿**Les** dan Uds. la medicina **a ellas** o **a ellos?**	*Are you giving the medicine to them* (fem.) *or to them* (masc.)*?*
—**Se** la damos **a ellos.**	*We are giving it to them* (masc.)*.*

Exercises

A. Mom is always doing things for us. Tell us how, using the information provided:

Modelo: Yo quiero *un abrigo.*   (comprar)
        Mamá *me lo* compra.

1. Papá quiere café.   (servir)
2. Nosotros necesitamos dinero.   (dar)
3. Tú quieres los periódicos.   (traer)
4. Yo quiero una blusa.   (prestar)
5. Mis hijos necesitan corbatas.   (comprar)
6. Papá quiere sopa.   (traer)
7. Uds. necesitan la medicina.   (dar)
8. Ud. quiere comer comida mexicana.   (hacer)

B. You keep changing your mind. First you say "yes" and then you say "no". Substitute pronouns for the italicized nouns:

Modelo: —¿Me compra Ud. *el abrigo?*
        —Sí, se lo compro.
        —No, no se lo compro.

1. ¿Me presta Ud. *su corbata?*
2. ¿Me compra Ud. *la blusa?*
3. ¿Les paga Ud. *los pasajes* a ellos?
4. ¿Está Ud. leyéndole *el periódico* a Inés?
5. ¿Nos va a traer Ud. *las medicinas?*
6. ¿Va a servirme Ud. *la comida* ahora?

5. **Pedir** contrasted with **preguntar**

A. **Pedir** means *to ask for* or *to request* (*something*):

—¿Qué te **piden** los muchachos?	*What do the boys ask you for?*

—Me **piden** la medicina para
su madre.

*They ask me for the medicine
for their mother.*

—¿Vas a **pedir**le dinero a tu
tío?

*Are you going to ask your
uncle for money?*

—No, voy a **pedír**selo a mi tía.
Ella es más generosa.

*No, I'm going to ask my aunt
(for it). She's more generous.*

—¿Cuánto **le** vas a **pedir?**

*How much are you going to
ask for?*

—Veinte dólares.

Twenty dollars.

B.   Preguntar means *to ask (a question)*:

—¿Qué vas a **preguntar**le a
René?

*What are you going to ask
René?*

—Voy a **preguntar**le si conoce
a mi primo.

*I'm going to ask him if he
knows my cousin.*

—¿Qué **le** vas a **preguntar** a
Ana?

*What are you going to ask
Ana?*

—Le voy a **preguntar** cuántos
hijos tiene.

*I'm going to ask her how many
children she has.*

Exercise

Tell us what these people are doing, using **pedir** or **preguntar,** as needed:

1. Mis hijos _____ dinero.
2. Yo le _____ qué quiere.
3. Ella le va a _____ si es el tío de Jorge.
4. Yo nunca le _____ nada. Ella no es muy generosa.
5. Le voy a _____ a Margarita si quiere ir allá.
6. ¿Qué le vas a _____ tú a Santa Claus?[1]
7. ¿Qué te _____ Carlos? ¿Dinero?
8. Yo nunca les _____ nada a mis primos, porque ellos no saben nada.

Vocabulary

COGNATES

generoso(a)   generous
la **medicina**   medicine
el **momento**   moment
el, la **presidente(a)**   president

---

[1]In most Latin American countries and in Spain, it is the custom to expect presents from the
Three Wise Men on January 6.

NOUNS

el **abrigo**   coat
la **comida**   food, dinner, meal
la **corbata**   tie
la **esposa**   wife
el **esposo, marido**   husband
los **hijos**   children (*sons and daughters*)
la **leche**   milk
la **madre, mamá**   mother, mom
el **padre, papá**   father, dad
el **pasaje**   ticket
el **periódico,** el **diario**   newspaper
el, la **primo(a)**   cousin
la **química**   chemistry
la **revista**   magazine

la **tía**   aunt
el **tío**   uncle

VERBS

creer   to believe
pagar   to pay
pedir   to ask for something, to request
preguntar   to ask (*a question*)
prestar   to lend
tomar   to drink

OTHER WORDS
AND EXPRESSIONS

allá   over there
¿para quién?   for whom?

EN EL LABORATORIO

The following material is to be used with the tape in the language laboratory.

I.   Vocabulary

Repeat each word after the speaker. When repeating words that are cognates, notice the difference in pronunciation between English and Spanish.

Cognates:	generoso la medicina el momento el presidente
Nouns:	el abrigo la comida la corbata la esposa
	el esposo el marido los hijos la leche
	la madre la mamá el padre el papá el pasaje
	el periódico el diario el primo la prima
	la química la revista la tía el tío
Verbs:	creer pagar preguntar prestar tomar
Other words and expressions:	allá ¿para quién?

II.   Structure Practice

A.   Give the Spanish equivalent of the demonstrative adjectives according to each noun mentioned by the speaker. Repeat the correct answer after the speaker's confirmation. Listen to the model:

Modelo: this / **mesa**
          esta mesa

1. this / these
2. that / those
3. that (*over there*) / those (*over there*)

B.   Change the verbs to the present progressive. Repeat the correct answer after the speaker's confirmation. Listen to the model:

Modelo: —Yo tomo café.
          —Yo estoy tomando café.

C. Repeat each sentence, then substitute the new indirect object pronouns in the sentence. Repeat the correct answer after the speaker's confirmation. Listen to the model:

Modelo: —Carmen me da el dinero.   (les)
—Carmen les da el dinero.

1. Pedro me trae los diarios.
   (nos / les / te / le)
2. Van a pedirte dinero.
   (me / nos / les / le)
3. Está escribiéndote una carta.
   (nos / le / me / les)

D. Repeat each sentence, changing the direct object to the corresponding direct object pronouns. Make all the necessary changes in the sentence. Repeat the correct answer after the speaker's confirmation. Listen to the model:

Modelo: —**Le** traen **el periódico.**
—**Se lo** traen.

E. Answer the questions, using the cue provided. Repeat the correct answer after the speaker's confirmation. Listen to the model:

Modelo: —¿Qué te pide Jorge?   (dinero)
—Me pide dinero.

1. (su dirección)
2. (500 dólares)
3. (no, a mi papá)
4. (si pueden ir al cine)
5. (la corbata)

III.   *Listening and Comprehension*

Listen carefully to the dialogue. It will be read twice.

(*Dialogue*)

Now the speaker will make statements concerning the conversation you just heard. After each statement, say whether it is true (**verdadero**) or false (**falso**). The speaker will confirm the correct answer.

LESSON 9

1. Possessive pronouns
2. Reflexive constructions
3. Command forms (**Ud.** and **Uds.**)
4. Uses of object pronouns with command forms

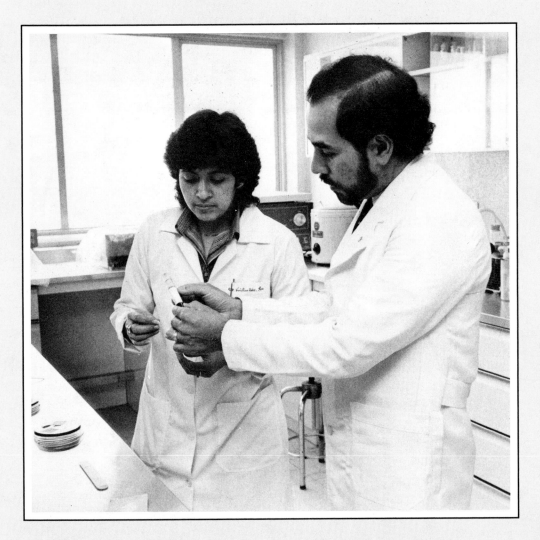

1. Possessive pronouns

Singular		Plural		
Masculine	*Feminine*	*Masculine*	*Feminine*	
el mío	la mía	los míos	las mías	mine
el tuyo	la tuya	los tuyos	las tuyas	yours (*familiar*)
el suyo	la suya	los suyos	las suyas	⎰ his, hers, yours (*formal*)
el nuestro	la nuestra	los nuestros	las nuestras	ours
el suyo	la suya	los suyos	las suyas	⎰ theirs, yours (*formal*)

A. The possessive pronouns in Spanish agree in gender and number with the thing possessed. They are generally used with the definite article:

—Aquí están los zapatos de ellos. ¿Dónde están **los nuestros?**   *Here are their shoes. Where are ours?*

—**Los nuestros** están en el dormitorio.   *Ours are in the bedroom.*

—Tus pantalones están aquí. ¿Dónde están **los míos?**   *Your trousers are here. Where are mine?*

—**Los tuyos** están en la tintorería.   *Yours are at the cleaners.*

—Mi vestido está allá. ¿Dónde está **el suyo?**   *My dress is over there. Where is yours?*

—**El mío** está en la cama.   *Mine is on the bed.*

EXCEPTION: After the verb **ser,** the definite article is omitted when ownership is indicated:

—¿Es **tuya** esta maleta?   *Is this suitcase yours?*

—Sí, esta maleta es **mía,** pero aquéllas son **tuyas.**   *Yes, this suitcase is mine, but those are yours.*

—¿Este talonario de cheques es **suyo,** señor Muñoz?   *Is this checkbook yours, Mr. Muñoz?*

—Sí, es **mío.** Gracias.   *Yes, it's mine. Thank you.*

B. Since the third-person forms of the possessive pronouns (**el suyo, la suya, los suyos, las suyas**) could be ambiguous, they may be replaced for clarification by the following:

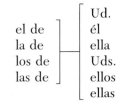

—Estos muebles son de Marta y Arturo, ¿no?

These (pieces of) furniture are Marta's and Arturo's, aren't they?

—Bueno, el sofá es **de ella,** pero la cama y el escritorio son **de él.**

Well, the sofa is hers, but the bed and the desk are his.

Exercises

A. Supply the correct possessive pronouns and read aloud. Follow the models.

Modelos: Yo tengo una cama. Es _____.
Yo tengo una cama. Es mía.

Juan tiene un libro. Es _____. (Es _____.)
Juan tiene un libro. Es suyo. (Es de él.)

1. Tú tienes un talonario de cheques. Es _____.
2. Juan tiene un escritorio. Es _____. (Es _____.)
3. Nosotras tenemos una maleta. Es _____.
4. Ud. tiene unos muebles. Son _____. (Son _____.)
5. Yo tengo un sofá. Es _____.
6. Uds. tienen dos lápices. Son _____. (Son _____.)
7. Yo tengo unos pantalones. Son _____.
8. Ud. tiene tres hijos. Son _____. (Son _____.)

B. Be an interpreter. Tell us how to say the following in Spanish:

1. This desk is mine. Where is yours, Mr. Britos?
2. These shoes aren't ours.
3. His pants are at the cleaners. Where are yours, Anita?
4. The books are hers, but the pens are theirs.
5. Your blouse is here, Mrs. Ortiz. Mine is in the bedroom.

2. Reflexive constructions

A reflexive construction, such as *I introduce myself*, consists of a reflexive pronoun and a verb. Reflexive pronouns refer to the same person the subject of the sentence does.

Subjects	Reflexive Pronouns	
yo	**me**	*myself, to (for) myself*
tú	**te**	*yourself, to (for) yourself* (**tú** form)
nosotros	**nos**	*ourselves, to (for) ourselves*
Ud.		*yourself, to (for) yourself*
Uds.		*yourselves, to (for) yourselves*
él	**se**	*himself, to (for) himself*
ella		*herself, to (for) herself*
		itself, to (for) itself
ellos, ellas		*themselves, to (for) themselves*

ATENCIÓN: Reflexive pronouns are positioned in the sentence in the same manner as object pronouns. They are placed in front of a conjugated verb: **Yo *me* levanto a las ocho;** or they may be attached to an infinitive or to a gerund: **Yo voy a levantar*me* a las ocho. Yo estoy levántando*me*.**

◆ Note that, with the exception of **se,** reflexive pronouns have the same forms as the direct and indirect object pronouns.

◆ The third-person singular and plural **se** is invariable.

Most verbs can be made reflexive in Spanish if they act upon the subject with the aid of a reflexive pronoun.

—Julia **le** prueba el vestido **a su hija.**   *Julia tries the dress **on her daughter.***

—Julia **se prueba** el vestido.   *Julia **tries on** the dress.*

Julia le prueba el vestido a su hija.

Julia se prueba el vestido.

A. Some commonly used reflexive verbs:

lavarse (*to wash oneself, to wash up*)	
Yo **me lavo**	*I wash (myself)*
Tú **te lavas**	*You wash (yourself)* (**tú** form)
Ud. **se lava**	*You wash (yourself)* (**Ud.** form)
Él **se lava**	*He washes (himself)*
Ella **se lava**	*She washes (herself)*
Nosotros **nos lavamos**	*We wash (ourselves)*
Uds. **se lavan**	*You wash (yourselves)*
Ellos **se lavan**	*They* (masc.) *wash (themselves)*
Ellas **se lavan**	*They* (fem.) *wash (themselves)*

Other verbs frequently used in the reflexive are:

> despertarse (e:ie)   *to wake up*
> levantarse   *to get up*
> vestirse (e:i)   *to get dressed*
> desvestirse (e:i)   *to get undressed*
> afeitarse   *to shave*
> bañarse   *to bathe*
> sentarse (e:ie)   *to sit down*
> acostarse (o:ue)   *to go to bed, to lie down*
> preocuparse (por)   *to worry (about)*

B. Some verbs are *always* used with reflexive pronouns in Spanish:

> acordarse (o:ue) (de)   *to remember*
> quejarse (de)   *to complain*
> suicidarse   *to commit suicide*

Notice that the use of a reflexive pronoun does not necessarily imply a reflexive action.

C. Some verbs change their meaning when they are used with reflexive pronouns:

acostar (o:ue) *to put to bed*	acostarse *to go to bed*
dormir (o:ue) *to sleep*	dormirse *to fall asleep*
ir *to go*	irse *to leave, to go away*
levantar *to lift, to raise*	levantarse *to get up*
probar (o:ue) *to try, to taste*	probarse *to try on*
poner *to put*	ponerse *to put on*
quitar *to take away, to remove*	quitarse *to take off* (i.e. clothing)

Notice the use of the reflexive in the following sentences:

—¿A qué hora **se levanta** Ud.,
señorita López?

—Generalmente **me levanto** a
las ocho, pero no **me acuesto**
hasta la medianoche.

What time do you get up, Miss
Lopez?

I generally get up at eight
o'clock, but I don't go to bed
until midnight.

—¿**Se acuerda** Ud. de Rosita?
—Sí, **me acuerdo** de ella.

Do you remember Rosita?
Yes, I remember her.

—¿Por qué no **te acuestas**,
querido?
—Primero voy a **acostar** a los
chicos.

Why don't you go to bed,
dear?
First I'm going to put the
children to bed.

—¿Por qué **te quitas** el abrigo?

—Porque tengo calor.

Why are you taking your coat
off?
Because I'm hot.

—¿Qué vas a hacer?
—**Me voy a lavar** las manos y
me voy.

What are you going to do?
I'm going to wash my hands
and I'm leaving.

ATENCIÓN: Notice that in Spanish, the definite article is used in place of the possessive adjective with articles of clothing or parts of the body.

Exercises

A. Describe what these people do. Use the present indicative of the verbs in parentheses.

1. Elena _____ (probarse) los zapatos.
2. Él _____ (acostarse) y Ud. _____ (acostar) a los muchachos.
3. Juan _____ (bañarse) y Luis _____ (vestirse).
4. Tú siempre _____ (dormirse) en la clase de química.
5. Nosotros no _____ (preocuparse) por eso.
6. Yo _____ (quitarse) los zapatos.
7. Debes _____ (desvestirse) antes de _____ (bañarse).
8. Nosotros vamos a _____ (sentarse) aquí.
9. ¿Por qué no _____ (afeitarse), querido?
10. Pepito, debes _____ (lavarse) las manos ahora.

B. We want to know the following:

1. ¿A qué hora se levanta Ud.?
2. ¿Siempre te despiertas temprano?
3. ¿Se acuerda Ud. de sus amigos?
4. ¿A qué hora se acuestan Uds.?
5. ¿Se queja el profesor de los estudiantes?

6. ¿Se van a poner Uds. los zapatos para salir?
7. ¿Cuántas horas duerme Ud.?
8. ¿Siempre pruebas la comida?

Summary of Personal Pronouns				
Subject	*Direct object*	*Indirect object*	*Reflexive*	*Object of prepositions*
yo	me	me	me	mí
tú	te	te	te	ti
usted (*f.*)	la			usted
usted (*m.*)	lo	le	-se	usted
él	lo			él
ella	la			ella
nosotros	nos	nos	nos	nosotros
ustedes (*f.*)	las			ustedes
ustedes (*m.*)	los	les	se	ustedes
ellos	los			ellos
ellas	las			ellas

3. Command forms (Ud. and Uds.)

A. To form the command for **Ud.** and **Uds.**,[1] first drop the **-o** of the first person singular of the present indicative, and then add the following endings to the stem:

  -ar verbs: **-e** (Ud.) and **-en** (Uds.)
  -er verbs: **-a** (Ud.) and **-an** (Uds.)
  -ir verbs: **-a** (Ud.) and **-an** (Uds.)

ATENCIÓN: Notice that the endings for the **-er** and **-ir** verbs are the same.

Infinitive	*First Person Present Ind.*	*Stem*	*Commands*	
			Ud.	*Uds.*
hablar	Yo hablo	**habl-**	hable	hablen
comer	Yo como	**com-**	coma	coman
abrir	Yo abro	**abr-**	abra	abran
cerrar	Yo cierro	**cierr-**	cierre	cierren
volver	Yo vuelvo	**vuelv-**	vuelva	vuelvan
pedir	Yo pido	**pid-**	pida	pidan
decir	Yo digo	**dig-**	diga	digan
traducir	Yo traduzco	**traduzc-**	traduzca	traduzcan

[1]The **tú** form will be studied in Lesson 18.

| | —¿Con quién debo hablar? | *With whom must I speak?* |
| | —**Hable** con la secretaria. | *Speak with the secretary.* |

—¿Vengo por la mañana o por la tarde?
Shall I come in the morning or in the afternoon?
—**Venga** por la mañana y **traiga** sus documentos.
Come in the morning and bring your documents.

—¿Cierro la puerta?
Shall I close the door?
—No, **cierre** la ventana, por favor.
No, close the window, please.

—¿Sigo derecho o doblo a la derecha?
Shall I continue straight ahead or shall I turn right?
—**Doble** a la izquierda.
Turn left.

B. The command forms of the following verbs are irregular:

	dar	estar	ser	ir
Ud.	dé	esté	sea	vaya
Uds.	den	estén	sean	vayan

—¿Podemos ir solas?
Can we go alone?
—No, no **vayan** solas. **Vayan** con sus padres.
No, don't go alone. Go with your parents.

—¡Le digo que quiero ver a mis hijos!
I'm telling you I want to see my children.
—Un momento, señora. ¡No **sea** tan impaciente!
One moment, madam. Don't be so impatient!

Exercises

A. Tell these people what to do, using the cues provided:

Modelos: ¿Hablo con el secretario?   (director)
No, hable con el director.

¿Hablamos con el secretario?   (director)
No, hablen con el director.

1. ¿Hago la lección número uno?   (la lección número dos)
2. ¿Cerramos las ventanas?   (las puertas)
3. ¿Compramos plumas?   (lápices)
4. ¿Damos nuestra dirección?   (mi dirección)

5. ¿Duermo aquí? (en el dormitorio)
6. ¿Estudiamos la lección cuatro? (la lección tres)
7. ¿Trabajamos hoy? (mañana)
8. ¿Vuelvo el lunes? (el martes)
9. ¿Sirvo café? (té)
10. ¿Pedimos refrescos? (sopa y postre)
11. ¿Doblo a la derecha? (a la izquierda)
12. ¿Estoy aquí a las ocho? (a las nueve)
13. ¿Salimos por la tarde? (por la noche)
14. ¿Traducimos la lección ocho? (la lección seis)
15. ¿Traigo la carne? (la ensalada)
16. ¿Vamos al cine? (al teatro)

B. Be an interpreter. Tell us how to say the following in Spanish:

1. Don't continue straight ahead. Turn left.
2. Don't be so impatient, ladies.
3. Wait one moment, Mr. Peña.
4. Go with the secretary.
5. Bring your documents, Miss Ruiz.

4. Uses of object pronouns with command forms

A. With all direct *affirmative* commands, the object pronouns are placed *after* the verb and are attached to it, thus forming only one word:

—¿Dónde pongo las maletas? *Where shall I put the suitcases?*
—**Póngalas** en la cama. *Put them on the bed.*

—¿Dónde sirvo el café? *Where shall I serve (the) coffee?*

—**Sírvalo** en la terraza. *Serve it on the terrace.*

—¿Qué les doy a las chicas? *What shall I give the girls?*
—**Déles** el postre. *Give them dessert.*

—¿Abrimos la puerta? *Shall we open the door?*
—Sí, **ábranla.** *Yes, open it.*

—¿Se lo digo a Ana? *Shall I tell (it to) Ana?*
—Sí, **dígaselo** a Ana. *Yes, tell (it to) Ana.*

—¿Dónde me siento? *Where shall I sit?*
—**Siéntese** aquí. *Sit here.*

Exercise

Answer the following questions according to the models.

Modelos: —¿Traigo las sillas?
              —**Sí, tráigalas, por favor.**

              —¿Traemos las sillas?
              —**Sí, tráiganlas, por favor.**

              —¿Le traigo el dinero?
              —**Sí, tráigamelo, por favor.**

              —¿Le traemos el dinero?
              —**Sí, tráiganmelo, por favor.**

1. ¿Traduzco la lección?
2. ¿Abrimos la puerta de la terraza?
3. ¿Cerramos las ventanas?
4. ¿Te servimos la sopa ahora?
5. ¿Me siento aquí?
6. ¿Hago el café?
7. ¿Le escribo la carta a Luis?
8. ¿Te compramos el vestido?
9. ¿Me baño?
10. ¿Nos acostamos ahora?
11. ¿Me visto?
12. ¿Nos desvestimos?
13. ¿Te traigo el té?
14. ¿Le doy el dinero a Marta?
15. ¿Le decimos tu número de teléfono a Pedro?

B.   With all *negative* commands, the object pronouns are placed *in front* of the verb:

—¿Nos levantamos ahora?	*Shall we get up now?*
—No, **no se levanten** todavía.	*No, don't get up yet.*
—Voy a traducir la lección al francés.	*I'm going to translate the lesson into French.*
—No, **no la traduzca** al francés. Tradúzcala al español.	*No, don't translate it into French. Translate it into Spanish.*
—¿Te traemos los vestidos?	*Shall we bring you the dresses?*
—No, **no me traigan** los vestidos. Tráiganme los abrigos.	*No, don't bring me the dresses. Bring me the coats.*
—¿Sirvo los refrescos?	*Shall I serve the sodas?*
—No, **no los sirva** todavía.	*No, don't serve them yet.*

—¿Te traemos las maletas?   *Shall we bring you the*
                                        suitcases?

—No, **no me las** traigan.   *No, don't bring them to me.*

Exercise

Someone gives the following commands; tell the people not to do what they ask:

Modelos: Traiga el escritorio.
            ¡No lo traiga!

            Tráigale el escritorio.
            ¡No se lo traiga!

1. Compre ese vestido.
2. Tráigale la camisa a Raúl.
3. Acuéstese.
4. Desvístase.
5. Cierren las ventanas.
6. Quéjense.
7. Levántese.
8. Aféitense.
9. Tráigale el café al señor.
10. Dígaselo a María.
11. Pónganse los zapatos.
12. Dele un cheque a Elena.

Vocabulary

COGNATES

el **documento** document
generalmente generally
impaciente impatient

el, la **secretario**(a) secretary
el **sofá** sofa
la **terraza** terrace

NOUNS

la **cama** bed
el **dormitorio** bedroom
el **escritorio** desk
la **maleta** suitcase
la **medianoche** midnight
los **muebles** furniture (*pieces of*)
los **padres** parents
el **pantalón,** los **pantalones**[1]
  pants, trousers

la **puerta** door
el **talonario de cheques**
  checkbook
la **tintorería** dry cleaners
la **ventana** window
el **vestido** dress
los **zapatos** shoes

[1]Both the singular and plural forms are used: **Me voy a poner** *el pantalón* (*los pantalones*).

VERBS

acordarse (o:ue) (de)   to remember

acostar(se) (o:ue)   to put to bed, to go to bed

afeitar(se)   to shave (oneself)

bañar(se)   to bathe

despertar(se) (e:ie)   to wake up

desvestir(se) (e:i)   to get undressed

doblar   to turn

dormirse   to fall asleep

irse   to leave, to go away

lavar(se)   to wash (oneself)

levantar(se)   to lift, to raise, to get up

ponerse   to put on

preocupar(se) (por)   to worry (about)

probar(se) (o:ue)   to try, to taste, to try on

quejarse (de)   to complain

quitar(se)   to take away, to take off

sentar(se) (e:ie)   to sit, to sit down

suicidarse   to commit suicide

vestir(se)   to dress, to get dressed

ADJECTIVES

querido(a)   dear

OTHER WORDS
AND EXPRESSIONS

a la derecha   to the right

a la izquierda   to the left

antes de   before

seguir (e:i) derecho   to continue straight ahead

tan   so

todavía   yet

EN EL LABORATORIO

The following material is to be used with the tape in the language laboratory.

I. Vocabulary

Repeat each word after the speaker. When repeating words that are cognates, notice the difference in pronunciation between English and Spanish.

Cognates:	el documento generalmente impaciente el secretario el sofá la terraza
Nouns:	la cama el dormitorio el escritorio la maleta la medianoche los muebles los padres el pantalón los pantalones la puerta el talonario de cheques la tintorería la ventana el vestido los zapatos
Verbs:	acordarse acostarse afeitarse bañarse despertarse desvestirse doblar dormirse irse lavarse levantarse ponerse preocuparse probarse quejarse (de) quitarse sentarse suicidarse vestirse
Adjectives:	querido
Other words and expressions:	a la derecha a la izquierda antes de seguir derecho tan todavía

II. Structure Practice

A. Answer the questions, using the cue provided. Repeat the correct answer after the speaker's confirmation. Listen to the model:

Modelo: —Mi blusa es verde. ¿Y la de Eva? (blanca)
—La suya es blanca.

1. (grande)
2. (aquí)
3. (rojos)
4. (también)
5. (en Honduras)
6. (de Guatemala)

B. Answer the questions, using the cue provided. Repeat the correct answer after the speaker's confirmation. Listen to the model:

Modelo: —¿A qué hora te levantas tú?   (a las seis)
        —Me levanto a las seis.

1. (no, tarde)   4. (aquí)
2. (en el dormitorio)   5. (no, de nada)
3. (no, por la noche)   6. (sí)

C. Change the following statements to commands. Repeat the correct answer after the speaker's confirmation. Listen to the model:

Modelo: —**Debe hablar** con la secretaria.
        —**Hable** con la secretaria.

III.   Listening and Comprehension

1. Listen carefully to the narration. It will be read twice.

   (*Narration*)

   Now the speaker will make some statements concerning the narration you just heard. After each statement, say whether it is true (**verdadero**) or false (**falso**). The speaker will confirm the correct answer.

2. Listen carefully to the dialogue. It will be read twice.

   (*Dialogue*)

   Now the speaker will make some statements concerning the conversation you just heard. After each statement, say whether it is true (**verdadero**) or false (**falso**). The speaker will confirm the correct answer.

1. The preterit of regular verbs
2. The preterit of **ser, ir,** and **dar**
3. Uses of **por** and **para**
4. Weather expressions

1. The preterit of regular verbs

A. Spanish has two simple past tenses: the preterit and the imperfect. (The imperfect will be studied in Lesson 11). The preterit of regular verbs is formed as follows. Note that the endings for **-er** and **-ir** verbs are identical.

-ar *Verbs*	-er *Verbs*	-ir *Verbs*
entrar (*to enter*)	**comer** (*to eat*)	**escribir** (*to write*)
entré	comí	escribí
entraste	comiste	escribiste
entró	comió	escribió
entramos	comimos	escribimos
entraron	comieron	escribieron

yo **entré**	*I entered; I did enter*
Ud. **comió**	*you ate; you did eat*
ellos **escribieron**	*they wrote; they did write*

B. The preterit tense is used to refer to actions or states that the speaker views as completed in the past. Spanish has no equivalent for the English *did*, when used as an auxiliary verb in questions and negative sentences.

—¿Quién te **prestó** esa bicicleta?	*Who lent you that bicycle?*
—Me la **prestó** Carlos ayer.	*Carlos lent it to me yesterday.*
—¿Dónde **comió** Ud. anoche?	*Where did you eat last night?*
—**Comí** en la cafetería.	*I ate at the cafeteria.*
—¿**Abrió** Ud. las ventanas?	*Did you open the windows?*
—No, no las **abrí.**	*No, I didn't open them.*
—¿A qué hora te **acostaste** anoche?	*What time did you go to bed last night?*
—Me **acosté** a las once.	*I went to bed at eleven.*

ATENCIÓN: **-ar** and **-er** stem-changing verbs are *not* stem-changing verbs in the preterit; they are regular: **Yo** *volví* **anoche y** *cerré* **la puerta.**

Exercises

A. Complete these sentences with the preterit of the verbs in parentheses:

1. ¿Dónde _____ (aprender) Ud. a hablar español?
2. ¿Qué _____ (decidir) Uds.? ¿Ir al hospital?

3. Yo no _____ (entender) su carta.
4. ¿Dónde _____ (comprar) tú esa bicicleta?
5. Lidia Y Gerardo no _____ (entrar) en la oficina.
6. ¿_____ (abrir) Ud. las puertas?
7. ¿Qué le _____ (preguntar) Uds. a la enfermera?
8. ¿A qué hora _____ (levantarse) tú ayer?
9. Carmen y yo _____ (tomar) café.
10. ¿Cuántas horas lo _____ (esperar) Ud.?

B. This is what people do generally. Tell us what everybody did yesterday:

Modelo: Yo como sándwiches.
 Yo comí sándwiches ayer.

1. Oscar habla con sus padres.
2. Tú ves a Sandra.
3. Le escriben una carta a Rosa.
4. Me baño por la tarde.
5. Cerramos las ventanas.
6. Gerardo se afeita por la mañana.
7. Me quito los zapatos.
8. No te entiendo.

2. The preterit of **ser, ir,** and **dar**

The preterit forms of **ser, ir,** and **dar** are irregular. Note that **ser** and **ir** have the same forms:

ser *(to be)*	ir *(to go)*	dar *(to give)*
fui	fui	di
fuiste	fuiste	diste
fue	fue	dio
fuimos	fuimos	dimos
fueron	fueron	dieron

—Ud. **fue** profesora en la
 Universidad de Arizona,
 ¿no?
—Sí, yo **fui** profesora de
 economía.

*You were a professor at the
 University of Arizona,
 weren't you?*
*Yes, I was a professor of
 economics.*

—¿Con quién **fue** Ud. al
 laboratorio ayer?
—**Fui** con mis padres.

*With whom did you go to the
 laboratory yesterday?*
I went with my parents.

—¿Quién le **dio** la medicina al niño?

Who gave the medicine to the boy?

—Se la **dio** el dentista.

The dentist gave it to him.

Exercise

Complete the following sentences with the preterit of the verbs **ir, ser,** or **dar,** as needed:

1. Yo _____ con mis padres al hospital.
2. Ella _____ mi profesora de economía el año pasado.
3. Nosotros no le _____ el dinero anoche.
4. ¿Le _____ a Ud. la medicina el dentista?
5. El doctor _____ al laboratorio.
6. Yo no te _____ el cuaderno.
7. Nosotros no _____ sus estudiantes.
8. ¿Le _____ Ud. la maleta a la enfermera?
9. ¿Quién _____ el primer presidente de los Estados Unidos?
10. ¿A dónde _____ tú ayer? ¿A la tienda?
11. Carlos y Roberto _____ al laboratorio anoche.
12. ¿Le _____ tú el diccionario a tu prima?
13. María y yo _____ a Santiago el año pasado.
14. Yo les _____ esos zapatos a mis hermanos.

3. Uses of **por** and **para**

A. The preposition **por** is used to indicate:

1. Motion (*through, along, by*):

   —¿**Por** dónde entró el ladrón?

   How (through where) did the burglar get in?

   —Entró **por** la ventana.

   He got in through the window.

   —¿A qué hora pasaste **por** mi casa ayer?

   At what time did you go by my house yesterday?

   —Pasé **por** tu casa a las tres.

   I went by your house at three o'clock.

2. Cause or motive of an action (*because of, on account of, on behalf of*):

   —¿Por qué no fueron Uds. a clase ayer?

   Why didn't you go to class yesterday?

   —No fuimos **por** la lluvia.

   We didn't go because of the rain.

3. Agency, means, manner, unit of measure (*by, for, per*):

—¿Vas a San Francisco **por** avión?	*Are you going to San Francisco by plane?*
—No, llevo el coche.	*No, I'm taking the car.*
—¿Cuál es el límite de velocidad en California?	*What's the speed limit in California?*
—Cincuenta y cinco millas **por** hora.	*Fifty-five miles per hour.*

4. *In exchange for:*

—¿Cuánto pagaste **por** ese abrigo?	*How much did you pay for that coat?*
—Pagué[1] cien dólares **por** él.	*I paid one hundred dollars for it.*

B. The preposition **para** is used to indicate:

1. Destination in space:

—¿A qué hora hay vuelos **para** México?	*What time are there flights to Mexico?*
—A las diez y a las doce de la noche.	*At ten and twelve P.M.*

2. Direction in time (*by, for*); a certain date in the future:

—¿Cuándo necesita Ud. las cartas?	*When do you need the letters?*
—Las necesito **para** mañana.	*I need them for tomorrow.*

3. Direction toward a recipient:

—¿**Para** quién es ese vestido?	*Who is that dress for?*
—Es **para** mi suegra.	*It's for my mother-in-law.*

4. *In order to;* purpose:

—¿**Para** qué necesita Ud. el dinero?	*What do you need the money for?*
—Lo necesito **para** pagar la cuenta del hospital.	*I need it (in order) to pay the hospital bill.*

Exercise

Complete the following sentences using **para** or **por,** as needed:

1. Salimos _____ México mañana. Vamos _____ avión.
2. Necesito el vestido _____ mañana.

---

[1]Verbs ending in **-gar** change **g** to **gu** before **e** in the first person of the preterit. (See verb paradigms in Appendix B, p. ●●●.)

3. Anoche Juan pasó _____ mi casa _____ verme.
4. Hoy no hay vuelos _____ Madrid.
5. El ladrón no entró _____ la ventana.
6. ¿Cuánto pagaste _____ esos zapatos?
7. El abrigo no es _____ mi suegra.
8. Conduzco mi coche a 55 millas _____ hora. Ése es el límite de velocidad.
9. No puedo conducir a mucha velocidad _____ la lluvia.
10. Pagué diez dólares _____ este libro.
11. Mi suegro se preocupa mucho _____ nosotros.
12. El dinero es _____ pagar las cuentas.

4. Weather expressions

In the following expressions, the verb **hacer** (*to make*) followed by a noun is used in Spanish, whereas the verb *to be* followed by an adjective is used in English:

> **Hace** (mucho) frío.   *It is (very) cold.*
> **Hace** (mucho) calor.   *It is (very) hot.*
> **Hace** (mucho) viento.[1]   *It is (very) windy.*
> **Hace** sol.[1]   *It is sunny.*

Hacer is not used in the following weather expressions:

> **llover** (o:ue) (*to rain*)   **llueve, está lloviendo** (*it rains, it's raining*)
> **nevar** (e:ie) (*to snow*)   **nieva, está nevando** (*it snows, it's snowing*)

Other words and expressions related to the weather are:

> la **lluvia**   *rain*
> la **niebla**   *fog*
> **está nublado**   *it's cloudy*

As in English, the impersonal verbs are used in Spanish in the infinitive, present or past participle, and third person singular forms only.

> —¿**Hace viento** hoy?   *Is it windy today?*
> —Sí, y también **está lloviendo**   *Yes, and it is raining a lot also.*
>   mucho.
>
> —¿Qué tiempo hace hoy,   *How's the weather today,*
>   Marta? ¿**Hace** buen[2] tiempo?   *Marta? Is it good (weather)?*
> —No, **hace** mal[2] tiempo. **Hace**   *No, we are having bad*
>   mucho **frío** y **está nevando**.   *weather. It is very cold and*
>   *it is snowing.*

---

[1]It is also correct to say: *hay* **viento,** *hay* **sol.**
[2]**Bueno** and **malo** drop the **o** before a masculine, singular noun.

Exercises

A. Study these words, and then complete the following sentences:

el **paraguas**   *umbrella*
el **impermeable**   *raincoat*
el **suéter**   *sweater*

1. ¿Necesitas un paraguas? Sí, porque _____.
2. ¿No necesitas un abrigo? No, porque _____.
3. ¿Quieres un impermeable? No, no está _____.
4. ¿Necesitas un suéter? No, hoy _____.
5. Está nevando. Lleve el _____.
6. Va a llover. Está _____.

B. How is the weather?

Vocabulary

COGNATES

la **bicicleta** bicycle	el **límite** limit
el, la **dentista** dentist	la **milla** mile
la **economía** economics	el **suéter** sweater
el **laboratorio** laboratory	

NOUNS

el **avión** plane
la **cuenta** bill
el **impermeable** raincoat
el, la **ladrón(ona)** thief, burglar,
    robber
la **lluvia** rain
la **niebla** fog
el **paraguas** umbrella
la **suegra** mother-in-law
el **suegro** father-in-law

VERBS

entrar to enter, to come in
llevar to take, to carry
llover (o:ue) to rain

nevar (e:ie) to snow
pasar (por) to go by

ADJECTIVES

nublado(a) cloudy
pasado(a) last

OTHER WORDS
AND EXPRESSIONS

anoche last night
ayer yesterday
el límite de velocidad speed
    limit
¿Qué tiempo hace hoy? How's
    the weather today?

EN EL LABORATORIO

The following material is to be used with the tape in the language laboratory.

I. Vocabulary

Repeat each word after the speaker. When repeating words that are cognates, notice the difference in pronunciation between English and Spanish.

Cognates:	la bicicleta el dentista la economía el laboratorio el límite la milla el suéter
Nouns:	el avión la cuenta el impermeable el ladrón la ladrona la lluvia la niebla el paraguas la suegra el suegro
Verbs:	entrar llevar llover nevar pasar
Adjectives:	nublado pasado
Other words and expressions:	anoche ayer el límite de velocidad ¿Qué tiempo hace hoy?

II. Structure Practice

A. Answer the questions, using the cues provided. Repeat the correct answer after the speaker's confirmation. Listen to the model:

Modelo: —¿Con quién trabajaron Uds. ayer? (con el director)
—Trabajamos con el director.

1. (con el gerente)
2. (al cine)
3. (cien dólares)
4. (en la cafetería)

5. (cuatro horas)
6. (el doctor Lozano)
7. (a las doce)
8. (a Teresa)

131

B. Answer the questions, using the cues provided. Repeat the correct answer after the speaker's confirmation. Listen to the model:

Modelo: —¿Por dónde entraron Uds.?   (la ventana)
        —Entramos por la ventana.

1. (sí)   5. (cincuenta dólares)
2. (mañana)   6. (avión)
3. (Pepito)   7. (estudiar)
4. (la niebla)   8. (mañana)

C. Answer the questions, using the cue provided. Repeat the correct answer following the speaker's confirmation. Listen to the model:

Modelo: —¿Dónde hace mucho frío?   (Alaska)
        —Hace mucho frío en Alaska.

1. (Oregón)
2. (Arizona)
3. (otoño)
4. (Chicago)
5. (sí)

III.   Listening and Comprehension

Listen carefully to the dialogue. It will be read twice.

(*Dialogue*)

Now the speaker will make statements concerning the conversation you just heard. After each statement, say whether it is true (**verdadero**) or false (**falso**). The speaker will confirm the correct answer.

TEST YOURSELF

Lesson 6

A. Some uses of the definite article

Give the Spanish equivalent:

1. Today is Wednesday.
2. Women want equality with men.
3. Freedom is important.
4. We're going to visit the jail next week.
5. I don't have classes on Fridays.

B. Stem-changing verbs (**o:ue**)

Answer the following questions:

1. ¿A qué hora vuelve Ud. a casa?
2. Cuando Uds. van a México, ¿vuelan o van en coche?
3. ¿Recuerdan Uds. los verbos irregulares?
4. ¿Cuántas horas duermes tú?
5. ¿Pueden Uds. ir a la iglesia hoy?

C. Affirmative and negative expressions

Change the following sentences to the affirmative:

1. Ellos no recuerdan nada.
2. No hay nadie en la escuela.
3. Yo no quiero volar tampoco.
4. No recibimos ningún regalo.
5. Nunca tiene éxito.

D. Uses of **tener que** and **hay que**

Give the Spanish equivalent:

1. To succeed, one must work.
2. You have to come back next week, Mr. Vega.
3. She has to work tomorrow.
4. One must start early.
5. Do we have to begin at eight?

E. Pronouns as object of a preposition

Give the Spanish equivalent:

1. Can you come with me?
2. Are you going to work with them?
3. The piano is for you, Anita.
4. The gift is not for me. It is for her.
5. No, Paco, I can't go with you.

Lesson 7

A. Stem-changing verbs (**e:i**)

Answer the following questions:

1. ¿Qué sirven Uds., sopa o ensalada?
2. ¿Qué pide Ud. para beber cuando va a un restaurante?
3. ¿Dice Ud. su edad?
4. ¿Sigue Ud. en la universidad?
5. ¿Uds. siempre piden postre?

B. Irregular first persons

Complete the sentences with the present indicative of the verbs in the following list. Use each verb once.

traer	conocer	traducir	hacer	saber
caber	salir	poner	conducir	ver

1. Yo _____ mi coche.
2. Yo siempre _____ con ella.
3. Yo _____ los documentos en el fichero.
4. Yo _____ del inglés al español.
5. Yo no _____ al maestro de mi hijo.
6. Yo no _____ aquí. Soy muy grande.
7. Yo _____ el postre.
8. Yo no _____ el regalo. ¿Dónde está?
9. Yo no _____ nadar.
10. Yo _____ la carne.

C. **Saber** contrasted with **conocer**

Give the Spanish equivalent:

1. I know your son.
2. He doesn't know French.

3. Can you (do you know how to) swim, Miss Vera?
4. Do you know the instructor?
5. Do the students know Cervantes' novels?

D. The impersonal **se**

Answer the following questions:

1. ¿Qué idioma se habla en los Estados Unidos?
2. ¿Cómo se dice *often* en español?
3. ¿A qué hora se cierra la biblioteca?
4. ¿Cómo se escribe su apellido?
5. ¿A qué hora se abren las tiendas?

E. Direct object pronouns

Complete the following sentences with the Spanish equivalent of the direct object pronouns in parentheses. Follow the models.

Modelos: Yo veo   (*him*)
   Yo lo veo.

   Yo quiero ver   (*him*)
   Yo quiero verlo.

1. Yo conozco   (*them*, fem.)
2. Uds. van a comprar   (*it*, masc.)
3. Nosotros no queremos ver   (*you*, familiar)
4. Ella sirve   (*it*, fem.)
5. ¿Ud. no conoce...?   (*me*)
6. Él escribe   (*them*, masc.)
7. Carlos va a visitar   (*us*)
8. Nosotros no vemos   (*you*, formal, sing., masc.)

Lesson 8

A. Demonstrative adjectives and pronouns

Give the Spanish equivalent:

1. I need these magazines and those (*over there*).
2. Do you want this notebook or that one?
3. I prefer these newspapers, not those (*over there*).
4. Do you want to buy this tie or that one, Dad?
5. I don't want to eat at this restaurant. I prefer that one (*over there*).
6. I don't understand that. (*neuter form*)

B. The present progressive

Complete the following sentences with the present progressive of **leer, decir, estudiar, tomar,** or **comer,** as needed:

1. Él _____ la lección.
2. Ella _____ en la cafetería.
3. Nosotros _____ el periódico.
4. Tú no _____ la verdad.
5. Yo _____ leche.

C. Indirect object pronouns

Answer the following questions according to the model.

Modelo: ¿Qué me vas a traer de México?   (un abrigo)
   Te voy a traer un abrigo.

1. ¿Qué te va a comprar Carlos?   (los pasajes)
2. ¿Qué le das tú a Luis?   (las revistas)
3. ¿En qué idioma les habla a Uds. el profesor?   (en español)
4. ¿Qué va a decirles Ud. a los niños?   (la verdad)
5. ¿Qué nos pregunta Ud.?   (la dirección de la oficina)
6. ¿A quién están escribiéndole Uds.?   (a nuestro padre)
7. ¿Cuándo le escribe Ud. a su esposo?   (los lunes)
8. ¿A quién le da Ud. la información?   (al presidente)
9. ¿En qué idioma me hablas tú?   (en inglés)
10. ¿Qué te compran tus hijos?   (nada)

D. Direct and indirect object pronouns used together

Give the Spanish equivalent:

1. The money? I'm giving it to you tomorrow, Mr. Peña.
2. I know you need the dictionary, Anita, but I can't lend it to you.
3. I need my coat. Can you bring it to me, Miss López?
4. The pens? She is bringing them to us.
5. When I need new shoes, my mother buys them for me.

E. **Pedir** contrasted with **preguntar**

Give the Spanish equivalent:

1. I'm going to ask her where she lives.
2. I always ask my husband for money.
3. She always asks how you are, Mrs. Nieto.
4. They are going to ask me for the chemistry books.
5. I want to ask him how old he is.

Lesson 9

A. Possessive pronouns

Answer the following questions in the negative, according to the model.

Modelo: —¿Estos pantalones son *de Juan?*
   —**No, no son de él.**

1. ¿Son *tuyas* estas maletas?
2. ¿Estos zapatos son *de Julia?*
3. ¿El vestido que está en la tintorería es *suyo*, señora?
4. ¿Es *de Uds.* esta cama?
5. ¿Este talonario de cheques es *de tus padres?*
6. ¿Son *tuyos* estos muebles?
7. ¿Es *de Uds.* este sofá?
8. ¿Es *nuestro* este escritorio?

B. Reflexive constructions

Give the Spanish equivalent:

1. I get up at seven, I bathe, I get dressed, and I leave at seven-thirty.
2. What time do the children wake up?
3. She doesn't want to sit down.
4. You always worry about your son, Mrs. Cruz.
5. Do you remember your teachers, Carlitos?
6. They are always complaining.
7. First she puts the children to bed, and then she goes to bed.
8. Do you want to try on this coat, miss?
9. Where are you going to put the money, ladies?
10. The students always fall asleep in this class.

C. The command forms: **Ud.** and **Uds.**

Complete the sentences with the command forms of the verbs in the following list, as needed, and read each sentence aloud. Use each verb once:

escribir	venir	dar	hablar	doblar
servir	cerrar	volver	seguir	ser
estar	poner	ir	abrir	traer

1. _____ la puerta, señor Benítez.
2. _____ español, señores.
3. _____ sus documentos, señorita.
4. _____ mañana por la mañana, señoras.

5. No _____ la ventana, señorita. Hace calor.
6. _____ a la izquierda, señores.
7. _____ derecho, señorita.
8. _____ su nombre y dirección, señores.
9. _____ en la oficina mañaná por la tarde, señores.
10. ¡No _____ tan impacientes, señoritas!
11. Señor Vega _____ a la casa del director.
12. _____ el martes, señora. El doctor no está.
13. _____ el café en la terraza, señorita.
14. _____ las maletas aquí, señores.
15. _____ las cartas mañana, señoras.

D. Uses of object pronouns with command forms

Give the Spanish equivalent:

1. Tell them the truth, Mr. Mena.
2. The dessert? Don't bring it to me now, Miss Ruiz.
3. Don't tell (it to) my secretary, please.
4. Bring the chairs, gentlemen. Bring them to the terrace.
5. Don't get up, Mrs. Miño.
6. The tea? Bring it to her at four o'clock in the afternoon, Mr. Vargas.

Lesson 10

A. Preterit of regular verbs / Preterit of **ser, ir,** and **dar**

Rewrite the following sentences according to the new beginnings. Follow the model.

Modelo: Voy al cine. (Ayer...)
 Ayer fui al cine.

1. Ella entra en la cafetería y come una ensalada. (Ayer...)
2. María le escribe a su suegra. (Ayer...)
3. Ella me presta su bicicleta. (El viernes pasado...)
4. Ellos son los mejores estudiantes. (El año pasado...)
5. Ellos te esperan cerca[1] del cine. (El sábado pasado...)
6. Mi dentista va a Buenos Aires. (El verano pasado...)
7. Le doy el impermeable. (Ayer por la mañana...)
8. Nosotros decidimos comprar la bicicleta. (El lunes pasado...)
9. Le pregunto la hora. (Anoche...)
10. Tú no pagas la cuenta. (Anoche...)

[1]**cerca (de)**   near

138

11. Somos los primeros.   (El jueves pasado...)
12. Me dan muchos problemas.   (Ayer...)
13. Mi suegro no bebe café.   (Anoche...)
14. Yo no voy al laboratorio.   (Ayer...)
15. Te damos el suéter.   (La semana pasada...)

B. Uses of **por** and **para**

Give the Spanish equivalent:

1. The thief went in through the window.
2. She went by my house.
3. She didn't come because of the rain.
4. There are flights to Mexico on Saturdays.
5. We are going by plane.
6. The speed limit is fifty-five miles per hour.
7. I need the lesson on economics for tomorrow.
8. Who is the umbrella for?
9. I need the money to pay the bill.
10. She paid two hundred dollars for that dress.

C. Weather expressions

Give the Spanish equivalent:

1. It is very windy today.
2. It is very cold, and it is also snowing.
3. It is very hot in Cuba.
4. How is the weather today?
5. Is it sunny or is it cloudy?
6. There are no flights because of the fog.

LESSON 11

1. Time expressions with **hacer** and **llevar**
2. Irregular preterits
3. **¿De quién...?** for *whose?*
4. The imperfect tense

1. Time expressions with **hacer** and **llevar**

A. Spanish uses the following formula to express how long something has been going on:

> **Hace** + length of time + **que** + *verb* (in the present tense)
> **Hace**   quince años   **que**   **vivo en esta ciudad.**
> I have been living in this city for fifteen years.

—¿Cuánto tiempo **hace que**
  Ud. trabaja para el gobierno? *How long have you been
  working for the government?*
—**Hace** tres años **que** trabajo *I have been working at that job
  en ese puesto. *for three years.*

—¿Cuánto tiempo **hace que** *How long have you lived here?*
  Uds. viven aquí?
—**Hace** un mes **que** vivimos *We have lived here for one
  aquí. *month.*

—¿Tienes hambre? *Are you hungry?*
—Sí, **hace** ocho horas **que** no *Yes, I haven't eaten for eight
  como. *hours.*

B. The verb **llevar** followed by a period of time and the *-ing* form of the verb is also used to express how long something has been going on:

> **Llevar** + length of time + *-ing* form
> **Llevo**   tres horas   **estudiando.**

—¿Cuánto tiempo **llevas** *How long have you been
  escribiendo?* *writing?*
—Llevo media hora *I've been writing for half an
  escribiendo. *hour.*

—¿Cuánto tiempo **llevan** Uds. *How long have you been
  estudiando español?* *studying Spanish?*
—**Llevamos** dos años *We have been studying Spanish
  estudiando español.* *for two years.*

Exercises

A. Answer the following questions according to the model:

Modelo: ¿Cuánto tiempo llevan Uds. trabajando?   (dos horas)
Llevamos dos horas trabajando.

1. ¿Cuánto tiempo hace que Ud. estudia español?   (tres meses)
2. ¿Cuánto tiempo lleva Ud. trabajando en este puesto?   (un año)

3. ¿Cuánto tiempo hace que Ud. no come?   (media hora)
4. ¿Cuánto tiempo llevan Uds. viviendo en esta ciudad?   (un mes)
5. ¿Cuánto tiempo hace que no llueve aquí?   (cuatro meses)
6. ¿Cuánto tiempo llevan ellos trabajando para el gobierno?   (un mes)
7. ¿Cuánto tiempo hace que el Presidente vive en Washington?   (un año)
8. ¿Cuánto tiempo hace que Uds. no van a clase?   (cinco días)

B.   Give the Spanish equivalent:

1. It has been raining for three days.
2. My father-in-law has been sick for a week.
3. How long have you been living here?
4. He has been working at this job for fifteen years.
5. We haven't slept for twenty-four hours.

2. Irregular preterits

The following Spanish verbs are irregular in the preterit:

tener:	tuve, tuviste, tuvo, tuvimos, tuvieron
estar:	estuve, estuviste, estuvo, estuvimos, estuvieron
poder:	pude, pudiste, pudo, pudimos, pudieron
poner:	puse, pusiste, puso, pusimos, pusieron
saber:	supe, supiste, supo, supimos, supieron
hacer:	hice, hiciste, hizo, hicimos, hicieron
venir:	vine, viniste, vino, vinimos, vinieron
querer:	quise, quisiste, quiso, quisimos, quisieron
decir:	dije, dijiste, dijo, dijimos, dijeron
traer:	traje, trajiste, trajo, trajimos, trajeron
conducir:	conduje, condujiste, condujo, condujimos, condujeron
traducir:	traduje, tradujiste, tradujo, tradujimos, tradujeron

ATENCIÓN: Notice that the third person singular of the verb **hacer** changes the **c** to **z** in order to maintain the soft sound of the **c** in the infinitive.

◆ All verbs ending in **-ducir** follow the same pattern as the verb **conducir:** **traducir,** *to translate;* **producir,** *to produce.*

—¿Llamaste por teléfono a Juan?   *Did you phone Juan?*

—No, porque él **vino** a mi casa.   *No, because he came to my house.*

—¿Qué **hiciste** ayer?	*What did you do yesterday?*
—Caminé por la ciudad.	*I walked around the city.*
—¿Dónde **pusieron** Uds. el dinero?	*Where did you put the money?*
—Lo **pusimos** en el banco.	*We put it in the bank.*
—Ayer **hubo** una fiesta en casa de Eva.	*Yesterday there was a party at Eva's house.*
—Sí, lo **supe** esta mañana.	*Yes, I found out (about it) this morning.*

ATENCIÓN: Notice that the preterit of **hay** (from the verb **haber**) is **hubo.**

Exercises

A. Complete the following paragraph with the preterit of the verbs in parentheses:

Isabel le escribe una carta a Teresa:

Toledo, 15 de julio de 19..

Querida Teresa:

    Ayer yo _____ (estar) en Madrid, pero no _____ (poder) ir a verte. Salí de Toledo por la mañana y _____ (conducir) por tres horas hasta llegar a Madrid. Allí _____ (tener) que ir al hospital para ver a Gustavo. Caminé por la ciudad y _____ (querer) llamarte por teléfono, pero no _____ (poder) encontrar uno. Como siempre, ayer _____ (hacer) mucho calor. _____ (Venir) de Madrid muy cansada. Esta mañana hablé por teléfono con Ramón. Él me _____ (decir) muchas cosas interesantes. ¡Ah...! Me _____ (poner) el vestido que compré en Madrid y salí con Jorge. El sábado vuelvo a Madrid para verte.

Tu amiga

Isabel

B. Change the underlined verbs to the preterit, to tell us what happened in the past:

1. Él tiene que ir al médico porque está enfermo.
2. ¿Uds. no pueden venir, o no quieren venir?
3. Ella viene aquí y no hace nada.
4. Ellos traen los libros y los ponen en el escritorio.
5. Hay una reunión en la universidad.
6. ¿Qué dices tú?
7. Yo traduzco las cartas.
8. Nosotros no lo sabemos.

3. ¿De quién...? for *whose?*

¿**De quién...**? is the interrogative form that is used in Spanish to express *whose.* It can be singular *or* plural:

—¿**De quién** es esta máquina de escribir?	*Whose typewriter is this?*
—Es del contador.	*It's the accountant's.*
—¿**De quiénes** son estos televisores?	*Whose TV sets are these?*
—Éste es de Pedro y ése es mío.	*This one is Pedro's, and that one is mine.*

Exercise

Be an interpreter. Tell us how to say the following in Spanish:

1. Whose typewriter is that?
2. Whose books are these? The accountant's?
3. Whose car is this?
4. Whose raincoat is this?
5. Whose umbrellas are these?

4. The imperfect tense

A. There are two simple past tenses in Spanish: the preterit, which you studied in Lessons 10 and 11, and the imperfect.

To form the imperfect tense, add the following endings to the stem of the verb:

The Imperfect Tense		
-ar *Verbs*	**-er *and* -ir *Verbs***	
hablar	comer	vivir
hablaba	comía	vivía
hablabas	comías	vivías
hablaba	comía	vivía
hablábamos	comíamos	vivíamos
hablaban	comían	vivían

◆ Notice that the endings of **-er** and **-ir** verbs are the same. Notice also that there is a written accent mark on the final **í** of **-er** and **-ir** verbs.

◆ The imperfect tense in Spanish is equivalent to three forms in English:

Yo **vivía** en Chicago. $\begin{cases} \textit{I used to live in Chicago.} \\ \textit{I was living in Chicago.} \\ \textit{I lived in Chicago.} \end{cases}$

◆ The Spanish imperfect is used to refer to habitual or repeated actions in the past, with no reference to when they began or ended.

—¿De qué te **hablaba** Pedro?	*What was Pedro talking to you about?*
—Me **hablaba** de la inflación.	*He was talking to me about inflation.*
—¿**Comían** ellos arroz con pollo?	*Did they used to eat chicken and rice?*
—Sí, lo **comían** de vez en cuando.	*Yes, they used to eat it once in a while.*
—¿Dónde **vivía** Ud. en esa época?	*Where did you live in those days?*
—Yo **vivía** en La Habana.	*I lived in Havana.*
—Yo siempre **depositaba** todo mi dinero en el banco.	*I would always deposit all my money in the bank.*
—Yo también **ahorraba** mi dinero, pero ahora lo gasto.	*I used to save my money too, but now I spend it.*

◆ The imperfect is also used to describe actions or events that the speaker views as in the process of happening in the past, again with no reference to when they began or ended.

Empezábamos a estudiar cuando él vino.	*We were beginning to study when he came.*

Exercise

Complete the following sentences with the imperfect tense of the verbs in this list. Use each verb once:

acostarse	preferir	servir	ahorrar
gastar	vivir	tener	hablar
poder	dar	dormir	depositar
comenzar			

1. Ellos no _____ ir a la universidad porque las clases _____ a las ocho de la mañana.
2. Mamá me _____ dinero para comprar café.
3. En esa época yo _____ en Montevideo.
4. ¿Tú _____ todo tu dinero en el banco o lo _____?
5. ¿Qué _____ Uds.? ¿Arroz con pollo o sopa?

6. Yo no _____ muy bien por la noche.
7. Papá siempre _____ su dinero.
8. Nosotros _____ muy temprano porque _____ que ir a trabajar.
9. Yo siempre _____ la sopa.
10. Nosotros _____ de la inflación de vez en cuando.

B. There are only three irregular verbs in the imperfect tense: **ser, ir,** and **ver.**

ser	ir	ver
era	iba	veía
eras	ibas	veías
era	iba	veía
éramos	íbamos	veíamos
eran	iban	veían

—¿Dónde vivías tú cuando **eras** niño?

Where did you live when you were a child?

—Yo vivía en Arizona cuando **era** niño.

I lived in Arizona when I was a child.

—Los vi esta mañana en la calle Quinta. ¿Adónde **iban** Uds.?

I saw you this morning on Fifth Street. Where were you going?

—**Íbamos** a la escuela.

We were going to school.

—¿Cecilia **veía** a sus abuelos todos los sábados?

Did Cecilia used to see her grandparents every Saturday?

—**Veía** a su abuela a veces, pero casi nunca **veía** a su abuelo.

She used to see her grandmother sometimes, but she hardly ever saw her grandfather.

Exercises

A. Change the verbs according to the new subjects. Make any additional changes needed:

1. Cuando yo **era** niña vivía con mis abuelos. (nosotros / tú / Gustavo / ellos / Uds.)
2. Ellos casi nunca **iban** a la escuela. (Yo / María / Nosotros / Tú / Uds.)
3. Nosotros **veíamos** que venía la inflación. (Ud. / Ellos / Yo / Tú / el Presidente)

B. Tell us what you used to do:

1. ¿Dónde vivía Ud. cuando era niño(a)?
2. ¿A qué escuela iba Ud.?
3. ¿Iban Uds. al cine a veces?
4. ¿Veía Ud. a sus abuelos todos los sábados?
5. ¿Hablaban Uds. español cuando eran niños?
6. Cuando Ud. era chico(a), ¿qué hacía los domingos?

Vocabulary

COGNATES

la **inflación**   inflation
La **Habana**   Havana

NOUNS

la **abuela**   grandmother
el **abuelo**   grandfather
los **abuelos**   grandparents
el **arroz**   rice
el, la **contador(a)**   accountant
la **fiesta**   party
el **gobierno**   government
la **máquina de escribir**
   typewriter
la **niña**   child, girl
el **niño**   child, boy
el **pollo**   chicken
el **puesto**   job
el **televisor**   TV set

VERBS

ahorrar   to save (*money*)
caminar   to walk
depositar   to deposit
gastar   to spend (*money*)

ADJECTIVES

todo(a)   all
todos(as)   every

OTHER WORDS
AND EXPRESSIONS

arroz con pollo   chicken with rice
a veces   sometimes
casi nunca   hardly ever
¿cuánto tiempo?   how long?
¿de quién?   whose?
de vez en cuando   once in a
   while
en esa época   in those days
llamar por teléfono   to phone
media hora   half an hour
por   around, by, through

EN EL LABORATORIO

The following material is to be used with the tape in the language laboratory.

I. Vocabulary

Repeat each word after the speaker. When repeating words that are cognates, notice the difference in pronunciation between English and Spanish.

Cognates:	la inflación La Habana
Nouns:	la abuela el abuelo los abuelos el arroz el contador la fiesta el gobierno la máquina de escribir la niña el niño el pollo el puesto el televisor
Verbs:	ahorrar caminar depositar gastar
Adjectives:	todo todos
Other words *and expressions:*	arroz con pollo a veces casi nunca ¿cuánto tiempo? ¿de quién? de vez en cuando en esa época llamar por teléfono media hora por

II. Structure Practice

A. Express how long the following has been going on, using the expression **hace...que** instead of **llevar.** Repeat the correct answer after the speaker's confirmation. Listen to the model:

Modelo: **Llevo** tres años viviendo en La Habana.
Hace tres años **que** vivo en La Habana.

B. Answer the following questions, using the cue provided. Repeat the correct answer after the speaker's confirmation. Listen to the model:

Modelo: —¿Qué tuviste que hacer ayer?   (estudiar español)
—Tuve que estudiar español.

1. (vestidos)
2. (anoche)
3. (los estudiantes)
4. (a las siete)
5. (en la mesa)
6. (nada)

149

C. Change the following to the imperfect to talk about what these people used to do:

Modelo: Mis abuelos **hablan** en español.
           Mis abuelos **hablaban** en español.

1. Yo voy a la universidad todos los días.
2. Nosotros no vemos a nuestros amigos.
3. Yo tengo un buen puesto.
4. Él es mi profesor.
5. Ellos comen arroz con pollo a veces.
6. Ud. me escribe de vez en cuando.

III.   *Listening and Comprehension*

Listen carefully to the dialogue that follows. It will be read twice.

(*Dialogue*)

Now the speaker will make statements concerning the conversation you just heard. After each statement, say whether it is true (**verdadero**) or false (**falso**). The speaker will confirm the correct answer.

LESSON 12

1. The past progressive
2. The preterit contrasted with the imperfect
3. Changes in meaning with the imperfect and preterit of **conocer, saber, querer,** and **poder**
4. **En** and **a** as the equivalent of *at*

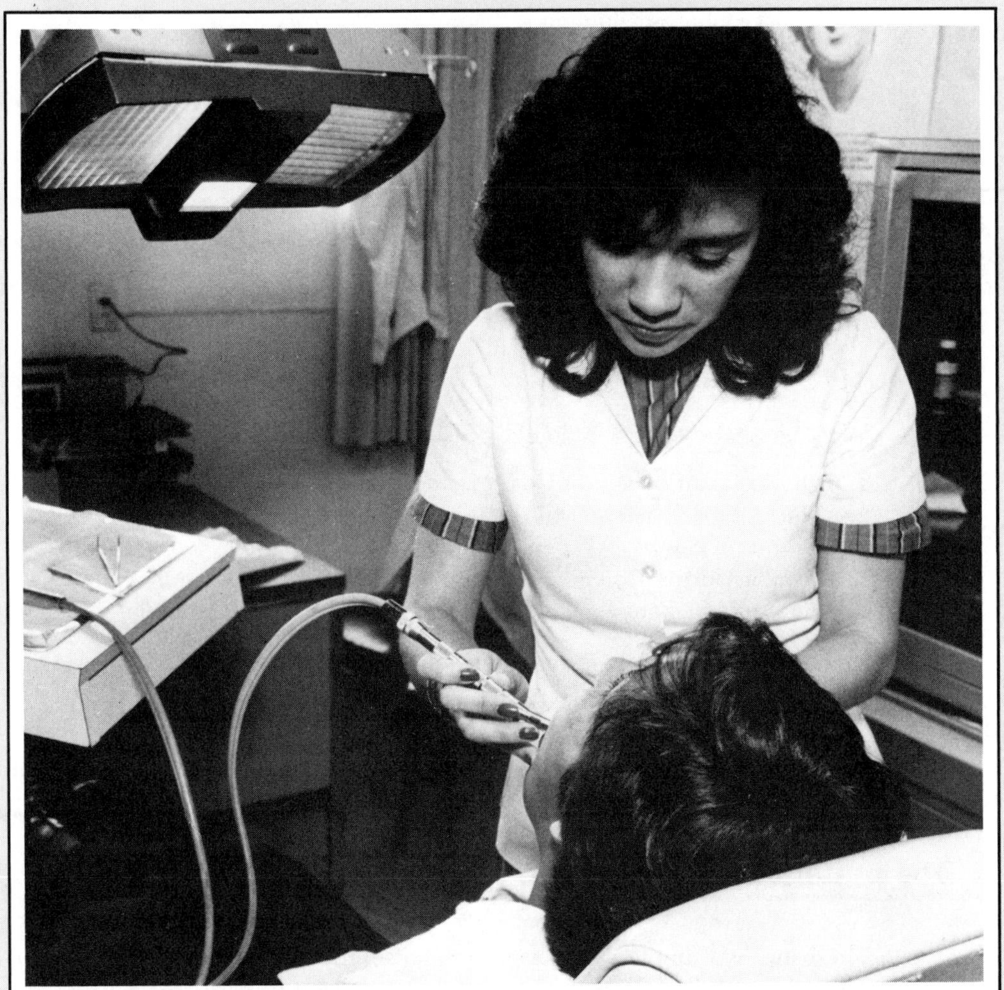

1. The past progressive

The past progressive indicates an action in progress in the past. It is formed with the imperfect tense of the verb **estar** and the -ing form of the main verb:

—¿En qué **estabas pensando** tú cuando tu coche chocó con el ómnibus?

What were you thinking about when your car collided with the bus?

—**Estaba pensando** en todas las cuentas que tengo que pagar.

I was thinking about all the bills (that) I have to pay.

—¿Qué **estaba haciendo** la secretaria cuando Ud. la llamó?

What was the secretary doing when you called her?

—**Estaba escribiendo** a máquina.

She was typing.

—¿Qué **estaban haciendo** Uds. cuando llegó el policía?

What were you doing when the policeman arrived?

—**Estábamos leyendo** el periódico.

We were reading the paper.

—¿A quién **estaban esperando** los niños?

Who were the children waiting for?

—**Estaban esperando** al señor García.

They were waiting for Mr. García.

Exercise

What were these people doing? Tell us, using the information provided:

1. ¿Qué estaban haciendo Uds. cuando llegó el policía?   (dormir)
2. ¿Qué estabas haciendo tú con esa pluma?   (escribir)
3. ¿En quién estaba Ud. pensando cuando yo le hablé?   (en mi padre)
4. ¿Estaba Ud. escribiendo a máquina cuando yo vine?   (no)
5. ¿Con quién estaba hablando Ud. por teléfono cuando yo lo (la) vi?   (con mi hermano)
6. ¿Qué estaban leyendo Uds.?   (el periódico)
7. Esta mañana mi auto chocó con un ómnibus. ¿En qué cree Ud. que yo estaba pensando?   (en los estudiantes)
8. ¿Estaban Uds. hablando de la inflación o de las cuentas que tienen que pagar?   (de la inflación)

2. The preterit contrasted with the imperfect

There are two simple past tenses in Spanish: the imperfect and the preterit. The difference between the two can be visualized this way:

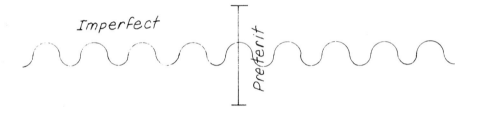

The continuous moving line of the imperfect represents an action or state as it was taking place in the past. We don't know when the action started or ended. The vertical line represents an event as a completed or finished unit in the past, and the preterit records such an action.

The following table summarizes the uses of the preterit and the imperfect:

Preterit	Imperfect
1. Records, narrates, and reports an independent act or event as a completed and undivided whole, regardless of its duration. 2. Sums up a condition or state viewed as a whole.	1. Describes an action in progress at a certain time in the past. 2. Indicates a continuous and habitual action: *used to . . .*[1] 3. Describes a physical, mental, or emotional state or condition in the past. 4. Expresses time in the past. 5. Is used in indirect speech.

THE PRETERIT:

—¿A qué hora **se acostó** Ud. anoche?

What time did you go to bed last night?

—Anoche **me acosté** a las once y media.

Last night I went to bed at eleven-thirty.

—Ayer **estuve** enferma.

Yesterday I was sick.

—Yo también.

Me, too.

THE IMPERFECT:

—Cuando **íbamos** al cine, vimos a María Ortiz.

As (when) we were going to the movies, we saw María Ortiz.

—¿Sí? Ella y yo siempre **íbamos** juntas de vacaciones.

Really? She and I always used to go on vacation together.

---

[1]Note that this use of the imperfect also corresponds to the English *would*, when used to describe a repeated action in the past: **Cuando yo era niña, comía pollo *todos los domingos.*** *When I was a child, I used to eat chicken every Sunday. (When I was a child, I would eat chicken every Sunday.)*

—¿Por qué te fuiste tan
temprano? **Eran** sólo las
ocho de la noche.

Why did you leave so early? It
was only eight o'clock in the
evening.

—Me fui porque no me **sentía**
muy bien.

I left because I wasn't feeling
very well.

—¿Qué dijo Eduardo?

What did Eduardo say?

—Dijo que Ana **estaba** en el
cine.

He said Ana was at the movies.

ATENCIÓN: In the first two exchanges above, **íbamos** describes an action in
progress; while in the fourth exchange, **sentía** describes a physical state.
These verbs in the imperfect act as background for completed actions in
the past, which are expressed by the preterit verbs **vimos, fui** and **dijo.**
Notice an example of indirect speech in the last exchange.

Exercises

A. Complete the following sentences with the preterit or the imperfect of
the verbs in parentheses, as needed:

1. Anoche él y yo _____ (ir) al cine juntos.
2. Cuando nosotros _____ (ser) chicos, _____ (ir) a casa de nuestros
   abuelos.
3. _____ (ser) las cuatro de la tarde cuando él _____ (llegar).
4. Ayer Roberto me _____ (decir) que _____ (necesitar) el coche.
5. La semana pasada yo _____ (estar) muy enfermo también.
6. Yo _____ (venir) por la calle Octava cuando _____ (ver) a los niños
   que _____ (ir) al cine.
7. Anoche ellos _____ (irse) porque no _____ (sentirse) bien.
8. Yo siempre los _____ (ver) cuando ellos _____ (ir) al teatro.
9. Ellos no _____ (estar) en casa anoche.
10. ¿Qué hora _____ (ser) cuando Uds. lo _____ (ver)?

B. We want to know about you. Answer the following questions:

1. ¿Dónde vivía Ud. cuando era niño(a)?
2. ¿Hablaba Ud. inglés o español con sus padres?
3. ¿A dónde iba todos los veranos?
4. ¿Veía Ud. a sus abuelos a menudo?
5. ¿A dónde fue Ud. anoche?
6. ¿A quién vio?
7. ¿Qué hora era cuando Ud. volvió a su casa ayer?
8. ¿Estuvo Ud. enfermo(a) ayer?
9. ¿Le dijo su profesor(a) que Ud. hablaba bien el español?
10. ¿Cómo se sentía Ud. hoy cuando salió de su casa?

3. Changes in meaning with the imperfect and preterit of conocer, saber, querer, and poder

In Spanish, a few verbs change their meaning when used in the preterit or the imperfect:

Preterit		Imperfect	
conocer		**conocer**	
conocí	*I met*	conocía	*I knew, I was acquainted with*
saber		**saber**	
supe	*I found out, I learned*	sabía	*I knew (a fact, how to)*
querer		**querer**	
no quise	*I refused*	no quería	*I didn't want to*
poder		**poder**	
pude	*I succeeded, I was able*	podía	*I could, I had the ability or chance*

—Mario, ¿**conocías** a la cuñada de Luisa?
—No, la **conocí** ayer.

Mario, did you know Louise's sister-in-law?
No, I met her yesterday.

—Rita, ¿**sabías** que teníamos examen hoy?
—No, lo **supe** esta mañana.

Rita, did you know that we had an exam today?
No, I found out this morning.

—¿Por qué no **fuiste** el domingo a la fiesta?
—Porque Carlos no **quiso** llevarme. Tuve que quedarme en casa.

Why didn't you go to the party on Sunday?
Because Carlos refused to take me. I had to stay home.

—Ramón, ayer me dijiste que **podías** ayudarme con la tarea y no viniste.

Raymond, yesterday you told me you could help me with the homework, and you didn't come.

—No **pude** salir porque mamá estaba enferma.

I wasn't able to go out because mother was sick.

Exercise

Be an interpreter, Tell us how to say the following in Spanish:

1. We met Julia's sister-in-law.
2. She said she couldn't help you with the homework.

3. My father-in-law wasn't able to take his wife to the party.
4. Yesterday they found out that they had an exam.
5. I didn't know your mother-in-law.
6. He refused to help me.
7. Did you know my address and my telephone number?

4. **En** and **a** as the equivalent of *at*

A. **En** is used in Spanish as the equivalent of *at* to indicate a certain place or location:

—¿Dónde están los chicos? ¿No están **en** casa?   *Where are the boys? Aren't they (at) home?*

—No, están **en** la estación de policía.   *No, they are at the police station.*

—¿Qué hacen allí?   *What are they doing there?*

—Tuvieron un accidente **en** la esquina de Domínguez y Figueroa.   *They had an accident at the corner of Domínguez and Figueroa.*

B. **A** is used in Spanish as the equivalent of *at*

1. To refer to a specific moment in time:

—¿Cuándo tuvieron el accidente?   *When did they have the accident?*

—Esta mañana **a** las once.   *This morning at eleven.*

2. To indicate direction towards a point after the verb **llegar:**

—¿Cuándo llegaron **al** aeropuerto?   *When did they arrive at the airport?*

—Llegaron **al** aeropuerto ayer.   *They arrived at the airport yesterday.*

Exercise

¿**En** or **a**? Which one will it be?

1. Ellos están _____ la universidad.
2. Hoy no voy a estar _____ casa.
3. Mamá llegó _____ aeropuerto _____ las diez y media.
4. Llegó _____ la estación de policía.
5. Estoy _____ la esquina de Montevideo y Séptima.
6. El accidente fue _____ las ocho.
7. ¿Están _____ el aeropuerto?
8. Tuvimos un accidente cuando llegamos _____ la esquina.

Vocabulary

COGNATES

el **accidente** accident	el **policía** policeman
el **aeropuerto** airport	la **policía** police (*force*)
la **estación** station	las **vacaciones**[1] vacation
el **examen** exam	

NOUNS

la **cuñada**   sister-in-law
el **cuñado**   brother-in-law
la **esquina**   corner
la **tarea**   homework

VERBS

ayudar (a)   to help
chocar (con)   to collide, to run into
pensar (en) (e:ie)   to think
quedarse   to stay, to remain
sentir(se) (e:ie)   to feel

OTHER WORDS
AND EXPRESSIONS

allí   there
en casa   at home
escribir a máquina   to type
ir de vacaciones   to go on vacation
juntos(as)   together
sólo, solamente   only

---

[1]**Vacaciones** is always used in the plural form in Spanish.

EN EL LABORATORIO

The following material is to be used with the tape in the language laboratory.

I. Vocabulary

Repeat each word after the speaker. When repeating words that are cognates, notice the difference in pronunciation between English and Spanish.

Cognates:	el accidente el aeropuerto la estación el examen el policía la policía las vacaciones
Nouns:	la cuñada el cuñado la esquina la tarea
Verbs:	ayudar chocar pensar (en) quedarse sentir sentirse
Other words and expressions:	allí en casa escribir a máquina ir de vacaciones juntos sólo solamente

II. Structure Practice

A. Change the following from the imperfect to the past progressive. Repeat the correct answer after the speaker's confirmation. Listen to the model:

Modelo: Yo **comía** en la cafetería.
Yo **estaba comiendo** en la cafetería.

B. Answer the questions, using the cues provided. Notice the use of the preterit or the imperfect. Repeat the correct answer after the speaker's confirmation. Listen to the model:

Modelo: —¿Qué hora era cuando él llegó?   (las nueve)
—**Eran** las nueve cuando él **llegó.**

1. (en casa)
2. (en México)
3. (esta mañana)
4. (en una fiesta)
5. (sí)
6. (que no podían venir)
7. (sí)
8. (no, pero vine)
9. (No)
10. (a Luisa)

III.   Listening and Comprehension

Listen carefully to the dialogue that follows. It will be read twice.

(*Dialogue*)

Now the speaker will make statements concerning the conversation you just heard. After each statement, say whether it is true (**verdadero**) or false (**falso**). The speaker will confirm the correct answer.

LESSON 13

1. The preterit of stem-changing verbs (**e:i** and **o:u**)
2. The expression **acabar de**
3. Special construction with **gustar, doler,** and **hacer falta**
4. **¿Qué?** and **¿cuál?** for *what?* used with **ser**

1. The preterit of stem-changing verbs (e:i and o:u)

Stem-changing verbs of the **-ir** conjugation, whether they change (e:ie) or (e:i) in the present indicative, change **e** to **i** in the third person singular and plural of the preterit:

sentir		pedir	
sentí	sentimos	pedí	pedimos
sentiste		pediste	
sintió	sintieron	pidió	pidieron

Stem-changing verbs of the **-ir** conjugation that change (**o:ue**) in the present indicative change the **o** to **u** in the third person singular and plural of the preterit:

dormir	
dormí	dormimos
dormiste	
durmió	durmieron

Some other verbs that follow the same pattern are:

preferir	elegir (*to choose*)
divertirse (*to have a good time*)	continuar
mentir (*to lie*)	despedirse (*to say goodbye*)
servir	seguir
repetir	morir (*to die*)

—Sra. López, ¿**sintió** Ud. dolor cuando le sacaron la muela?

Mrs. López, did you feel (any) pain when they took out your tooth?

—No, no sentí nada.

No, I didn't feel anything.

—¿Cuántas horas **durmió** Ud. anoche?

How many hours did you sleep last night?

—Yo dormí seis horas, pero Ana y Luis sólo **durmieron** tres.

I slept six hours, but Ana and Luis slept only three.

—¿A quién le **pidieron** Uds. los documentos?

Whom did you ask for the documents?

—Se los pedimos al director.

We asked the director (for them).

Exercise

Complete the sentences with the preterit of the verb in parentheses:

1. Ellos _____ (despedirse) de Eva en el aeropuerto.
2. Ayer yo no _____ (sentir) dolor cuando me sacaron la muela.
3. Ella no me _____ (mentir). Me dijo la verdad.
4. ¿_____ (servir) ellos los refrescos o los _____ (servir) tú?
5. El hijo de Carmen no _____ (conseguir) el puesto.
6. Pedro _____ (morir) en el accidente de anoche.
7. ¿Dónde _____ (dormir) Uds. anoche? Yo _____ (dormir) en el sofá.
8. ¿A quién le _____ (pedir) Ud. la maleta?
9. María _____ (elegir) el vestido rojo.
10. Ellos _____ (divertirse) mucho en la fiesta ayer.

2. The expression acabar de

Acabar de means *to have just*. This formula is used in Spanish:

| *subject* + **acabar** (present tense) + **de** + *infinitive* |
| Pedro   acaba   de   llegar. |

—¿Tiene Elena un puesto?   *Does Elena have a job?*
—Sí, **acaba de encontrar** uno.   *Yes, she has just found one.*

—¿Quieres un poco de sopa?   *Do you want some soup?*
—No, gracias. **Acabo de**   *No, thanks. I have just eaten.*
   comer.

◆ Notice that the conjugation of **acabar** is regular.

Exercise

Tell us what everybody has just done by completing the following sentences with the correct form of **acabar de** + *infinitive:*

1. Juan _____ a esta ciudad.   *(has just arrived)*
2. Yo _____ esta casa.   *(have just bought)*
3. Ellas _____ un puesto.   *(have just found)*
4. Él _____ un poco de carne.   *(has just eaten)*
5. Elena _____.   *(has just gotten dressed)*
6. Uds. _____ a la oficina.   *(have just gone)*
7. Elena _____ la carta.   *(has just written)*
8. Tú _____ la revista.   *(have just read)*

9. Yo _____. *(have just bathed)*
10. Ellos _____ el periódico. *(have just lent me)*
11. Nosotros _____ las maletas. *(have just found)*
12. Marta y Ana _____. *(have just gotten up)*

3. Special construction with **gustar, doler,** and **hacer falta**

A.   The verb **gustar** means *to like (something or somebody).* A special construction is required to translate the English *to like.* This is done by making the English direct object the subject of the Spanish sentence. The English subject then becomes the indirect object of the Spanish sentence.

English:	*I like your suit.*	
	subj. d.o.	
Spanish:	**Me gusta tu traje.**	
	i.o. subj.	
Literally:	*Your suit is pleasing (appeals) to me.*	

The two most commonly used forms of **gustar** are: (1) the third-person singular **gusta** if the subject is singular or if **gustar** is followed by one or more infinitives; and (2) the third-person plural **gustan** if the subject is plural.

Indirect Object

Pronouns

Me			ese edificio
Te	gusta		
Le			comer y beber
Nos			
Les	gustan		esos modelos

Note that the verb **gustar** agrees with the subject of the sentence—that is, the person or thing *being liked.*

Me gust**a el café.**   Le gust**an las chicas altas.**

Note that the person who does the liking is the *indirect object.*

Me gusta el café.   **Le** gustan las chicas altas.
I.O.   I.O.

—¿**Les gusta** el café?   *Do you like coffee?*
—Sí, **nos gusta** mucho el café,   *Yes, we like coffee very much,*
   pero **nos gusta** más el té.   *but we like tea better.*

ATENCIÓN: Note that the words **más** (*better*) and **mucho** immediately follow **gustar.**

B. The verbs **doler** (*to hurt, to ache*) and **hacer falta** (*to need*) have the same construction as **gustar:**

—¿Qué **les hace falta,** señoras?   *What do you need, ladies?*
—**Nos hace falta** otra toalla y   *We need another towel and*
   jabón.   *soap.*

—¿Por qué estás tomando   *Why are you taking aspirins?*
   aspirinas?
—Porque **me duele** la cabeza.   *Because my head hurts.*

ATENCIÓN: In Spanish, the definite article is used instead of the possessive adjective with parts of the body.

Exercises

A. Answer the following questions:

1. ¿Qué le duele?
2. ¿Qué le hace falta a Ud.?
3. ¿Qué te gusta más, el piano o la radio?
4. ¿Les hacen falta a Uds. más toallas?
5. ¿Le duele a Ud. la cabeza?
6. ¿Te gusta caminar?
7. ¿Cuándo toman Uds. aspirinas?
8. ¿Les gusta a Uds. el español?

B. Tell us which you and these people like.

Modelo: (**José**) el café
          Le gusta el café.

1. (Elsa) ese modelo.
2. (nosotros) el español
3. (yo) esa corbata
4. (ellos) comer y beber
5. (tú) las fiestas
6. (Uds.) los refrescos

C. Be an interpreter. Tell us how to say the following in Spanish:

1. They like those buildings.
2. I need a suit.
3. I like this model.
4. We don't like to take aspirin.

5. Does your head hurt, madam?
6. Do you need towels or soap?

4. ¿Qué? and ¿cuál? for *what* used with **ser**

A.   When asking for a definition, use ¿qué? to translate *what:*

—¿**Qué** es un termómetro?   *What is a thermometer?*
—Un termómetro es un   *A thermometer is an instrument*
instrumento que usamos   *we use to measure*
para medir la temperatura.   *temperature.*

B.   When asking for a choice, use ¿cuál? to translate *what.* ¿Cuál? carries the idea of selection from among many objects or ideas:

—¿**Cuál** es su número de   *What is your social security*
seguro social?   *number?*
—Mi número de seguro social   *My social security number is*
es 243-50-8139.   *243-50-8139.*

—¿**Cuáles** son sus ideas sobre   *What are your ideas about the*
la economía?   *economy?*
—Yo no sé nada de economía.   *I don't know anything about*
                                  the economy.

Exercise

Qué or **cual**? Which one will it be?

1. ¿———— es su número de seguro social?
2. ¿———— es un termómetro? ¿Un instrumento para medir la temperatura?
3. ¿———— son sus ideas sobre la economía?
4. ¿———— es su estado civil?
5. ¿———— es un impermeable? ¿Es algo para la lluvia?
6. ¿———— es su número de teléfono?

Vocabulary

COGNATES

la **aspirina** aspirin	el **modelo** model
la **idea** idea	la **temperatura** temperature
el **instrumento** instrument	el **termómetro** thermometer

NOUNS

la **cabeza**   head
el **dolor**   pain
el **edificio**   building
el **jabón**   soap
la **muela**   tooth (*molar*)
el **regalo**   present, gift
la **toalla**   towel
el **traje**   suit
la **velocidad**   speed

VERBS

despedirse (e:i)   to say goodbye
divertirse (e:ie)   to have a good time
doler (o:ue)   to hurt, to ache
elegir (e:i)   to choose, to select
encontrar (o:ue)   to find

gustar   to like, to be pleasing
medir (e:i)   to measure
mentir (e:ie)   to lie
morir (o:ue)   to die
sacar   to take out
tomar   to take
usar   to use

ADJECTIVE

otro(a)   other, another

OTHER WORDS
AND EXPRESSIONS

acabar de   to have just
hacer falta   to need, to lack
sobre   about
un poco de   some, a little

EN EL LABORATORIO

The following material is to be used with the tape in the language laboratory.

I. Vocabulary

Repeat each word after the speaker. When repeating words that are cognates, notice the difference in pronunciation between English and Spanish.

Cognates:	la aspirina la idea el instrumento el modelo la temperatura el termómetro
Nouns:	la cabeza el dolor el edificio el jabón la muela el regalo la toalla el traje la velocidad
Verbs:	despedirse divertirse doler elegir encontrar gustar medir mentir morir sacar tomar usar
Adjectives:	otro otra
Other words and expressions:	acabar de hacer falta sobre un poco de

II. Structure Practice

A. Change the verbs according to the new subjects. Repeat the correct answer after the speaker's confirmation. Listen to the model:

Modelo: Yo no lo conseguí.   (ella)
Ella no lo consiguió.

1. (él)
2. (ellos)
3. (Ana)
4. (Ud.)
5. (Uds.)
6. (Ud.)
7. (Luis)
8. (ellos)
9. (Carlos)
10. (los niños)

B. Answer each question, using the expression **acabar de** + *infinitive*. Repeat the correct answer after the speaker's confirmation. Listen to the model:

Modelo: ¿Ya comiste?
Sí, acabo de comer.

C. Restate each statement or question, using **gusta más** to replace **preferir.**
Repeat the correct answer.

Modelo: Yo **prefiero** este traje.
Me gusta más este traje.

1. Tú prefieres ir al cine.
2. Él prefiere ese modelo.
3. Ella prefiere esas habitaciones.
4. Nosotros preferimos tomar café.
5. Uds. prefieren ese hotel.
6. Yo prefiero viajar en avión.

D. Restate each statement or question, using the expression *hacer falta* to
replace *necesitar:*

Modelo: Nosotros **necesitamos** dinero.
Nos hace falta dinero.

1. Yo necesito toallas.
2. Él necesita un coche.
3. Ellos necesitan un escritorio.
4. ¿Tú necesitas lápices?
5. Nosotros necesitamos una casa más grande.

III. Listening and Comprehension

Listen carefully to the dialogue that follows. It will be read twice.

(*Dialogue*)

Now the speaker will make statements concerning the conversation you just
heard. After each statement, say whether it is true (**verdadero**) or false
(**falso**). The speaker will confirm the correct answer.

1. **Hace** meaning *ago*
2. The past participle
3. The present perfect tense
4. The past perfect (pluperfect) tense

1. **Hace** meaning *ago*

In sentences in the preterit and in some cases the imperfect, **hace** + *period of time* is equivalent to the English *ago.* [1]

Llegué **hace dos años.**   *I arrived two years ago.*

When **hace** is placed at the beginning of the sentence, the construction is as follows:

> **Hace** + period of time + **que** + verb (*preterit*)
> **Hace** + **dos años**   + **que** + **llegué.**

—¿Cuánto tiempo **hace que** llegó?   *How long ago did you arrive?*

—Llegué **hace dos horas.**   *I arrived two hours ago.*

—¿Cuánto tiempo **hace que** Uds. se casaron?   *How long ago did you get married?*

—**Hace un año que** nos casamos.   *We got married a year ago.*

Exercises

A. Tell us something about yourself:

1. ¿Cuánto tiempo hace que comenzó la clase?
2. ¿Cuánto tiempo hace que Ud. comió?
3. ¿Cuánto tiempo hace que Uds. empezaron a estudiar español?
4. ¿Cuánto tiempo hace que Uds. terminaron la lección trece?
5. ¿Cuánto tiempo hace que Ud. vino a esta ciudad?
6. ¿Cuánto tiempo hace que sus padres se casaron?

B. Be an interpreter. Tell us how to say the following in Spanish:

1. They bought the building five years ago.
2. I took two aspirins two hours ago.
3. How long ago did you arrive, Mr. Pérez?
4. We came to this city a month ago.

---

[1]Sometimes the imperfect may be used with **hacer** to mean *ago: Hace dos años,* **yo vivía en Buenos Aires.** (*Two years ago, I lived in Buenos Aires.*)

2. The past participle

A. Forms

The past participle of regular verbs is formed by adding the following endings to the stem of the verb:

Past Participle Endings		
-ar *Verbs*	**-er** *Verbs*	**-ir** *Verbs*
habl- **ado**	ten- **ido**	ven- **ido**

The following verbs have irregular past participles in Spanish:

abrir	**abierto**	morir	**muerto**
cubrir	**cubierto**	poner	**puesto**
decir	**dicho**	ver	**visto**
escribir	**escrito**	volver	**vuelto**
hacer	**hecho**	romper	**roto**

B. Past participles used as adjectives

In Spanish, most past participles may be used as adjectives. As such, they agree in number and gender with the nouns they modify:

—¿Tuviste un accidente?	*Did you have an accident?*
—Sí, y tengo **la pierna rota.**	*Yes, and I have a broken leg.*
—¿Y el brazo?	*And your arm?*
—No, **el brazo** no está **roto.**	*No, my arm is not broken.*
—¿**Las ventanas** están **abiertas?**	*Are the windows open?*
—No, están **cerradas.**	*No, they are closed.*

Exercises

A. Give the past participles of the following verbs:

1. dormir	6. cubrir	11. caminar	16. abrir
2. romper	7. recibir	12. pedir	17. ver
3. estar	8. hacer	13. decir	18. volver
4. comer	9. cerrar	14. comprar	19. aprender
5. poner	10. ser	15. morir	20. escribir

B. Using the elements from the two columns and the verb **estar,** create descriptive sentences. You may use a verb more than once:

Modelo: ventanas / cerrar
Las ventanas **están cerradas.**

los hombres	servir
Pedro y yo	romper
el libro	cerrar
la carta	morir
los instrumentos	cubrir
las puertas	escribir (en español)
el café	hacer (de madera)
la mesa	abrir

3. The present perfect tense

The present perfect tense is formed by using the present tense of the auxiliary verb **haber** and the past participle of the verb to be conjugated.

This tense is equivalent to the use, in English, of the auxiliary verb *have* + past participle, as in *I have spoken.*

Present of **haber**[1] (*to have*)	
he	hemos
has	
ha	han

The Present Perfect Tense			
	hablar	**tener**	**venir**
yo	**he** hablado	**he** tenido	**he** venido
tú	**has** hablado	**has** tenido	**has** venido
Ud. él ella	**ha** hablado	**ha** tenido	**ha** venido
nosotros	**hemos** hablado	**hemos** tenido	**hemos** venido
Uds. ellos ellas	**han** hablado	**han** tenido	**han** venido

[1]Note that the English verb *to have* has two equivalents in Spanish: **haber** (used only as an auxiliary verb) and **tener.**

—¿**Ha terminado** Ud. su
lección de matemáticas?
—No, no la **he terminado**
todavía.

*Have you finished your math
lesson?*
No, I haven't finished it yet.

—¿Cuántas veces **ha venido**
ella a este lugar?
—Ella **ha venido** muchas veces.
—¿De qué **han hablado** Uds.?
—**Hemos hablado** de negocios.

*How many times has she come
to this place?*
She has come many times.
What have you talked about?
We have talked about business.

—¿Qué les **ha dicho** el
gerente?
—El gerente nos **ha dicho** que
tenemos que terminar el
trabajo para mañana.

*What has the manager said to
you?*
*The manager has told us that
we have to finish the work
for tomorrow.*

ATENCIÓN: Note that when the past participle is part of a perfect tense, it is
invariable and cannot be separated from the auxiliary verb **haber**:

Siempre **ha escrito** las cartas a máquina.
*He has **always** typed the letters.*

Exercise

Tell us what you and these people have or haven't done:

1. Ellos / terminar / lecciones
2. Ella / venir / a estudiar matemáticas
3. Yo / siempre / hacer bien / trabajo
4. Nosotros / escribirlo / dos veces
5. Tú / nunca / abrir / esa ventana
6. Ud. / no decírselo

4. The past perfect (pluperfect) tense

The past perfect tense is formed by using the imperfect tense of the auxiliary
verb **haber** and the past participle of the verb to be conjugated.

This tense is equivalent to the use, in English, of the auxiliary verb *had* +
past participle, as in *I had spoken.*

Imperfect of **haber**	
había	habíamos
habías	
había	habían

The Past Perfect Tense			
	estudiar	beber	ir
yo	había estudiado	había bebido	había ido
tú	habías estudiado	habías bebido	habías ido
Ud. él ella	había estudiado	había bebido	había ido
nosotros	habíamos estudiado	habíamos bebido	habíamos ido
Uds. ellos ellas	habían estudiado	habían bebido	habían ido

—¿No trajiste las sábanas?　　　*Didn't you bring the sheets?*
—Ernesto ya las **había traído.**　*Ernesto had already brought*
　　　　　　　　　　　　　　　　them.

—¿De qué **había hablado** el　　*What had Dr. Peña talked*
　doctor Peña?　　　　　　　　　*about?*
—El Dr. Peña **había hablado**　　*Dr. Peña had talked about his*
　de sus experimentos con　　　*experiments with tropical*
　plantas tropicales.　　　　　　*plants.*

—¿Para qué **habían venido**　　*Why (what for) had they come?*
　ellos?
—**Habían venido** para ver al　　*They had come to see the*
　administrador.　　　　　　　　*administrator.*

Exercise

Using the verbs provided, complete these dialogues in the pluperfect tense:

hablar/salir
1. —¿Habló el profesor de sus experimentos con plantas tropicales?
　　—No, él ya _____ de eso.
　　—¿Jorge vino a la clase?
　　—No, él ya _____ para México.

casarse/decir
2. —¡Yo no sabía que tú _____!
　　—¿No te lo dijo Ernesto? Yo se lo _____ a él.

comprar
3. —¿Uds. compraron las sábanas para Eva y Luis?
　　—No, nosotros ya les _____ otro regalo.

escribir/escribir
4. —¿A quién le _____ Uds. sobre ese problema?
　　—Le _____ al administrador.

Vocabulary

COGNATES

el, la **administrador(a)** administrator   la **planta** plant
el **experimento** experiment   **tropical** tropical
las **matemáticas** mathematics

NOUNS

el **brazo** arm
el **lugar** place
los **negocios** business
la **pierna** leg
la **sábana** sheet
el **trabajo** work, job
la **vez** time (*in a series*)

VERBS

casarse (con) to get married
cubrir to cover
romper to break
terminar, acabar to finish

EN EL LABORATORIO

The following material is to be used with the tape in the language laboratory.

I. Vocabulary

Repeat each word after the speaker. When repeating words that are cognates, notice the difference in pronunciation between English and Spanish.

Cognates:	el administrador el experimento las matemáticas la planta tropical
Nouns:	el brazo el lugar los negocios la pierna la sábana el trabajo la vez
Verbs:	acabar casarse cubrir romper terminar
Other words and expressions:	todos todas

II. Structure Practice

A. Answer each question, using the cues provided below. Repeat the correct answer after the speaker's confirmation. Listen to the model:

1. tres meses
2. quince minutos
3. cinco años
4. dos semanas
5. cuatro horas

B. Answer each question using each past participle as an adjective. Repeat the correct answer after the speaker's confirmation. Listen to the model:

Modelo: —¿Terminaste la carta?
           —Sí, ya *está terminada.*

C. Change each sentence to the present perfect tense. Repeat the correct answer following the speaker's confirmation. Listen to the model:

Modelo: Yo compro los regalos.
           Yo *he comprado* los regalos.

D. Change the verbs according to the new subjects. Repeat the correct answer after the speaker's confirmation. Listen to the model:

Yo no lo había hecho todavía.
(Uds. / Nosotras / Tú / Eva / Ellos / Ud.)

III.   Listening and Comprehension

Listen carefully to the narration that follows. It will be read twice.

(*Narration*)

Now the speaker will make statements concerning the narration you just heard. After each statement, say whether it is true (**verdadero**) or false (**falso**). The speaker will confirm the correct answer.

LESSON 15

1. Uses of **hacía...que**
2. The future tense
3. The conditional tense
4. Some uses of the prepositions **a, de,** and **en**

1. Uses of **hacía...que**

Hacía...que is used:

1. To describe a situation that had been going on for a period of time and was still going on at a given moment in the past:

—¿Cuánto tiempo **hacía que** Ud. vivía allí?	*How long had you been living there?*
—**Hacía diez años que** vivía allí.	*I had been living there for ten years.*

2. To describe a situation that had been going on in the past when something else happened:

—¿Cuánto tiempo **hacía que** esperabas cuando él llegó?	*How long had you been waiting when he arrived?*
—**Hacía dos horas y media que** esperaba cuando él llegó.	*I had been waiting for two and a half hours when he arrived.*

ATENCIÓN: Notice that in the **hacía...que** construction, the verb that follows it is in the imperfect tense:

—¿Cuánto tiempo **hacía que estudiabas?**	*How long had you been studying?*
—**Hacía tres años que estudiaba.**	*I had been studying for three years.*

Exercise

Be an interpreter. Tell us how to say the following in Spanish:

1. She had been living there for two months when she met him.
2. How long had you been waiting there?
3. They had been studying for four years.
4. I had been working for two weeks when she arrived.
5. How long had you known him?

2. The future tense

A. The English equivalent of the Spanish future is *will* or *shall* + a verb. As you have already learned, Spanish also uses the construction **ir a** + infinitive or the present tense with a time expression to express future actions or states, very much like the English present tense or the expression *going to*.

Vamos a ir al cine esta noche.	*We're going (We'll go) to*
or: **Iremos** al cine esta noche.	*the movies tonight.*

Anita **toma** el examen mañana.	*Anita is taking (will take)*
or: Anita **tomará** el examen mañana.	*the exam tomorrow.*

ATENCIÓN: The Spanish future is *not* used to express willingness, as is the English future. In Spanish this is expressed with the verb **querer**.
¿Quieres llamar a Tomás? *Will you call Tomás?*

Most Spanish verbs are regular in the future. The infinitive serves as the stem of almost all Spanish verbs. The endings are the same for all three conjugations.

The Future Tense			
Infinitive		*Stem*	*Endings*
trabajar	yo	trabajar-	**é**
aprender	tú	aprender-	**ás**
escribir	Ud.	escribir-	**á**
hablar	él	hablar-	**á**
decidir	ella	decidir-	**á**
entender	nosotros	entender-	**emos**
caminar	Uds.	caminar-	**án**
perder	ellos	perder-	**án**
recibir	ellas	recibir-	**án**

ATENCIÓN: Notice that all the endings, except the one for the **nosotros** form, have written accent marks.

—**¿Irán** Uds. a la conferencia sobre la civilización y la cultura de México?	*Will you go to the lecture on the civilization and the culture of Mexico?*
—Sí, **iremos** todos, sin falta.	*Yes, we'll all go without fail.*
—¿Cree Ud. que el paciente **mejorará** pronto?	*Do you think the patient will improve soon?*
—Yo creo que sí.	*I think so.*
—¿Cuándo **estarán** listos los análisis?	*When will the tests be ready?*
—**Estarán** listos mañana por la tarde.	*They will be ready tomorrow afternoon.*

Exercise

This is what generally happens. Now tell us what *will happen* in the future:

1. Nosotros somos los primeros.
2. Los pacientes mejoran pronto.
3. Los alumnos entienden la lección.
4. Los análisis están listos.
5. Él no entiende los problemas de la economía.
6. Tú aprendes español.
7. Yo compro las sábanas.
8. Uds. deciden a dónde ir.
9. Nosotros escribimos sobre la cultura y la civilización de México.
10. Ella va a clase sin falta.
11. Nosotros caminamos por la ciudad.
12. ¿Van Uds. a la conferencia?

B. A few verbs are irregular in the future tense. These verbs use a modified form of the infinitive as a stem. The endings are the same as the ones for regular verbs:

Infinitive	Stem	Future Tense		
decir	dir-	yo	**dir-**	é
hacer	har-	tú	**har-**	ás
saber	sabr-	Ud.	**sabr-**	á
poder	podr-	ella	**podr-**	á
poner	pondr-	nosotros	**pondr-**	emos
venir	vendr-	Uds.	**vendr-**	án
tener	tendr-	ellos	**tendr-**	án
salir	saldr-	ellas	**saldr-**	án

—¿Les has dicho que habrá una reunión?
Have you told them that there will be a meeting?

—No, se la **diré** después.
No, I'll tell (it to) them later.

—¿Cuándo **sabrán** Uds. el resultado de los análisis?
When will you know the result(s) of the tests?

—Lo **sabremos** la semana próxima.
We will know (it) next week.

—¿**Vendrá** hoy el mecánico a arreglar el coche?
Will the mechanic come today to fix the car?

—Sí, **vendrá** por la tarde.
Yes, he will come in the afternoon.

ATENCIÓN: The future of **hay** is **habrá**.

Exercise

Using the verbs provided, complete these dialogues in the future tense:

decir/decir/tener/saber
1. —¿Qué le _____ Ud. al paciente?
    —Le _____ que _____ que venir mañana.
    —¿Cuándo _____ el resultado de los análisis?
    —Esta tarde.

poder/venir/salir
2. —¿ _____ el mecánico arreglar el coche?
    —Sí, él me ha dicho que _____ mañana.
    —Muy bien, porque nosotros _____ para la capital por la noche.

hacer/haber/poner
3. —¿Qué _____ Uds. el domingo?
    —Iremos a la fiesta que _____ en el Club.
    —¿Qué te _____ para ir a la fiesta?
    —El traje azul.

3. The conditional tense

A. The conditional tense in Spanish is equivalent to the conditional in English, expressed by *would* plus *verb.*[1] Like the future tense, the conditional uses the infinitive as the stem and has only one set of endings for all three conjugations:

The Conditional Tense			
Infinitive		*Stem*	*Endings*
trabajar	yo	trabajar-	ía
aprender	tú	aprender-	ías
escribir	Ud.	escribir-	ía
ir	él	ir-	ía
ser	ella	ser-	ía
dar	nosotros	dar-	íamos
servir	Uds.	servir-	ían
estar	ellos	estar-	ían
preferir	ellas	preferir-	ían

[1]The conditional is never used in Spanish as an equivalent of *used to:* **Cuando era pequeño siempre *iba* a la playa.** *When I was little I would always go to the beach.*

—¿**Vendería** Ud. su casa por
cincuenta mil dólares?

*Would you sell your house for
fifty thousand dollars?*

—No, yo no la **vendería** a ese
precio.

*No, I wouldn't sell it at that
price.*

—¿**Preferirían** Uds. ir conmigo
a Europa?

*Would you prefer to go with
me to Europe?*

—Sí, **preferiríamos** ir contigo.

*Yes, we would prefer to go
with you.*

The conditional is also used to describe a future action in relation to the past:

—Mi sobrino **dijo** que
trabajaría en una estación de
servicio el verano próximo.

*My nephew said he would work
at a service station next
summer.*

—¡Buena idea!

Good idea!

Exercise

These people don't agree with Ana's ideas. Using the cues in parentheses,
say what they wouldn't do:

Modelo: Ana va a vender su casa.   (Yo)
        Yo no la *vendería.*

1. Ana va a comprar el coche por ese precio.   (Nosotros)
2. Ana va a escribirle.   (Yo)
3. Ana va a trabajar en la estación de servicio.   (Uds.)
4. Ana va a servir los refrescos.   (Ellos)
5. Ana va a arreglar el coche.   (Tú)
6. Ana va a ir con Pedro.   (Elsa)

B. The same verbs that are irregular in the future are also irregular in the
conditional. The conditional endings are added to the modified form of
the infinitive:

Infinitive	Stem	Conditional Tense		
decir	dir-	yo	**dir-**	ía
hacer	har-	tú	**har-**	ías
saber	sabr-	Ud.	**sabr-**	ía
poder	podr-	ella	**podr-**	ía
poner	pondr-	nosotros	**pondr-**	íamos
venir	vendr-	Uds.	**vendr-**	ían
tener	tendr-	ellos	**tendr-**	ían
salir	saldr-	ellas	**saldr-**	ían

ATENCIÓN: The conditional of **hay** is **habría**.

| —¿Lo **harían** Uds.? | *Would you do it?* |
| —No, no lo **haríamos.** | *No, we wouldn't do it.* |

| —¿**Saldrías** conmigo? | *Would you go out with me?* |
| —No, no **saldría** contigo. | *No, I wouldn't go out with you.* |

| —¿**Podría** él llegar a tiempo? | *Would he be able to arrive on time?* |

| —No, no **podría** llegar a tiempo. | *No, he wouldn't be able to arrive on time.* |

Exercises

A. What did these people say they would do?

Modelo: Dice que lo **hará.**   (Dijo)
Dijo que lo haría.

1. Digo que vendré.   (Dije)
2. Decimos que saldremos.   (Dijimos)
3. Dices que lo pondrás en el banco.   (Dijiste)
4. Ud. dice que lo sabrá mañana.   (Ud. dijo)
5. Dicen que se lo dirán hoy.   (Dijeron)
6. Dice que habrá una reunión.   (Dijo)
7. Digo que no podré ir.   (Dije)
8. Dices que lo tendrás listo hoy.   (Dijiste)

B. Be an interpreter. Tell us how to say the following in Spanish:

1. Would the men arrive on time?
2. My mother wouldn't do it.
3. They wouldn't know what to say.
4. Would you like to go to Europe?
5. Would the mechanic be at the service station?
6. We wouldn't tell (it to) him.
7. Did she say there would be a meeting?
8. I said that she wouldn't be able to work.

4. Some uses of the prepositions **a, de,** and **en**

A. The preposition **a** (*to, at, in*) is used:

1. To introduce the direct object when it is a person,[1] animal, or anything that is given personal characteristics:

---

[1]When the direct object is not a definite person, the personal **a** is not used: **Busco un buen maestro.**

Esperamos **a** los niños.
Llevé **a** mi perro al veterinario.

2. To indicate the time of day:

El análisis estará listo **a** las cinco.

3. After verbs of motion when they are followed by an infinitive, a noun, or a pronoun:

Siempre venimos **a** ver a mi sobrino.

4. After the verbs **enseñar, aprender, comenzar,** and **empezar** when they are followed by an infinitive:

Voy a **empezar a** arreglar el carro.
Él dijo que me **enseñaría a** conducir.

5. After the verb **llegar:**

Llegaremos a Lima mañana sin falta.

B. The preposition **de** (*of, from, about*) indicating possession, the material something is made of, and origin, is used:

1. To refer to a specific time of the day or night:

Dijeron que vendrían a las ocho **de** la noche.

2. With the superlative:

Mi sobrina es la más inteligente **de** la familia.

3. As a synonym of **sobre** or **acerca de** (*about*):

Hablaban **de** los precios de las casas.

C. The preposition **en** (*at, in, on, inside, over*) is used:

1. To refer to a definite place:

Mi coche está **en** la gasolinera.

2. As a synonym of **sobre** (*on*):

Los libros están **en** la mesa.

3. To indicate means of transportation:

Siempre viajábamos **en** autobús.

ATENCIÓN: In México and in most Spanish-speaking countries of Latin America, "**por avión**" is used:

Vamos **por** avión.
Vamos **por** tren.
but
Vamos **en** autobús.
Vamos **en** automóvil.

Exercise

Complete the following sentences using **a, de,** or **en,** as needed:

1. Llegaremos _____ Lima _____ las ocho _____ la mañana.
2. Esperaremos _____ la doctora para ver los análisis.
3. Los niños están _____ casa.
4. Oscar siempre me está hablando _____ su perro.
5. ¿_____ qué hora van _____ empezar _____ estudiar?
6. Vienen _____ enseñarnos _____ conducir.
7. No me gusta viajar _____ avión.
8. Llevé _____ mi perro al veterinario.
9. Esa niña es la más alta _____ la clase.
10. Los libros están _____ el escritorio.

Vocabulary

COGNATES

la **civilización**   civilization
la **cultura**   culture
Europa   Europe
el **mecánico**   mechanic

el, la **paciente**   patient
el **resultado**   result
el, la **veterinario(a)**   veterinary

NOUNS

el **análisis**   test
la **conferencia**   lecture
la **estación de servicio, gasolinera**
  service station
el, la **niño(a)**   child
el **perro**   dog
el **precio**   price
la **sobrina**   niece
el **sobrino**   nephew

VERBS

arreglar   to fix, to arrange
enseñar   to teach
mejorar   to improve
valer   to be worth
vender   to sell

OTHER WORDS AND EXPRESSIONS

a tiempo   on time
después   later, afterwards
estar listo(a)   to be ready
pronto   soon
sin falta   without fail
yo creo que sí   I think so

EN EL LABORATORIO

The following material is to be used with the tape in the language laboratory.

I. Vocabulary

Repeat each word after the speaker. When repeating words that are cognates, notice the difference in pronunciation between English and Spanish.

Cognates:	la civilización la cultura Europa el mecánico el paciente el resultado el veterinario
Nouns:	el análisis la conferencia la estación de servicio la gasolinera la fecha el niño la niña el perro el precio la sobrina el sobrino
Verbs:	arreglar enseñar mejorar valer vender
Other words and expressions:	a tiempo después estar listo pronto sin falta yo creo que sí

II. Structure Practice

A. Answer each question, using the cues provided. Repeat the correct answer after the speaker's confirmation.

1. tres horas
2. cinco años
3. dos meses
4. quince minutos
5. una semana

B. Change each sentence, using the future tense instead of the expression **ir a** + **infinitive**. Repeat the correct answer after the speaker's confirmation. Listen to the model:

Modelo: Vamos a salir muy tarde.
    Saldremos muy tarde.

C. Answer each question, always selecting the second alternative. Repeat the correct answer after the speaker's confirmation. Listen to the model:

Modelo: —¿Comprarías un coche o una casa?
—**Compraría** una casa.

D. Answer the following questions in complete sentences, using the cue words provided. Repeat the correct answer after the speaker's confirmation.

1. María
2. las ocho
3. autobús
4. la mesa
5. Europa
6. hospital
7. Carlos
8. Sí

III.   Listening and Comprehension

Listen carefully to the narration that follows. It will be read twice.

(*Narration*)

Now the speaker will make statements concerning the narration you just heard. After each statement, say whether it is true (**verdadero**) or false (**falso**). The speaker will confirm the correct answer.

TEST YOURSELF

Lesson 11

A. Time expressions with **hacer** and **llevar**

Give two Spanish equivalents for each of the sentences. Follow the models.

Modelos: How long have you lived in California?
      a) **¿Cuánto tiempo hace que vive en California?**
      b) **¿Cuánto tiempo lleva viviendo en California?**

      I have been living in California for two months.
      a) **Hace dos meses que vivo en California.**
      b) **Llevo dos meses viviendo en California.**

1. How long have you been working in Lima?
2. We have been working in Lima for five years.
3. How long have they been waiting?
4. They have been waiting for three hours.
5. How long has she been studying Spanish?
6. She has been studying Spanish for two years.

B. Irregular preterits

Rewrite the sentences according to the new beginnings. Follow the model.

Modelo: Tenemos que salir.   (Ayer)
      Ayer tuvimos que salir.

1. María está muy ocupada.   (Ayer)
2. No pueden venir.   (Anoche)
3. Pongo el dinero en el banco.   (La semana pasada)
4. No haces nada.   (El domingo pasado)
5. Ella viene con Juan.   (Ayer)
6. No queremos venir a clase.   (La semana pasada)
7. Yo no digo nada.   (Anoche)
8. Traemos la máquina de escribir.   (Ayer)
9. Yo conduzco mi coche.   (Anoche)
10. Ellos traducen las lecciones.   (Ayer)

C. **¿De quién...?** for *Whose?*

Ask who these items belong to. Follow the model.

Modelo: esta máquina de escribir
¿De quién es esta máquina de escribir?

1. ese paraguas
2. esos revólveres
3. estos zapatos
4. este dinero
5. aquella silla

D. The imperfect tense

Answer the following questions according to the model.

Modelo: ¿Qué querían ellos?   (arroz con pollo)
Querían arroz con pollo.

1. ¿Dónde vivían Uds. cuando eran chicos?   (en Alaska)
2. ¿Qué idioma hablabas tú cuando eras chico(a)?   (inglés)
3. ¿A quién veías siempre cuando eras chico(a)?   (a mi abuela)
4. ¿En qué banco depositaban Uds. el dinero?   (en el Banco de América)
5. ¿A qué hora se acostaban los niños?   (a las nueve)
6. ¿A dónde iba Rosa?   (a su trabajo)
7. ¿Qué compraba Ud.?   (café)
8. ¿En qué gastaban Uds. su dinero?   (en libros)

Lesson 12

A. The past progressive

Complete the sentences with the past progressive of the following verbs, as needed. Use each verb once: **hacer, hablar, estudiar, comer, pensar, leer, trabajar, escribir**

1. Nosotros _____ arroz con pollo cuando llegó Elsa.
2. ¿Qué _____ Uds. cuando yo llamé?
3. Elena _____ a máquina cuando llegó el doctor Vargas.
4. Yo _____ por teléfono con mi cuñado.
5. ¿En qué _____ tú cuando yo te hablé?
6. Ud. _____ el periódico cuando yo vine.
7. Los niños _____ la lección.
8. Roberto _____ en el garaje cuando yo lo vi.

B. The preterit contrasted with the imperfect

Give the Spanish equivalent:

1. We went to bed at eleven last night.
2. She was very busy when I saw her.
3. We used to go to Buenos Aires.
4. It was ten-thirty when I called my sister-in-law.
5. She said she wanted to read.

C. Changes in meaning with imperfect and preterit of **conocer, saber, querer,** and **poder**

Complete the sentences with the preterit or the imperfect of the verbs **conocer, saber, querer,** and **poder** as needed:

1. Yo no _____ a los abuelos de María. Los _____ ayer.
2. Nosotros no _____ que ella era casada. Lo _____ anoche.
3. Pedro dijo que no _____ venir, pero vino a eso de las dos.
4. Ellos no _____ llamarte por teléfono porque estaban trabajando. Por eso no te llamaron.
5. Mamá no vino a la reunión porque no _____ venir.
6. Yo no _____ ir a la fiesta, pero cuando _____ que Carlos iba a ir, decidí ir también.

D. **En** and **a** for *at*

Write sentences using these items. Follow the model.

Modelo: Yo / estar / universidad / anoche
       Yo estuve en la universidad anoche.

1. Nosotros / llegar / aeropuerto / seis y media
2. Mi cuñada / estar / casa
3. Ellos / estar / esquina de Unión y Figueroa
4. El accidente / ser / las doce
5. Yo / estar / la estación de policía / ayer

Lesson 13

A. Preterit of stem-changing verbs (**e:i** and **o:u**)

Rewrite the sentences according to the new beginnings. Follow the model.

Modelo: Él no pide dinero. (Ayer)
      Ayer él no pidió dinero.

1. Él siente mucho dolor. (Ayer)

2. Marta no duerme bien. (Anoche)
3. No le pido nada. (Ayer)
4. Ella te miente. (La semana pasada)
5. Ellos sirven los refrescos. (El sábado pasado)
6. No lo repito. (Ayer)
7. Ella sigue estudiando. (Anoche)
8. Tú no consigues nada. (El lunes pasado)

B. The expression **acabar de**

Answer the following questions according to the model:

Modelo: ¿Ya llegó Juan?
             Sí, acaba de llegar.

1. ¿Ya encontraste el termómetro?
2. ¿Ya le tomaste la temperatura?
3. ¿Ya compraron ellos los instrumentos?
4. ¿Ya midieron Uds. la ventana?
5. ¿Ya te bañaste?
6. ¿Ya llegaron los estudiantes?

C. Special construction with **gustar, doler,** and **hacer falta**

Complete the following sentences with the appropriate forms of **gustar, doler,** and **hacer falta,** as needed:

1. No _____ esos edificios. Prefiero aquéllos.
2. ¿Qué _____, señora? ¿Jabón?
3. A Marta _____ la cabeza. ¿Tienes aspirinas?
4. A nosotros no _____ dinero. No necesitamos comprar nada.
5. ¿_____ a Ud. este modelo, o prefiere el otro?
6. _____ toallas. ¿Puede traérmelas, por favor?
7. _____ una muela. Tengo que ir al dentista.
8. ¿No _____ caminar? ¡Podemos ir en coche!

D. **¿Qué?** and **¿cuál?** for *what?* used with **ser**

Give the Spanish equivalent:

1. What is freedom?
2. What is your address?
3. What is a thermometer?
4. What is your telephone number?
5. What are his ideas about this?

Lesson 14

A. Hace meaning *ago*

Write two sentences for each set of items. Follow the model.

Modelo: Un año / yo / conocer / él
       Hace un año que yo lo conocí.
      Yo lo conocí hace un año.

1. tres meses / nosotros / llegar / a California
2. dos horas / el niño / tomar / un poco / leche
3. dos días / ellos / terminar / el trabajo
4. veinte años / ella / ver / él
5. quince días / tú / venir / a esta ciudad

B. The past participle

Complete the following chart:

Infinitive	Past Participle
1. trabajar	1. trabajado
2. recibir	2. _____
3. _____	3. vuelto
4. usar	4. _____
5. escribir	5. _____
6. _____	6. ido
7. aprender	7. _____
8. _____	8. abierto
9. cubrir	9. _____
10. comer	10. _____
11. _____	11. visto
12. hacer	12. _____
13. ser	13. _____
14. _____	14. dicho
15. cerrar	15. _____
16. _____	16. muerto
17. _____	17. roto
18. dormir	18. _____
19. estar	19. _____
20. _____	20. puesto

C. Past participles used as adjectives:

Give the Spanish equivalent:

1. The article is written.
2. He has a broken leg.
3. The door is open.
4. Are the books closed?
5. The work is finished.

D. The present perfect tense

Complete the sentences with the present perfect of the following verbs. Use each verb once: **hablar, hacer, abrir, venir, decir, terminar, escribir, tener, poner, romperse, casarse**

1. Yo _____ muchas veces a este lugar.
2. ¿_____ Uds. la lección de matemáticas?
3. Nosotros todavía no _____ de negocios con el gerente del hotel.
4. Ellos me _____ que tengo que venir el sábado y el domingo.
5. ¿No _____ (tú) las cartas todavía?
6. Hoy nosotros no _____ nada, porque no _____ tiempo.
7. ¿Quién _____ las puertas?
8. ¿Dónde _____ Ud. las sillas?
9. Elena y Carlos no _____ todavía.
10. Yo _____ el brazo.

E. The past perfect tense

Give the Spanish equivalent:

1. I had already brought the sheets.
2. We had written to him about our experiments with tropical plants.
3. They had broken the pencils.
4. He had already seen the administrator.
5. Had you covered the tables, Miss Peña?

Lesson 15

A. Uses of **hacía...que**

Answer the following questions according to the model.

Modelo: ¿Cuánto tiempo hacía que Ud. vivía allí? (tres años)
Hacía tres años que yo vivía allí.

1. ¿Cuánto tiempo hacía que Ud. no comía? (diez horas)
2. ¿Cuánto tiempo hacía que Uds. lo esperaban cuando él llegó? (media hora)

3. ¿Cuánto tiempo hacía que estudiabas español cuando fuiste a Madrid? (dos meses)
4. ¿Cuánto tiempo hacía que la paciente no bebía? (dos horas)
5. ¿Cuánto tiempo hacía que Uds. trabajaban para el gobierno? (quince años)

B. The future tense

Answer the following questions according to the model.

Modelo: ¿Cuándo comprarán Uds. un coche?   (el año próximo)
   Compraremos un coche el año próximo.

1. ¿Cuál será el tema de la conferencia?   (la civilización y la cultura de Europa)
2. ¿Cuándo estarán listos los análisis?   (la semana que viene)
3. ¿Qué idioma enseñará Ud.?   (el español)
4. ¿Dónde estarán Uds. para esa fecha?   (en Chile)
5. ¿Qué le dirán Uds. al veterinario?   (que sí)
6. ¿Qué harás tú el domingo?   (nada)
7. ¿Cuándo sabremos el resultado?   (pronto)
8. ¿Quién arreglará el coche?   (el mecánico)
9. ¿Quiénes podrán venir?   (mis sobrinos)
10. ¿Dónde pondrás el dinero?   (en el banco)
11. ¿Cuándo volverán los niños de México?   (el sábado)
12. ¿Con quién vendrá Ud. a la reunión?   (con la señorita Vargas)
13. ¿Qué tendrán que hacer Uds.?   (estudiar para el examen)
14. ¿Cuándo me dará Ud. las cartas?   (mañana sin falta)
15. ¿Con quiénes saldrán Uds. el sábado?   (con Raúl y Mario)

C. The conditional tense

Complete the sentences with the conditional tense of the following verbs: **servir, poner, quejarse, haber, trabajar, seguir, vender, levantarse, preferir, ir.** Use each verb once.

1. Él dijo que nosotros _____ a Europa el verano próximo.
2. ¿Ellos _____ su casa a ese precio? Yo creo que sí.
3. ¿Dijo Ud. que _____ una reunión esta tarde?
4. Yo no _____ el café en la terraza.
5. Tú no _____ en una estación de servicio.
6. ¿_____ Ud. su dinero en ese banco?
7. ¿Qué _____ Uds.: ir a México o ir a Guatemala?
8. ¿_____ Uds. estudiando español?
9. ¿_____ tú a las tres de la mañana?
10. Nosotros no _____ del profesor.

D. Some uses of the prepositions **a, de,** and **en**

Give the Spanish equivalent:

1. We won't arrive at the university on time.
2. Did you take your dog to the vet, Mary?
3. Later we will travel by plane.
4. She's at the hospital. She's improving.
5. What are they talking about?

LESSON 16

1. The present subjunctive
2. The subjunctive with verbs of volition
3. The absolute superlative

1. The present subjunctive

Uses of the subjunctive

A.   While the indicative mood is used to express events that are factual and definite, the subjunctive mood is used to refer to events or conditions that the speaker does not view as part of reality or of his or her own experience. Expressions of volition, doubt, surprise, fear, and so forth are naturally followed by actions that occur only in the speaker's mind.

Except for its use in main clauses to express commands, the Spanish subjunctive is most often used in subordinate or dependent clauses.

The subjunctive is also used in English, although not as often as in Spanish. For example:

> *I suggest that he **arrive** tomorrow.*

The expression that requires the use of the subjunctive is in the main clause, *I suggest.* The subjunctive appears in the subordinate clause, *that he **arrive** tomorrow.* The subjunctive mood is used because the action of arriving is not real; it is only what is *suggested* that he do.

B.   There are four main concepts that call for the use of the subjunctive in Spanish:

1. *Volition:* demands, wishes, advice, persuasion, and other impositions of will

> Ella **quiere** que yo le **escriba.**
> Te **aconsejo** que no **vayas** a ese banco.
> Deseo que **vengas** con nosotros.

2. *Emotion:* pity, joy, fear, surprise, hope, desire, etc.

> Espero que Uds. **puedan** venir.
> Siento mucho que Luisa **esté** enferma.

3. *Doubt, disbelief, and denial:* uncertainty, negated facts

> **Dudo** que **paguen** un 10 por ciento de interés.
> **No es verdad** que él **sea** médico.
> Ella **niega** que Juan **sea** su esposo.

4. *Unreality:* expectations, indefiniteness, nonexistence

> **¿Hay alguien** que **hable** alemán?
> **No hay nadie** que lo **sepa.**

Formation of the present subjunctive

The present subjunctive is formed by adding the following endings to the stem of the first person singular of the present indicative, after dropping the **-o**:

The Present Subjunctive of Regular Verbs		
-ar *Verbs*	**-er** *Verbs*	**-ir** *Verbs*
trabajar	**comer**	**vivir**
trabaje	coma	viva
trabajes	comas	vivas
trabaje	coma	viva
trabajemos	comamos	vivamos
trabajen	coman	vivan

ATENCIÓN: Notice that the endings for **-er** and **-ir** verbs are the same.

The following table shows you how to form the first person singular of the present subjunctive from the infinitive of the verb:

Verb	First Person Singular (Indicative)	Stem	First Person Singular (Present Subjunctive)
hablar	hablo	**habl-**	hable
aprender	aprendo	**aprend-**	aprenda
escribir	escribo	**escrib-**	escriba
decir	digo	**dig-**	diga
hacer	hago	**hag-**	haga
traer	traigo	**traig-**	traiga
venir	vengo	**veng-**	venga
conocer	conozco	**conozc-**	conozca

Exercise

Give the present subjunctive of the following verbs:

1. **yo:** comer, venir, hablar, hacer, salir, ponerse
2. **tú:** decir, ver, traer, trabajar, escribir, acostarse
3. **él:** vivir, aprender, salir, estudiar, levantarse
4. **nosotros:** escribir, caminar, poner, desear, tener, afeitarse
5. **ellos:** salir, hacer, llevar, conocer, ver, bañarse

Subjunctive forms of stem-changing verbs

1. **-ar** and **-er** verbs maintain the basic pattern of the present indicative. That is, their stems undergo the same changes in the present subjunctive:

recomendar (*to recommend*)		recordar (*to remember*)	
recomiende	recomendemos	recuerde	recordemos
recomiendes		recuerdes	
recomiende	recomienden	recuerde	recuerden

entender (*to understand*)		mover (*to move*)	
entienda	entendamos	mueva	movamos
entiendas		muevas	
entienda	entiendan	mueva	muevan

2. **-ir** verbs change the unstressed **e** to **i** and the unstressed **o** to **u** in the first person plural:

mentir (*to lie*)		dormir (*to sleep*)	
mienta	mintamos	duerma	durmamos
mientas		duermas	
mienta	mientan	duerma	duerman

Verbs that are irregular in the subjunctive

dar	estar	haber	saber	ser	ir
dé	esté	haya	sepa	sea	vaya
des	estés	hayas	sepas	seas	vayas
dé	esté	haya	sepa	sea	vaya
demos	estemos	hayamos	sepamos	seamos	vayamos
den	estén	hayan	sepan	sean	vayan

Exercise

Give the present subjunctive of the following verbs:

1. **yo:**   dormir, mover, cerrar, sentir, ser
2. **tú:**   mentir, volver, ir, dar, recordar

3. **ella:**   estar, saber, perder, dormir, ser
4. **nosotros:**   pensar, recordar, dar, morir, cerrar
5. **ellos:**   ver, preferir, dar, ir, saber

2. The subjunctive with verbs of volition

A. All impositions of will, as well as indirect or implied commands, require
the subjunctive in subordinate clauses. The subject in the main clause
must be different from the subject in the subordinate clause.
    Some verbs of volition:

querer	**aconsejar**	**sugerir**	**rogar**
mandar	**pedir**	**necesitar**	**recomendar**

Note the sentence structure for the use of the subjunctive in Spanish.

Yo **quiero**	que	*Ud.* **estudie.**
main clause		subordinate clause
I want		*you* to study.

—Mañana tengo examen de   *I have an exam in physical*
  geografía física.   *geography tomorrow.*
—Pues te aconsejo que   *Well, I advise you to study.*
  estudies.

—Mi familia y yo tenemos que   *My family and I have to move*
  mudarnos a otra casa.   *to another house.*
—Yo les sugiero que no **se**   *I suggest that you don't move*
  muden hasta fin de mes.   *until the end of the month.*

—¿Qué quiere que yo **haga?**   *What do you want me to do?*
—Quiero que Ud. me **traiga**   *I want you to bring me those*
  esos paquetes.   *packages.*

ATENCIÓN: If there is no change of subject, the infinitive is used:

—¿Qué quiere **hacer** Ud.?   *What do you want to do?*
—Yo quiero **traer** esos   *I want to bring those packages.*
  paquetes.

Exercise

Tell us what you or other people want someone else to do. Use the present
subjunctive of the verbs in parentheses:

1. Yo te sugiero que _____ (hacer) el trabajo hoy.
2. Nosotros queremos que Ud. _____ (sentarse).

3. ¿Ud. me aconseja que yo _____ (mudarse) a fin de mes?
4. Ellos necesitan que él _____ (traer) los paquetes.
5. Él me pide que yo lo _____ (ayudar).
6. Uds. les dicen a ellas que _____ (abrir) la puerta.
7. Ellos prefieren que nosotros no _____ (ir) hasta las nueve.
8. La doctora Rivas quiere que Ud. _____ (venir) por la tarde.
9. El profesor nos recomienda que _____ (estudiar) geografía física.
10. Yo no quiero que Uds. me _____ (dar) nada.

B. Sometimes the main clause that contains the verb of volition is omitted in Spanish. However, the expression of the speaker's will is easily understood:

¿Qué quiere Ud. que **haga** el niño?	*What do you want the boy to do?*
(Quiero) Que **se lave** la cara.	*I want him to wash his face.*
¿Va Ud. a hacer el trabajo?	*Are you going to do the work?*
No. Que lo **haga** Jorge.	*No. Let Jorge do it.*

Exercise

Respond, following the model.

Modelo: ¿Quién va a hacerlo? ¿Ud.?
  ¡Yo no! ¡Que lo haga ella!

1. ¿Quién va a salir? ¿Ud.?
2. ¿Quién va a comer? ¿Ud.?
3. ¿Quién va a ir? ¿Ud.?
4. ¿Quién va a hablar? ¿Ud.?
5. ¿Quién va a traerlo? ¿Ud.?

Modelo: ¿No va a entrar Ud.?
  No, ¡que entren ellos!

1. ¿No va a dormir Ud.?
2. ¿No va a volver Ud.?
3. ¿No va a trabajar Ud.?
4. ¿No va a venir Ud.?
5. ¿No va a beber Ud.?

3. The absolute superlative

In Spanish, when a high degree of a given quality is expressed without comparing it to the same quality of another person or thing, there are two ways of expressing this:

A. By modifying the adjective with an adverb (**muy, sumamente**):

—¿Cómo es tu novia? | *What is your girlfriend like?*
—Es **muy** inteligente y | *She is very intelligent and*
sumamente buena. | *extremely kind.*

B. By adding the suffix **-ísimo** (**-a, -os, -as**) to the adjective. If the word ends in a vowel, the vowel is dropped before adding the suffix. Notice that the **í** of the suffix always has a written accent:

alto	alt-	ísimo	altísimo
ocupada	ocupad-	ísima	ocupadísima
lentos	lent-	ísimos	lentísimos
buenas	buen-	ísimas	buenísimas
difícil	dificil-	ísimo	dificilísimo

—¿Fuiste a Madrid el verano | *Did you go to Madrid last*
pasado? | *summer?*
—Sí, es una ciudad **bellísima,** | *Yes, it is a very beautiful city,*
pero es **dificilísimo** conducir | *but it is extremely difficult*
allí. | *to drive there.*

—¿Pueden ir al correo con | *Can you go to the post office*
nosotros? | *with us?*
—No, estamos **ocupadísimas.** | *No, we are extremely busy.*

Exercise

Change the following sentences using the absolute superlative:

1. Mi novia es muy bella.
2. Mi novio es sumamente alto.
3. Ellos están muy ocupados.
4. Es muy fácil llegar al correo.
5. Ellas son muy buenas.
6. La enfermera está sumamente ocupada.
7. Ellos son muy lentos.
8. Las clases son sumamente difíciles allí.

Vocabulary

COGNATES

la **familia**   family
físico(a)   physical
la **geografía**   geography

NOUNS

la **cara**   face
el **correo,** la **oficina de correos**
    post office
el **paquete**   package

VERBS

aconsejar   to advise
lavar(se)   to wash (oneself)
mudarse   to move
recomendar (e:ie)   to recommend
sugerir (e:ie)   to suggest

ADJECTIVES

bello(a)   pretty
bueno(a)   kind
lento(a)   slow
ocupado(a)   busy

OTHER WORDS
AND EXPRESSIONS

fin de mes   the end of the month
hasta   until
sumamente   extremely, highly

EN EL LABORATORIO

The following material is to be used with the tape in the language laboratory.

I. Vocabulary

Repeat each word after the speaker. When repeating words that are cognates, notice the difference in pronunciation between English and Spanish.

Cognates:	la familia físico la geografía
Nouns:	la cara el correo la oficina de correos el paquete
Verbs:	aconsejar lavarse mudarse recomendar sugerir
Adjectives:	bello bueno lento ocupado
Other words and expressions:	fin de mes hasta sumamente

II. Structure Practice

A. Tell us what Carmen wants everybody to do. Use the present subjunctive with the cue words provided. Repeat the correct answer after the speaker's confirmation. Listen to the model:

Modelo: —¿Qué quiere Carmen que yo haga?   (escribir una carta)
—Carmen quiere que Ud. escriba una carta.

1. ir al correo
2. traer el paquete
3. lavar el auto
4. dar dinero
5. mudarse
6. lavarse la cara
7. cerrar la ventana
8. comprarle un libro

B. Repeat each sentence, changing **muy** + adjective to the absolute superlative. Repeat the correct answer after the speaker's confirmation. Listen to the model:

Modelo: Mi novio es muy alto.
Mi novio es altísimo.

209

III.   Listening and Comprehension

1. Listen carefully to the narration that follows. It will be read twice.

   (*Narration*)

   Now the speaker will make statements concerning the narration you just heard. After each statement, say whether it is true (**verdadero**) or false (**falso**). The speaker will confirm the correct answer.

2. Listen carefully to the dialogue that follows. It will be read twice.

   (*Dialogue*)

   Now the speaker will make statements concerning the conversation you just heard. After each statement, say whether it is true (**verdadero**) or false (**falso**). The speaker will confirm the correct answer.

LESSON 17

1. The subjunctive to express emotion
2. The subjunctive with some impersonal expressions
3. Formation of adverbs

1. The subjunctive to express emotion

In Spanish, the subjunctive is always used in the subordinate clause when the verb in the main clause expresses any kind of emotion, such as fear, joy, pity, hope, pleasure, surprise, anger, regret, and sorrow. Some verbs of emotion are **temer** (*to fear*), **alegrarse** (**de**) (*to be glad*), **sentir** (**e:ie**) (*to regret*), **esperar** (*to hope*).

—¿Vas a ir a la barbería hoy?	*Are you going to the barbershop today?*
—No. **Temo** que el barbero **tenga** muchos clientes.	*No. I'm afraid the barber will have many customers.*
—¿Cuándo vienen tus padres?	*When are your parents coming?*
—**Espero** que ellos **lleguen** mañana.	*I hope they will arrive tomorrow.*

ATENCIÓN: The subject of the subordinate clause must be different from that of the main clause. If there is no change of subject, the infinitive is used instead:

—¿Vas a terminar el trabajo para las cinco?	*Are you going to finish the work by five?*
—Temo no **poder** terminarlo tan pronto. (**Yo temo** in main clause. **Yo no puedo** in subordinate clause.)	*I'm afraid I can't finish it so soon.*
—¿Cuándo se van Uds.?	*When are you leaving?*
—Esperamos **irnos** esta noche. (**Nosotros esperamos** in main clause. **Nosotros nos vamos** in subordinate clause.)	*We hope to leave tonight.*

Exercise

Complete the following sentences with the subjunctive or infinitive of the verbs in parentheses, as needed:

1. Espero que los niños _____ (cortarse) el pelo hoy.
2. Me alegro de _____ (estar) aquí.
3. Temen no _____ (poder) terminar para la una.
4. Ella espera _____ (salir) esta noche.
5. Uds. esperan que el barbero no _____ (tener) muchos clientes.
6. Siento mucho que ellos no _____ (volver) mañana.
7. Espero que no _____ (llover) hoy pues tengo que salir.

8. Espero que ellos lo _____ (traer).
9. Siento _____ (estar) tan enferma.
10. Temo que Ud. no _____ (tener) trabajo pronto.
11. Temo no _____ (recordar) su dirección.
12. Me alegro de que nosotros _____ (poder) terminar hoy.

2. The subjunctive with some impersonal expressions

In Spanish, some impersonal expressions that convey emotion, uncertainty, unreality, or an indirect or implied command are followed by a verb in the subjunctive. This occurs only when the verb of the subordinate clause has an expressed subject. The most common expressions are:

conviene   *it is advisable*
es difícil   *it is unlikely*
es importante   *it is important*
es (im)posible   *it is (im)possible*
es lástima   *it is a pity*
es mejor   *it is better*
es necesario   *it is necessary*
¡ojalá!   *if only . . . !* or *I hope . . .*
puede ser   *it may be*

—¿Viene hoy el plomero? — *Is the plumber coming today?*
—**Es difícil** que **venga** hoy. — *It is unlikely that he'll come today.*

—¿Cuándo quiere Ud. que yo escriba las cartas? — *When do you want me to write the letters?*
—**Es importante** que las **escriba** hoy. — *It is important that you write them today.*

—¿Cuándo quiere Ud. que los estudiantes tomen el examen? — *When do you want the students to take the exam?*
—**Es mejor** que lo **tomen** en seguida. — *It is better that they take it right away.*

—**Es lástima** que Ud. no **pueda** hacerlo. — *It is a pity you can't do it.*
—Sí, pero no tengo tiempo. — *Yes, but I don't have time.*

—¿Crees que va a llover mañana? — *Do you think it's going to rain tomorrow?*
—Espero que no llueva porque **es posible** que Enrique me **lleve** a la playa. — *I hope it won't rain, because it's possible that Enrique will take me to the beach.*

ATENCIÓN:

1. When the impersonal expression implies certainty, the indicative is used:

¿Vienen ellos hoy?	*Are they coming today?*
Sí, **es seguro** que **vienen** hoy.	*Yes, it is certain that they'll come today.*

2. In Spanish, when a sentence is completely impersonal (that is, when no subject is stated), the above expressions are followed by the infinitive:

¿Cuándo vamos a firmar el contrato?	*When are we going to sign the contract?*
Conviene **firmarlo** esta semana.	*It is advisable to sign it this week.*

Exercise

Be an interpreter. Tell us how to say the following in Spanish:

1. It is unlikely that the plumber will come today.
2. It is important that the students take the test right away.
3. It's a pity that your mother is so sick.
4. It is necessary to finish the job, but I don't have time.
5. I hope he doesn't say anything.
6. It is certain that it is going to rain tonight.
7. It is better to see the client now.
8. It is advisable to sign the contract this week.
9. Well, is it possible to do it today?
10. It is impossible to go to the beach now.

3. Formation of adverbs

A. Most Spanish adverbs are formed by adding **-mente** (the equivalent of *-ly* in English) to the adjective:

especial	*special*	especial**mente**	*specially, especially*
reciente	*recent*	reciente**mente**	*recently*

B. If the adjective ends in **-o**, change the ending to **-a** before adding **-mente**:

lent**o**	*slow*	lent**amente**	*slowly*
rápid**o**	*rapid*	rápid**amente**	*rapidly*

C. If two or more adverbs are used together, both change the **-o** to **-a**, but only the last adverb takes the **-mente** ending.

lenta y cuidados**amente**   *slowly and carefully*

D. If the adjective has a written accent mark, the adverb retains it:

fácil   fácilmente

Traigo estos libros **especialmente** para Ud. Gracias.	*I'm bringing these books especially for you. Thanks.*
El niño escribe la carta **lenta** y **cuidadosamente.**	*The child is writing the letter slowly and carefully.*
¡Pero la escribe muy bien!	*But he is writing it very well!*

Exercise

Be an interpreter. Tell us how to say the following in Spanish:

1. She reads slowly.
2. Do it carefully, Miss Peña.
3. The chair is especially for you, sir.
4. She is going to do it rapidly but carefully.
5. When did you see her, sir? Recently?
6. The lesson? We can translate it easily.

Vocabulary

COGNATES

el **barbero**	barber	**importante**	important
el **contrato**	contract	**posible**	possible
especial	special	**reciente**	recent

NOUNS

el **cliente** customer
la **playa** beach
el **plomero** plumber
el **tiempo** time

VERBS

alegrarse (**de**) to be glad
esperar to hope
firmar to sign
sentir (**e:ie**) to regret
temer to fear

ADJECTIVES

cuidadosa(**a**) careful
rápido(**a**) fast

OTHER WORDS
AND EXPRESSIONS

conviene it is advisable
cortarse el pelo to get a haircut
en seguida right away
es difícil it's unlikely
es lástima it is a pity
es seguro it is certain
esta noche tonight
¡ojalá! if only . . . !, I hope . . .
pues well
tan so

EN EL LABORATORIO

The following material is to be used with the tape in the language laboratory.

I. Vocabulary

Repeat each word after the speaker. When repeating words that are cognates, notice the difference in pronunciation between English and Spanish.

Cognates:	el barbero el contrato especial importante posible reciente
Nouns:	el cliente la playa el plomero el tiempo
Verbs:	alegrarse esperar firmar sentir temer
Adjectives:	cuidadoso rápido
Other words and expressions:	conviene cortarse el pelo en seguida es difícil es lástima es seguro esta noche ojalá pues tan

II. Structure Practice

A. Restate each of the following sentences, inserting the cue at the beginning and making any necessary changes. Repeat the correct answer after the speaker's confirmation. Listen to the model:

Modelo: El cliente firma el contrato.   (Espero)
　　　　　Espero que el cliente firme el contrato.

1. (Temo)
2. (Espero)
3. (Siento)
4. (Temo)
5. (Me alegro)
6. (Espero)

B. Restate each of the following sentences, inserting the cue at the beginning and making any necessary changes. Repeat the correct answer after the speaker's confirmation. Listen to the model:

Modelo: Él conduce muy rápido.   (Es difícil)
　　　　　Es difícil que él conduzca muy rápido.

1. (No conviene)
2. (Es necesario)
3. (Es imposible)
4. (Es mejor)

5. (Puede ser)
6. (Ojalá)
7. (Es lástima)
8. (Es importante)

C. Give the adverb that corresponds to each adjective. Repeat the correct answer after the speaker's confirmation. Listen to the model:

Modelo: especial
especialmente

III. *Listening and Comprehension*

1. Listen carefully to the dialogue that follows. It will be read twice.

(*Dialogue*)

Now the speaker will make statements concerning the conversation you just heard. After each statement, say whether it is true (**verdadero**) or false (**falso**). The speaker will confirm the correct answer.

2. Listen carefully to the dialogue that follows. It will be read twice.

(*Dialogue*)

Now the speaker will make statements concerning the conversation you just heard. After each statement, say whether it is true (**verdadero**) or false (**falso**). The speaker will confirm the correct answer.

1. Other uses of the subjunctive
2. The familiar command
3. Diminutive suffixes

1. Other uses of the subjunctive

A. The subjunctive to express doubt, uncertainty and disbelief

In Spanish, the subjunctive mood is always used in the subordinate clause when the main clause expresses doubt, uncertainty or disbelief.

1. Doubt or uncertainty:

—¿Viene tu hermana a la oficina hoy? | *Is your sister coming to the office today?*
—**Dudo** que ella **venga** hoy. | *I doubt that she's coming today.*

—¿Está Ud. seguro de que el jefe sale mañana? | *Are you sure (that) the boss is leaving tomorrow?*
—No, **no estoy seguro** de que **salga** mañana. | *No, I'm not sure (that) he's leaving tomorrow.*

ATENCIÓN: The verb **dudar** (in the affirmative) takes the subjunctive in the subordinate clause even when there is no change of subject:

—¿Puedes ir conmigo al médico? | *Can you go to the doctor's with me?*
—**(Yo) dudo** que (yo) **pueda** ir contigo hoy. | *I doubt that I can go with you today.*

When the speaker expresses no doubt and is certain of the reality, the indicative is used:

—¿Viene tu hermana hoy? | *Is your sister coming today?*
—**No dudo** que ella **viene.** | *I don't doubt (I'm sure) that she's coming.*

—¿Está Ud. seguro de que él sale mañana? | *Are you sure (that) he's leaving tomorrow?*
—Sí, estoy seguro de que él **sale** mañana. | *Yes, I'm sure (that) he's leaving tomorrow.*

2. The verb **creer** (*to believe, to think*) is followed by the subjunctive when used in negative sentences in which it expresses disbelief. It is followed by the indicative in affirmative sentences in which it expresses belief. In the interrogative, if doubt is strongly implied, the subjunctive should also be used.

—¿Cuántos cuartos tiene la casa? | *How many rooms does the house have?*
—**Creo** que **tiene** veinte y cinco cuartos. | *I think it has twenty-five rooms.*
—¡Vamos! **No creo** que **tenga** veinte y cinco cuartos. | *Come on! I don't believe it has twenty-five rooms.*

—¿**Cree** Ud. que ella **tenga**   *Do you think she is forty years*
cuarenta años?   *old?*
—No, creo que **tiene** muchos   *No, I think she is much older.*
más.

B. The subjunctive to express denial

When the main clause denies what is said in the subordinate clause, the subjunctive is used.

—¿Es verdad que tu padre   *Is it true that your father is in*
está preso?   *jail?*
—No, **no es verdad** que mi   *No, it isn't true that my father*
padre **esté** preso.   *is in jail.*

ATENCIÓN: When the main clause does not deny what is said in the subordinate clause, the indicative is used.

—¿Es verdad que tu padre   *Is it true that your father is in*
está preso?   *jail?*
—Sí, **es verdad** que mi padre   *Yes, it is true that my father is*
está preso.   *in jail.*

C. The subjunctive to express unreality

The subjunctive is always used when the subordinate clause refers to someone or something that is indefinite, unspecified, or non-existent:

—¿Qué clase de casa necesitan   *What kind of house do they*
ellos?   *need?*
—Ellos necesitan una casa que   *They need a house that is big*
sea grande y que **quede**   *and (that is) located near the*
cerca del centro.   *downtown area.*

—Buscamos un profesor que   *We're looking for a professor*
hable tres idiomas.   *who speaks three languages.*
—Pues yo busco un profesor   *Well, I'm looking for a*
que **sepa** inglés.   *professor who knows*
                                      English.

—¿Hay alguien aquí que **sepa**   *Is there anybody here who*
hacer traducciones?   *knows how to do*
                                      translations?

—No, no hay nadie que **sepa**   *No, there is no one who knows*
hacer traducciones.   *how to do translations.*

ATENCIÓN: If the subordinate clause refers to existent, definite, or specific persons or things, the indicative is used:

—¿Dónde viven ellos?   *Where do they live?*
—Ellos viven en una casa que   *They live in a house that is big*
es grande y que **queda** cerca   *and that is located near the*
del centro.   *downtown area.*

—¿Tienen Uds. secretaria?	*Do you have a secretary?*
—Sí, tenemos una secretaria que **habla** tres idiomas y que **sabe** escribir muy bien a máquina.	*Yes, we have a secretary who speaks three languages and who can (knows how to) type very well.*
—Aquí hay alguien que **sabe** hacer traducciones.	*There is someone here who knows how to do translations.*
—¡Fantástico!	*Fantastic!*

Exercise

Complete the sentences, using either the present indicative or the present subjunctive of the verbs in the following list, as needed. Read each sentence aloud:

tener	saber	querer
poder	ser	escribir
entender	servir	venir
salir	hablar	estar
abrirse	quedar	ir

1. Dudo que la maestra _____ a la escuela hoy, niños, porque está muy enferma.
2. No estoy seguro de que (nosotros) _____ terminar el trabajo para esta tarde.
3. Dudo que (yo) _____ a la reunión esta noche.
4. Estamos seguros de que Uds. _____ la situación.
5. No creo que el avión _____ el sábado por la noche.
6. Creo que el banco _____ a las nueve de la mañana.
7. ¡Vamos! No es verdad que el jefe _____ preso.
8. Es verdad que la casa de Tomás _____ sólo tres cuartos.
9. Tengo una secretaria que _____ cuatro idiomas.
10. ¿Hay alguien aquí que _____ escribir a máquina?
11. María busca una casa que _____ cerca del centro.
12. Busca una esposa que _____ inteligente.
13. En esta ciudad no hay ningún restaurante que _____ comida italiana.
14. Aquí hay tres personas que _____ hacer traducciones del inglés al español. ¡Fantástico!
15. Necesito una pluma que _____ bien.

2. The familiar command

The affirmative command

A. The affirmative command for **tú** has exactly the same form as the third person singular of the present indicative:

Verb	Present Indicative Third Person Singular	Familiar Command (tú Form)
hablar	él habla	**habla**
comer	él come	**come**
abrir	él abre	**abre**
cerrar	él cierra	**cierra**
volver	él vuelve	**vuelve**
pedir	él pide	**pide**
traer	él trae	**trae**

—¿Qué pido? — *What shall I order?*
—**Pide** un coctel para mí y una limonada para ti. — *Order a cocktail for me and a lemonade for you.*

—**Cierra** las ventanas y **apaga** las luces antes de salir.[1] — *Close the windows and turn off the lights before going out.*
—Muy bien. **Espérame** en el coche. — *Very well. Wait for me in the car.*

—¿Puedo jugar afuera? — *May I play outside?*
—No, **quédate** adentro. Hace mucho frío. — *No, stay inside. It's very cold.*

ATENCIÓN: Remember that direct, indirect, and reflexive pronouns are always attached to an affirmative command.

B. Eight Spanish verbs have irregular affirmative command forms of **tú**:

decir:	**di** (*say, tell*)	salir:	**sal** (*go out, leave*)
hacer:	**haz** (*do, make*)	ser:	**sé** (*be*)
ir:	**ve** (*go*)	tener:	**ten** (*have*)
poner:	**pon** (*put*)	venir:	**ven** (*come*)

—Carlitos, **ven** aquí. **Haz**me un favor. **Ve** y **di**le a tu mamá que quiero hablar con ella. — *Carlitos, come here. Do me a favor. Go and tell your mom I want to speak with her.*

—¿Dónde pongo las plantas? — *Where shall I put the plants?*
—**Pon**las en la mesa. — *Put them on the table.*

—Marcos, **sé** bueno y **sal** con los niños esta tarde. Necesito trabajar. — *Marcos, be nice (kind) and go out with the kids this afternoon. I need to work.*
—Bueno. Pero ¿cuándo vas a terminar ese trabajo? — *Okay. But when are you going to finish that job?*

[1]The infinitive, not the *-ing* form, is used after a preposition in Spanish.

| —**Ten** paciencia. Estará listo mañana por la tarde. | *Have patience. It will be ready tomorrow afternoon.* |

The negative command

The negative command for **tú** uses the corresponding form of the present subjunctive:

—Tengo mil dólares para gastar en mis vacaciones.	*I have a thousand dollars to spend on my vacation.*
—**No lleves** dinero. Lleva cheques de viajero.	*Don't take money. Take travelers' checks.*
—Tengo que ir a la oficina de correos. **No me esperes** para cenar.	*I have to go to the post office. Don't wait for me to (have) dinner.*
—**No vayas** hoy. Ve mañana.	*Don't go today. Go tomorrow.*
—**No te bañes** todavía. No hay agua caliente.	*Don't bathe yet. There is no hot water.*
—**No me digas** que otra vez tengo que bañarme con agua fría.	*Don't tell me that I have to bathe with cold water again.*

ATENCIÓN: Remember that all object pronouns are placed *before* a negative command.

Exercises

A. Answer the following questions according to the model.

> *Modelo:* ¿Traigo las plantas?
> **Sí, tráelas, por favor.**

1. ¿Pido el coctel?
2. ¿Hago la limonada?
3. ¿Apago la luz?
4. ¿Te espero en el coche?
5. ¿Me quedo aquí?
6. ¿Juego afuera?
7. ¿Vengo con Eva?
8. ¿Lo pongo adentro?
9. ¿Se lo digo?
10. ¿Voy con Alberto?
11. ¿Salgo temprano?
12. ¿Me baño con agua fría?
13. ¿Abro las ventanas?
14. ¿Cierro las puertas?
15. ¿Traigo los cheques de viajero?

B. Make the following commands negative:

1. Gasta todo el dinero.
2. Vete.
3. Dile que venga con nosotros.
4. Sal con Roberto.
5. Ven esta tarde.
6. Pídele que salga con los chicos.
7. Dile que necesitas trabajar.
8. Báñate con agua caliente.
9. Hazlo otra vez.
10. Pon las plantas en la habitación.
11. Sé bueno.
12. Ten paciencia.
13. Quédate con ella.
14. Dale el dinero al médico.
15. Llévala al cine.

C. Give the Spanish equivalent, using the **tú** form:

1. Tell him what kind of house you want.
2. Go to the post office.
3. Don't have supper now.
4. Do me a favor.
5. Wash your hands before going out.

3. Diminutive suffixes

To express the idea of size, and also to denote affection, different suffixes are used in Spanish. The most common suffixes are **-ito(a)** and **-cito(a)**. There are no set rules for forming the diminutive, but usually if the word ends in **-a** or **-o,** the vowel is dropped and **-ito(a)** is added:

niño	niñ + **ito** =	**niñito**	(*little boy*)
niña	niñ + **ita** =	**niñita**	(*little girl*)
abuelo	abuel + **ito** =	**abuelito**	(*grandpa*)
Ana	An + **ita** =	**Anita**	(*Annie*)

If the word ends in a consonant other than **-n** or **-r,** the suffix **ito(a)** is added:

árbol + **ito** =	**arbolito**	(*little tree*)
Luis + **ito** =	**Luisito**	(*Louie*)

If the word ends in **-e, -n** or **-r,** the suffix **-cito(a)** is added:

coche	+ **cito** =	**cochecito**	(*little car*)
mujer	+ **cita** =	**mujercita**	(*little woman*)
Carmen	+ **cita** =	**Carmencita**	

—Hola, **abuelito**. ¿Me trajiste   *Hello, grandpa. Did you bring*
el **arbolito** de Navidad?   *me the little Christmas tree?*
—Sí, **Tomasito**.   *Yes, Tommy.*

—Me gusta tu **cochecito**.   *I like your little car.*
—Gracias, **Carmencita**.   *Thanks, Carmen.*

Exercise

Give the diminutive corresponding to each of the following:

1. primo   6. hermana
2. escuela   7. favor
3. árbol   8. Juan
4. Raúl   9. Adela
5. coche   10. mamá

Vocabulary

COGNATES

el **coctel** cocktail	el **favor** favor
el **cheque** check	la **limonada** lemonade
fantástico(a) fantastic	la **paciencia** patience

NOUNS

el **agua** (*f.*)[1]   water
el **árbol**   tree
el **centro**   downtown
la **clase**   kind, type
el **cuarto**, la **habitación**   room
el, la **jefe(a)**   boss, chief
la **luz**   light
la **traducción**   translation
el, la **viajero(a)**   traveler

VERBS

apagar   to turn off
buscar   to look for
cenar   to have supper, to dine
dudar   to doubt
jugar[2]   to play (*a game*)
quedar   to be located

ADJECTIVES

caliente   hot
frío(a)   cold
seguro(a)   sure

OTHER WORDS AND EXPRESSIONS

adentro   inside
afuera   outside
antes de   before
cerca (de)   near, next to
estar preso(a)   to be in jail
otra vez   again
¡vamos!   come on!

---

[1]When a feminine singular noun begins with a stressed **a** or **ha**, the article **el** (**un**) is used.
[2]Present indicative: **juego, juegas, juega, jugamos, juegan**

EN EL LABORATORIO

The following material is to be used with the tape in the language laboratory.

I. Vocabulary

Repeat each word after the speaker. When repeating words that are cognates, notice the difference in pronunciation between English and Spanish.

Cognates:	el coctel el cheque fantástico el favor la limonada la paciencia
Nouns:	el agua el árbol el centro la clase el cuarto la habitación el jefe la jefa la luz la traducción el viajero
Verbs:	apagar buscar cenar dudar jugar quedar
Adjectives:	caliente frío seguro
Other words and expressions:	adentro afuera antes de cerca de estar preso otra vez vamos

II. Structure Practice

A. Restate each of the following sentences, inserting the cue at the beginning and making any necessary changes. Repeat the correct answer after the speaker's confirmation. Listen to the model:

Modelo: No dudo que ella viene hoy.   (Dudo)
         Dudo que ella venga hoy.

1. (No estoy seguro)
2. (No creo)
3. (No es verdad)
4. (Buscamos)
5. (Necesito una secretaria)
6. (No hay nadie)

B. Change the following commands from the negative to the affirmative. Repeat the correct answer after the speaker's confirmation. Listen to the model:

Modelo: No hables inglés.
         Habla inglés.

C. Change the following commands from the affirmative to the negative. Repeat the correct answer after the speaker's confirmation. Listen to the model:

Modelo: Ponlo en la mesa.
            No lo pongas en la mesa.

III.   *Listening and Comprehension*

1. Listen carefully to the narration that follows. It will be read twice.

   (*Narration*)

   Now the speaker will make statements concerning the narration you just heard. After each statement, say whether it is true (**verdadero**) or false (**falso**). The speaker will confirm the correct answer.

2. Listen carefully to the dialogue that follows. It will be read twice.

   (*Dialogue*)

   Now the speaker will make statements concerning the conversation you just heard. After each statement, say whether it is true (**verdadero**) or false (**falso**). The speaker will confirm the correct answer.

LESSON 19

1. The subjunctive after conjunctions implying uncertainty or unfulfillment
2. The present perfect subjunctive
3. Uses of the present perfect subjunctive

1. The subjunctive after conjunctions implying uncertainty or unfulfillment

A. The subjunctive is used after conjunctions of time when the main clause refers to the future or is a command. Some conjunctions of time are **tan pronto como, en cuanto** (both meaning *as soon as*), **hasta que** (*until*), and **cuando** (*when*).

—Eva, ¿cuándo va a llamarte el doctor?
Eva, when is the doctor going to call you?

—Me llamará **tan pronto como sepa** el resultado de los análisis.
He is going to call me as soon as he finds out the result of the tests.

—Carlos, ¿a qué hora vamos a empezar la asamblea?
Carlos, at what time are we going to begin the assembly?

—La vamos a empezar **en cuanto lleguen** todos los empleados.
We are going to begin (it) as soon as all the employees arrive.

—Tomás, ¿cuándo vamos a salir para el aeropuerto?
Thomas, when are we going to leave for the airport?

—No podemos salir **hasta que** el carro **esté** arreglado.
We can't leave until the car is fixed.

—**Cuando llegue** Carlos, dígale que saque copia de estas cartas y las eche al correo.
When Carlos arrives, tell him to photocopy these letters and mail them.

—Muy bien, se lo diré **cuando venga.**
OK, I'll tell him when he arrives.

ATENCIÓN: If the action already happened or if there is no indication of a future action, the indicative is used after the conjunction of time.

—Eva, ¿cuándo te llamó el doctor?
Eva, when did the doctor call you?

—Me llamó **tan pronto como supo** el resultado de los análisis.
He called me as soon as he found out the result of the tests.

—Carlos, ¿a qué hora vamos a empezar la asamblea?
Carlos, at what time are we going to begin the assembly?

—Siempre empezamos **en cuanto llegan** todos los empleados.
We always begin as soon as all the employees arrive.

—Pedro, ¿cuándo salieron Uds. para el aeropuerto?
Pedro, when did you leave for the airport?

—No pudimos salir **hasta que**
el coche **estuvo** arreglado.

*We were not able to leave until
the car was fixed.*

B. There are some conjunctions that by their very meaning imply uncertainty or condition and are therefore *always* followed by the subjunctive. Some of them are **con tal que** (*provided that*), **sin que** (*without*), **en caso de que** (*in case*), **a menos que** (*unless*), **para que** (*in order that*), and **antes de que** (*before*).

—¿Va Ud. a firmar el
testamento hoy?

*Are you going to sign the will
today?*

—No puedo firmarlo **sin que**
mi abogado lo **lea.**

*I can't sign it without my
lawyer reading it.*

—¿Piensa Ud. vender su casa?

*Are you thinking of selling
your house?*

—Voy a venderla **a menos que**
pueda alquilarla.

*I'm going to sell it unless I can
rent it.*

Exercise

Complete the sentences with the subjunctive or the indicative of the verbs in the following list, as needed. Use each verb only once. Read each sentence aloud.

arreglar	venir	dar
llegar	pedir	irse
firmar	llover	salir
preguntar	necesitar	ver
traer	estar	

1. Vamos a echar las cartas al correo tan pronto como el jefe las _____.
2. Siempre cierro las ventanas cuando _____.
3. Me llamó tan pronto como _____ de la asamblea.
4. No puede salir sin que ellos lo _____.
5. No me lo dirán a menos que se lo _____.
6. No podré alquilarlo hasta que Ud. me _____ el dinero.
7. Le dimos el carro tan pronto como nos lo _____.
8. Dígale al empleado que saque copia del testamento en cuanto _____ terminado.
9. Siempre espero hasta que él _____ del trabajo.
10. Te llamaré por teléfono cuando _____ a casa.
11. Voy a llamar al abogado antes de _____ a su casa.
12. Trae el coche mañana para que lo _____ el mecánico.
13. En caso de que nosotros lo _____, trae mañana el carro.
14. Firmaré el informe con tal que tú lo _____ temprano.

2. The present perfect subjunctive

The present perfect subjunctive is formed with the present subjunctive of the auxiliary verb **haber** and the past participle of the main verb.

The Present Perfect Subjunctive		
Present Subjunctive of **haber** +		*Past Participle of the Main Verb*
yo	haya	amado
tú	hayas	comido
Ud. él ella	haya	vivido
nosotros	hayamos	hecho
Uds. ellos ellas	hayan	puesto

Exercise

Conjugate the following verbs in the present perfect subjunctive for each subject given:

1. **yo:** hacer, venir, comer, levantarse
2. **tú:** trabajar, poner, decir, acostarse
3. **ella:** escribir, cerrar, abrir, sentarse
4. **nosotros:** morir, hablar, llegar, vestirse
5. **ellos:** romper, vender, alquilar, bañarse

3. Uses of the present perfect subjunctive

The present perfect subjunctive is used in sentences in which the main clause calls for the use of the subjunctive in the subordinate clause. It is used in the same way the present perfect is used in English.

—¿Ya han pagado Uds. la cuenta del teléfono?

—No recuerdo...no, **no creo** que la **hayamos pagado** todavía.

Have you already paid the phone bill?

I don't remember . . . No, I don't think we've paid it yet.

—Estoy tan ocupado que no he tenido tiempo de revisar los informes.	*I'm so busy (that) I haven't had time to check the reports.*
—**Espero** que por lo menos su ayudante los **haya visto**.	*I hope at least your assistant **has seen** them.*
—Hubo un accidente en la autopista. Chocaron dos autobuses, y **temo** que **hayan muerto** todos los pasajeros.	*There was an accident on the freeway. Two buses collided and I fear all the passengers **have died**.*
—¡Qué horrible![1] **Ojalá** que algunos **hayan sobrevivido**.	*How horrible! I hope some (of them) **have survived**.*

Exercise

Complete the sentences with the present perfect subjunctive of the verbs in the following list, as needed: **estar, ir, sobrevivir, conseguir, pagar, chocar, poder, revisar, morir, llegar**. Use each verb only once:

1. No creo que ellos _____ la cuenta.
2. Siento que tú _____ tan ocupado.
3. Espero que Uds. _____ los informes.
4. Ojalá que mi ayudante _____ a la oficina.
5. No es verdad que _____ dos autobuses.
6. Temo que ninguno de los pasajeros del avión _____.
7. Dudo que él _____ vender la casa a ese precio.
8. Ojalá que no _____ todos los pasajeros en el accidente.
9. No creo que todos los empleados _____ a la reunión.
10. Siento que tú no _____ el puesto.

Vocabulary

COGNATES

la **asamblea**	assembly	el, la **pasajero(a)**	passenger
horrible	horrible	el **testamento**	testament, will

NOUNS

el, la **abogado(a)** lawyer, attorney	el **carro, coche** car
la **autopista** freeway	el, la **empleado(a)** employee
el, la **ayudante** assistant	el **informe** report

[1]The Spanish equivalent of *how + adjective* is **qué** + *adjective*.

VERBS

alquilar   to rent
revisar, chequear   to check
sobrevivir   to survive

OTHER WORDS
AND EXPRESSIONS

a menos que   unless
antes de que   before

echar al correo   to mail
en caso de que   in case
en cuanto, tan pronto como   as
   soon as
hasta que   until
para que   in order that
por lo menos   at least
sacar copia   to photocopy

EN EL LABORATORIO

The following material is to be used with the tape in the language laboratory.

I. Vocabulary

Repeat each word after the speaker. When repeating words that are cognates, notice the difference in pronunciation between English and Spanish.

Cognates:	la asamblea horrible el pasajero el testamento
Nouns:	el abogado la autopista el ayudante el carro el coche el empleado el informe
Verbs:	alquilar revisar chequear sobrevivir
Other words and expressions:	a menos que antes de que echar al correo en caso de que en cuanto tan pronto como hasta que para que por lo menos sacar copia

II. Structure Practice

A. Restate each of the following sentences, inserting the cue at the beginning and making any necessary changes. Repeat the correct answer after the speaker's confirmation. Listen to the model:

Modelo: Siempre me llama tan pronto como llega.   (Me va a llamar)
Me va a llamar tan pronto como llegue.

1. (Le voy a hablar)
2. (Se lo va a dar)
3. (Van a trabajar)
4. (Lo echaré)
5. (Sacaré)
6. (Se lo diré)

B. Restate each of the following sentences, inserting the cue at the beginning and making any necessary changes. Use the present perfect subjunctive. Listen to the model:

Modelo: El abogado ha llegado.   (Espero)
Espero que el abogado haya llegado.

<table>
<tr><td>1. Ojalá</td><td>6. Es imposible</td></tr>
<tr><td>2. Dudo</td><td>7. Temo</td></tr>
<tr><td>3. No creo</td><td>8. Es una lástima</td></tr>
<tr><td>4. No es verdad</td><td>9. No es posible</td></tr>
<tr><td>5. Dudan</td><td>10. Puede ser</td></tr>
</table>

III.   Listening and Comprehension

1. Listen carefully to the dialogue that follows. It will be read twice.

   (*Dialogue*)

   Now the speaker will make statements concerning the conversation you just heard. After each statement, say whether it is true (**verdadero**) or false (**falso**). The speaker will confirm the correct answer.

2. Listen carefully to the dialogue that follows. It will be read twice.

   (*Dialogue*)

   Now the speaker will make statements concerning the conversation you just heard. After each statement, say whether it is true (**verdadero**) or false (**falso**). The speaker will confirm the correct answer.

LESSON 20

1. The imperfect subjunctive
2. Uses of the imperfect subjunctive
3. *If* clauses

1. The imperfect subjunctive

The imperfect subjunctive is the simplest past tense of the subjunctive. It is formed in the same way for all verbs, regular and irregular. The **-ron** ending of the third person plural of the preterit is dropped and the following endings are added to the stem: **-ra, -ras, -ra, -ramos, -ran.**[1]

	The Imperfect Subjunctive		
Verb	*Preterit, Third Person Plural*	*Stem*	*Imperfect Subjunctive*
hablar	hablaron	**habla-**	que yo habla- ra
comer	comieron	**comie-**	que tú comie- ras
vivir	vivieron	**vivie-**	que Ud. vivie- ra
traer	trajeron	**traje-**	que él traje- ra
ir	fueron	**fue-**	que ella fue- ra
saber	supieron	**supie-**	que nosotros supié- ramos
decir	dijeron	**dije-**	que Uds. dije- ran
poner	pusieron	**pusie-**	que ellos pusie- ran
estar	estuvieron	**estuvie-**	que ellas estuvie- ran

◆ Notice the written accent mark in the first person plural form.

Exercise

Give the imperfect subjunctive of the following verbs:

1. **yo:**   alquilar, aprender, abrir, cerrar, acostarse
2. **tú:**   salir, sentir, temer, recordar, ponerse
3. **Ud.:**   llevar, romper, morir, revisar, volar, alegrarse
4. **nosotros:**   esperar, traer, pedir, volver, servir, vestirse
5. **ellos:**   tener, ser, dar, estar, poder, irse

2. Uses of the imperfect subjunctive

A. The imperfect subjunctive is always used in the subordinate clause when the verb of the main clause is in the past:

—Señorita Peña, ayer le **dije**   *Miss Peña, yesterday I told you*
que **archivara** las solicitudes   *to file the job applications.*
de empleo.

---

[1]See Appendix B: Verbs, for the other set of endings of the imperfect subjunctive, the **-se** endings.

—Pero el jefe de personal me
pidió que las **dejara** en su
escritorio.

But the personnel director
asked me to leave them on
his desk.

—Carlitos, te **dije** que **te**
lavaras la cara y las manos
antes de hacer la tarea.

Carlitos, I told you to wash
your face and hands before
doing your (the) homework.

—Ya me las lavé.

I already washed them.

B. The imperfect subjunctive is also used when the verb of the main clause
is in the present, but the subordinate clause refers to the past:

—**Es** una lástima que no
asistieras ayer a la
conferencia de la Dra. Ruiz.

It's a pity that you didn't
attend Dr. Ruiz's lecture
yesterday.

—No pude, porque tuve que ir
al consulado a recoger mi
pasaporte.

I wasn't able to (make it)
because I had to go to the
consulate to pick up my
passport.

ATENCIÓN: The imperfect subjunctive form of **querer** (**quisiera**) is used as a
polite form of request:

Quisiera pedirle un favor.   *I would like to ask you a favor.*

Exercises

A. Complete the sentences with the imperfect subjunctive of the following
verbs, as needed: **escribir, asistir, sacar, archivar, lavarse, venir, reco-**
ger, firmar. Use each verb once.

1. El jefe de personal nos dijo que _____ los documentos.
2. Sentí mucho que Ud. no _____ a la conferencia el sábado pasado.
3. Le pedí a papá que _____ mi pasaporte en el consulado.
4. Ella no les dijo que _____ las cartas.
5. Es una lástima que el plomero no _____ ayer.
6. El director me pidió que _____ copias de las solicitudes de empleo.
7. El profesor quería que nosotros _____ a máquina las lecciones.
8. Tú no me dijiste que _____ la cara y las manos antes de hacer la
   tarea.

B. Be an interpreter. Tell us how to say the following in Spanish:

1. They wanted me to leave my car.
2. I told you not to play with him, Robert.
3. I'm sorry you were sick yesterday, Mr. Vera.
4. We asked them to attend the lecture.
5. He told us to get dressed.
6. I'm glad you were able to come last Friday.

3. *If* clauses

In Spanish, the imperfect subjunctive is used in a clause introduced by **si** (*if*) when it refers to statements considered contrary to fact, hypothetical, or unlikely to happen. The resultant clause usually has a verb in the conditional:

Si yo fuera Ud....	*If I were you . . .*
Si yo **tuviera** dinero, iría de vacaciones con Uds.	*If I had money, I would go on vacation with you.*
¿No te lo puede prestar tu padre?	*Can't your father lend it to you?*
No, porque si mi padre me lo **prestara,** tendría que devolvérselo antes de septiembre, y yo necesito el dinero para pagar la matrícula.	*No, because if my father were to lend it to me, I would have to give it back to him before September, and I need the money to pay for registration.*
Si los muchachos **vinieran** hoy, podríamos ir a la playa o al parque.	*If the boys (young men) came today, we could go to the beach or to the park.*
Sí, pero ellos no llegan hasta mañana por la tarde.	*Yes, but they are not arriving until tomorrow afternoon.*

ATENCIÓN:

1. The present subjunctive is *never* used with an if-clause.
2. When an if-clause is *not* contrary to fact or hypothetical, or when there is a possibility that it will happen. the indicative is used.
   Si los muchachos **vienen** hoy, podemos ir a la playa.

Exercises

A. Complete the following sentences with the present indicative or the imperfect subjunctive of the verbs in parentheses, as needed:

1. Si yo _____ (tener) tiempo, te llevaré al cine.
2. Si tú _____ (poder), ¿lo harías?
3. Si Federico me _____ (devolver) el dinero, podré pagar la matrícula.
4. Si ella _____ (venir), iríamos a la playa.
5. Si el jefe me _____ (dar) una semana de vacaciones, iría a Francia.
6. Nosotros visitaríamos a nuestros abuelos si (nosotros) no _____ (estar) enfermos.
7. Compraré la casa si _____ (conseguir) el dinero.
8. Si yo _____ (ser) tú, no conduciría a esa velocidad.

9. Mamá dice que me va a comprar el vestido si _____ (salir) temprano de la oficina.
10. Si ellos lo _____ (saber), te lo dirían.

B. Be an interpreter. Tell us how to say the following in Spanish:

1. I would help you if I could, Charlie.
2. If she has time, she'll take you to the movies.
3. If you study, you will learn.
4. We would go on vacation if we had the money.
5. I would attend the lecture if I weren't sleepy.
6. We are going to go to the park if she comes back early.

Vocabulary

COGNATES

el **consulado** consulate	el **parque** park
Francia France	el **personal** personnel

NOUNS

el **empleo** job
la **matrícula** registration
la **solicitud** application

VERBS

archivar to file
asistir to attend
dejar to leave (*behind*)
devolver (o:ue) to return (*something*), to give back
recoger to pick up

EN EL LABORATORIO

LESSON 20

The following material is to be used with the tape in the language laboratory.

I. Vocabulary

Repeat each word after the speaker. When repeating words that are cognates, notice the difference in pronunciation between English and Spanish.

Cognates:	el consulado Francia el parque el pasaporte el personal
Nouns:	el empleo la matrícula la solicitud
Verbs:	archivar asistir dejar devolver recoger

II. Structure Practice

A. Restate each of the following sentences, inserting the cue at the beginning and making any necessary changes. Repeat the correct answer after the speaker's confirmation. Listen to the model:

Modelo: Ella quiere que yo vaya con él.   (Ella quería)
Ella quería que yo fuera con él.

1. Fue una lástima
2. No creí
3. Esperaba
4. Dudábamos
5. No había nadie
6. Necesitaba
7. No quería
8. No creían

B. Restate each of the following sentences, inserting the cue at the beginning and making any necessary changes. Repeat the correct answer after the speaker's confirmation. Listen to the model:

Modelo: Iré si tengo tiempo.   (Iría)
Iría si tuviera tiempo.

1. Le hablaría
2. Lo compraríamos
3. Lo harían
4. Se lo diría
5. Vendríamos
6. Me alegraría
7. Lo compraría
8. Lo haríamos

III.   Listening and Comprehension

1. Listen carefully to the narration that follows. It will be read twice.

   (*Narration*)

   Now the speaker will make statements concerning the narration you just heard. After each statement, say whether it is true (**verdadero**) or false (**falso**). The speaker will confirm the correct answer.

2. Listen carefully to the dialogue that follows. It will be read twice.

   (*Dialogue*)

   Now the speaker will make statements concerning the conversation you just heard. After each statement, say whether it is true (**verdadero**) or false (**falso**). The speaker will confirm the correct answer.

TEST YOURSELF

Lesson 16

A. The subjunctive

Complete the sentences with the Spanish equivalent of the verbs in parentheses. Use the present subjunctive. Follow the model:

Modelo: ...que yo _____ (*speak*)
...que yo hable

1. ...que nosotros _____ (*advise*)
2. ...que yo _____ (*wash*)
3. ...que Uds. _____ (*write*)
4. ...que tú _____ (*live*)
5. ...que él _____ (*say*)
6. ...que Ud. _____ (*close*)
7. ...que ellos _____ (*come*)
8. ...que ella _____ (*get up*)
9. ...que yo _____ (*ask for, request*)
10. ...que Uds. _____ (*do*)
11. ...que Ana _____ (*bring*)
12. ...que Ud. _____ (*recommend*)
13. ...que nosotros _____ (*move*)
14. ...que yo _____ (*go*)
15. ...que Luis _____ (*shave*)
16. ...que nosotros _____ (*sleep*)
17. ...que ella _____ (*give*)
18. ...que ellos _____ (*know*)
19. ...que yo _____ (*go out*)
20. ...que tú _____ (*have*)

B. The subjunctive with verbs of volition

Give the Spanish equivalent:

1. She wants me to bring the packages.
2. I prefer that we go to the post office.
3. At what time do you want me to be there tomorrow, Mr. Acevedo?
4. Ask him to help you, Mrs. Portillo.
5. Tell them not to be afraid.
6. (Let) your boyfriend do it.
7. (Let) them come in.

8. He wants me to be his girlfriend.
9. Do you need them to give you the money today, Mr. Ortiz?
10. I don't want you to do anything, Johnny.

C. The absolute superlative

Answer the following questions according to the model.

Modelo: ¿Es inteligente el hijo de Yolanda?
    ¡Ah, sí! Es inteligentísimo.

1. ¿Es alto Roberto?
2. ¿Están Uds. ocupadas?
3. ¿Son lentos los niños?
4. ¿Es buena la profesora?
5. ¿Es difícil esta lección?
6. ¿Es bella la ciudad donde viven Uds.?
7. ¿Es fácil la geografía física?
8. ¿Estás ocupado este fin de semana?

Lesson 17

A. The subjunctive to express emotion

Give the Spanish equivalent:

1. I hope you can get a haircut this afternoon, Robbie.
2. I'm glad your mother is feeling better, Mr. Gómez.
3. I'm afraid we can't meet until Monday, Miss Herrero.
4. We're glad to be here today.
5. She hopes to leave tomorrow morning.
6. I hope you can come to the meeting, Mr. Peña.
7. We're afraid we can't finish the job tonight.
8. I'm sorry you are so sick, Mrs. Treviño.

B. The subjunctive with impersonal expressions

Complete the following sentences with the subjunctive, the indicative, or the infinitive of the verb in parentheses, as needed:

1. Es difícil que ellos _____ (tener) tiempo hoy.
2. Es necesario _____ (estudiar) mucho.
3. Es mejor _____ (escribir) ahora mismo.
4. Es verdad que nosotros _____ (terminar) mañana.
5. Es lástima que el plomero no _____ (estar) aquí ahora.
6. Es importante _____ (hacer) bien el trabajo.
7. Es seguro que ellos _____ (llegar) el lunes.
8. Es posible _____ (firmar) los contratos hoy.

C. Formation of adverbs

Write the adverbs corresponding to the following adjectives:

1. feliz
2. especial
3. rápido
4. fácil
5. lento y cuidadoso

Lesson 18

A. The subjunctive to express doubt and unreality

Change the following sentences according to the model.

Modelo: Estoy seguro de que el jefe *viene* hoy.   (Dudo)
Dudo que el jefe venga hoy.

1. Dudo que el café ya *esté* frío.   (Estoy seguro de que)
2. Creo que Pedro *va* con nosotros.   (No creo que)
3. Es verdad que María *está* muy enferma.   (No es verdad que)
4. Tengo una casa que *queda* cerca del centro.   (Busco)
5. ¿Hay alguien aquí que *sepa* escribir a máquina?   (Aquí hay una chica que)
6. Hay muchas personas que *quieren* hacer traducciones.   (No hay muchas personas que)
7. No creo que él se *levante* a las cuatro de la mañana.   (Creo que)
8. Necesito una casa que *tenga* seis cuartos.   (Vivo en una casa que)

B. The affirmative familiar command (**tú** form)

Change the commands from the **Ud.** (*formal*) form to the **tú** (*informal*) form. Follow the model.

Modelo: Salga con los niños.
Sal con los niños.

1. Venga acá, por favor.
2. Hable con la maestra.
3. Dígame su dirección.
4. Lávese la cara.
5. Póngase el abrigo.
6. Tráiganos agua caliente.
7. Termine el trabajo.
8. Hágame el favor.
9. Apague la luz.
10. Vaya a su habitación.

11. Salga temprano.
12. Quédese afuera.
13. Tenga paciencia.
14. Sea buena.
15. Cene con nosotros.

C. The negative familiar command (**tú** form)

Give the Spanish equivalent:

1. Don't tell (it to) him.
2. Don't go out now.
3. Don't get up.
4. Don't do the translations.
5. Don't drink the lemonade.
6. Don't break it (*masc.*).
7. Don't talk to them.
8. Don't go downtown.
9. That dress? Don't put it on!
10. Don't do that.

D. Diminutive suffixes

Complete the following sentences with the Spanish equivalent of the words in parentheses:

1. Yo ya compré el _____ de Navidad.   (*little tree*)
2. Mi _____ se llama _____.   (*little sister / little Theresa*)
3. ¿Puedes hacerme un _____ para mi _____?   (*little dress / little daughter*)
4. Fuimos a Disneylandia con _____.   (*Johnny*)
5. Tenemos un _____ muy bueno.   (*little car*)

Lesson 19

A. The subjunctive after conjunctions implying uncertainty or unfulfillment

Give the Spanish equivalent:

1. I'll speak to him as soon as I see my lawyer.
2. Stay here in case he calls, Miss González.
3. He wrote to me as soon as he arrived.
4. We are going to wait until he comes.
5. I can't go without my parents knowing (it).
6. We'll buy the car when we have the money.

B. The present perfect subjunctive

Complete the following sentences with the Spanish equivalent of the verbs in parentheses. Use the present perfect subjunctive. Follow the model.

Modelo: ...que él _____ (*speak*)
que él haya hablado

1. ...que yo _____ (*see*)
2. ...que Uds. _____ (*do*)
3. ...que tú _____ (*learn*)
4. ...que ellos _____ (*sign*)
5. ...que Ud. _____ (*fix*)
6. ...que nosotros _____ (*file*)
7. ...que Ana _____ (*return*)
8. ...que Luis _____ (*go to bed*)

C. Uses of the present perfect subjunctive

Write sentences using the following items. Follow the model.

Modelo: Yo / alegrarse / tú / venir
Yo me alegro de que tú hayas venido.

1. Ellos / sentir / Uds. / estar enfermos
2. Rosa / no creer / yo / hacerlo
3. Nosotros / temer / él / morir
4. No es verdad / nosotros / escribir / esa carta
5. Ojalá / papá / poder / venir

Lesson 20

A. The imperfect subjunctive (forms)

Complete the sentences with the Spanish equivalent of the verbs in parentheses. Use the imperfect subjunctive. Follow the model.

Modelo: ...que yo _____ (*live*)
que yo viviera

1. ...que nosotros _____ (*attend*)
2. ...que tú _____ (*leave behind*)
3. ...que ellos _____ (*wash themselves*)
4. ...que yo _____ (*pick up*)
5. ...que Ud. _____ (*can*)
6. ...que Carlos _____ (*bring*)

7. ...que Uds. _____ (*give back*)
8. ...que ella _____ (*have*)

B. Uses of the imperfect subjunctive

Change the following sentences according to the models.

Modelo 1: Me dice que hable con él.
Me dijo que hablara con él.

Modelo 2: Siento que tú estés enferma.   (ayer)
Siento que tú estuvieras enferma ayer.

1. Le pido que venga en seguida.
2. Me alegro de que puedas terminarlo.   (anoche)
3. No creo que ella lo haga.
4. No es verdad que mi hermano esté preso.   (el año pasado)
5. Tenemos que ella no sepa escribir a máquina.
6. Dudo que la conferencia sea hoy.   (el sábado pasado)

C. *If*-clauses

Complete the following sentences:

1. Yo compraría una casa si...
2. Iremos a verte si...
3. Yo iría al médico si...
4. Mañana saldremos si...
5. Ellos nos ayudarían si...
6. Nosotros se lo diremos si...
7. Yo dormiría si...
8. Vamos a comer algo si...

Appendices

Appendix A: Pronunciation

1. Spanish sounds

A. The vowels

There are five distinct vowels in Spanish: **a, e, i, o, u.** Each vowel has only one basic sound, which is produced with considerable muscular tension. The pronunciation of each vowel is constant, clear, and brief.

The sound is never prolonged; in fact, the length of the sound is practically the same whether it is produced in a stressed or an unstressed syllable.[1]

To produce the English stressed vowels that most closely resemble Spanish, the speaker changes the position of the tongue, lips, and lower jaw during the production of the sound, so that the vowel actually starts as one sound, and then *glides* into another. In Spanish, however, the tongue, lips, and jaw keep a constant position during the production of the sound.

English: banana   *Spanish:* banana

The stress falls on the same vowel and syllable in both Spanish and English, but the stressed English *a* is longer in comparison to Spanish stressed **a.**

English: banana   *Spanish:* banana

Also notice that the stressed English *a* has a sound different from the other *a*'s in the word, while the Spanish **a** sound remains constant and is similar to the other **a** sounds in the Spanish word.

a   in Spanish has a sound somewhat similar to the English *a* in the word *father:*

alta	palma	cama	alma
casa	Ana	Panamá	apagar

e   is pronounced like the English *e* in the word *met:*

mes	este	ese	teme
entre	deje	encender	prender

i   has a sound similar to the English *ee* in the word *see:*

fin	sí	dividir	difícil
ir	sin	Trini	

---

[1] In a stressed syllable the prominence of the vowel is indicated by its loudness.

o   is similar to the English *o* in the word *no*, but without the glide:

toco	poco	corto	solo
como	roto	corro	loco

u   is pronounced like the English *oo* sound in the word *shoot* or the *ue* sound in the word *Sue:*

su	Úrsula	un	sucursal
Lulú	cultura	luna	Uruguay

C. Diphthongs and triphthongs

When unstressed **i** or **u** falls next to another vowel in a syllable, it unites with it to form a *diphthong*. Both vowels are pronounced as one syllable. Their sounds do not change; they are only pronounced more rapidly and with a glide. For example:

traiga	Lidia	treinta	siete	oigo	adiós
Aurora	agua	bueno	antiguo	ciudad	Luis

A *triphthong* is the union of three vowels, a stressed vowel between unstressed **i** or **u**, in the same syllable. For example:

Paraguay   estudiáis

NOTE: Stressed **i** and **u** do not form diphthongs with other vowels, except in the combinations **iu** and **ui**. For example:

rí-o   sa-bí-ais

In syllabication, diphthongs and triphthongs are considered as a single vowel; their components cannot be separated.

B. The consonants

Consonant sounds are produced by regulating the flow of air through the mouth with the aid of two speech organs. As the diagrams illus-

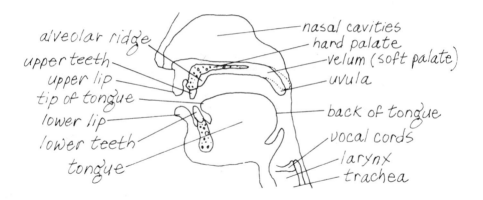

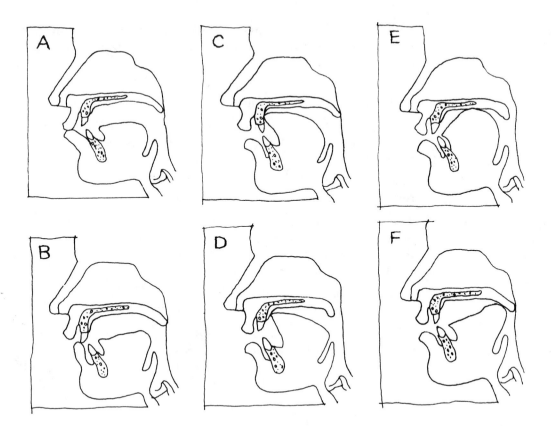

trate, different speech organs can be used to control the air flow. The point of articulation will differ accordingly.

In Spanish the air flow can be controlled in different ways. One such way is called a *stop*, because in the articulation of the sound the air is stopped at some point while passing through the oral cavity.

When we bring the speech organs close together, but without closing the air flow completely, we produce a friction sound called a *fricative*, such as the *ff* and the *th* in the English words *offer* and *other*.

p   Spanish **p** is produced by bringing the lips together as a stream of air passes through the oral cavity (see diagram A). It is pronounced in a manner similar to the English *p* sound, but without the puff of air that comes out after the English sound is produced:

pesca	pude	puedo	parte	papá
postre	piña	puente	Paco	

k   Spanish **k** sound, represented by the letters **k, c** (before **a, o, u,** or *a consonant*), and **qu,** is produced by touching the velum with the back of the tongue, as in diagram B. The sound is somewhat similar to the English *k* sound but without the puff of air:

| casa | comer | cuna | clima | acción |
| quinto | queso | aunque | kiosko | kilómetro |

t   The Spanish **t** sound is produced by touching the back of the upper front teeth with the tip of the tongue, as in diagram C. It has no puff of air as in the English *t:*

| todo | antes | corto | Guatemala | diente |
| resto | tonto | roto | tanque | |

d   The Spanish consonant **d** has two different sounds depending on its position. At the beginning of an utterance and after **n** or **l**, the tip of the tongue presses the back of the upper front teeth to produce what is called a *voiced dental stop* (see diagram C):

| día | doma | dice | dolor | dar |
| anda | Aldo | caldo | el deseo | un domicilio |

In all other positions the sound of **d** is similar to the *th* sound in the English word *they*, but softer. This sound is called a *voiced dental fricative* (see diagram C). To produce it, place the tip of the tongue behind the front teeth:

| medida | todo | nada | nadie | medio |
| puedo | moda | queda | nudo | |

g   The Spanish consonant **g** also represents two sounds. At the beginning of an utterance or after **n**, it is a *voiced velar stop* (see diagram B), identical to the English g sound in the word *guy:*

| goma | glotón | gallo | gloria |
| gorrión | garra | guerra | angustia |

In all other positions, except before **e** or **i**, it is a *voiced velar fricative* (see diagram B), similar to the English g sound in the word *sugar*. To produce it, move the back of the tongue close to the velum, as in diagram F:

| lago | alga | traga | amigo |
| algo | Dagoberto | el gorrión | la goma |

j   The sound of Spanish **j** (or **g** before **e** and **i**) is called a *voiceless velar fricative*. To produce it, position the back of the tongue close to the velum (see diagram F). (In some Latin American countries the sound is similar to a strongly exaggerated English *h* sound.):

| gemir | juez | jarro | gitano | agente |
| juego | giro | bajo | gente | |

b, v   There is no difference in sound between Spanish **b** and **v**. Both letters are pronounced alike. At the beginning of an utterance or after **m** or **n**, **b** and **v** have a sound called a *voiced bilabial stop* (see diagram A), which is identical to the English *b* sound in the word *boy:*

vivir	beber	vamos	barco	enviar
hambre	batea	bueno	vestido	

When pronounced between vowels the Spanish **b** and **v** sound is a *voiced bilabial fricative* (see diagram A). To produce this sound, bring the lips together but do not close them, letting some air pass through.

y, ll   At the beginning of an utterance or after **n** or **l**, Spanish **y** and **ll** have a sound similar to the English *dg* in the word *edge*, but somewhat softer (see diagram E):

el llavero	el yeso	llama
un yelmo	su yunta	yema

In all other positions the sound is a *voiced palatal fricative* (see diagram E), similar to the English *y* sound in the word *yes:*

oye	trayectoria	milla
trayecto	mayo	bella

NOTE: Spanish **y** when it stands alone or is at the end of a word is pronounced like the vowel **i:**

rey	doy	voy
hoy	buey	estoy
y	muy	soy

r, rr   Spanish **r** is produced by tapping the alveolar ridge with the tongue only once and very briefly (see diagram D). The sound is similar to the English *tt* sound in the word *gutter* or the *dd* sound in the word *ladder:*

crema	aroma	cara	arena	aro
harina	toro	oro	eres	portero

Spanish **r** in an initial position and after **n**, **l**, or **s**, and also **rr** in the middle of a word are pronounced with a very strong trill. This trill is produced by bringing the tip of the tongue near the alveolar ridge and letting it vibrate freely while the air passes through the mouth:

rama	carro	Israel	cierra	roto
perro	alrededor	rizo	corre	Enrique

s Spanish **s** is represented in most of the Spanish world by the letters **s, z,** and **c** before **e** or **i.** The sound is very similar to the English sibilant *s* in the word *sink:*

sale	sitio	presidente	signo
salsa	seda	suma	vaso
sobrino	ciudad	cima	canción
zapato	zarza	cerveza	centro

When it is in final position, Spanish **s** is less sibilant than in other positions. In many regions of the Spanish world there is a tendency to aspirate word-final **s** and even to drop it altogether:

eres	somos	estas	mesas	libros
vamos	sillas	cosas	rezas mucho	

h The letter **h** is silent in Spanish, unless it is combined with the **c** to form **ch:**

hoy	hora	hidra	hemos
humor	huevo	horror	hortelano

ch Spanish **ch** is pronounced like the English *ch* in the word *chief:*

hecho	chico	coche	Chile
mucho	muchacho	salchicha	

f Spanish **f** is identical in sound to the English *f:*

difícil	feo	fuego	forma
fácil	fecha	foto	fueron

l To produce the Spanish **l** sound, touch the alveolar ridge with the tip of the tongue as for the English *l.* Try to keep the rest of the tongue fairly low in the mouth:

dolor	lata	ángel	lago	sueldo
los	pelo	lana	general	fácil

m Spanish **m** is pronounced like the English *m* in the word *mother:*

mano	moda	mucho	muy
mismo	tampoco	multa	cómoda

n In most cases, Spanish **n** has a sound similar to the English *n* (see diagram D):

nada	nunca	ninguno	norte
entra	tiene	sienta	

The sound of Spanish **n** is often affected by the sounds that occur around it. When it appears before **b**, **v**, or **p**, it is pronounced like an **m:**

tan bueno	toman vino	sin poder
un pobre	comen peras	siguen bebiendo

Before **k**, **g**, and **j**, Spanish **n** has a voiced velar nasal sound, similar to the English *ng* in the word *sing:*

un kilómetro	incompleto	conjunto	mango
tengo	enjuto	un comedor	

ñ   Spanish **ñ** is a voiced palatal sound (see diagram E), similar to the English *ny* sound in the word *canyon:*

señor	otoño	ñoño	uña
leña	dueño	niños	años

x   Spanish **x** has two pronunciations depending on its position. Between vowels the sound is similar to an English *gs:*

examen	exacto	boxeo	éxito
oxidar	oxígeno	existencia	

When Spanish **x** occurs before a consonant it sounds like *s:*

expresión	explicar	extraer	excusa
expreso	exquisito	extremo	

NOTE: When the x appears in the word **México** or in other words of Mexican origin that are associated with historical or legendary figures or name places, it is pronounced like the letter **j.**

2. Rhythm

Rhythm is the melodic variation of sound intensity that we usually associate with music. Spanish and English each regulate these variations in speech differently, because they have different patterns of syllable length. In Spanish the length of the stressed and unstressed syllables remains almost the same, while in English stressed syllables are considerably longer than unstressed ones:

student	estudiante
composition	composición
police	policía

Since the length of the Spanish syllables remains constant, the greater the number of syllables in a given word or phrase, the longer the phrase will be.

Pronounce the following words trying to keep stressed and unstressed syllables the same length, and enunciating each syllable clearly. (Remember that stressed and unstressed vowels are pronounced alike.)

Úr-su-la	los-za-pa-tos
la-su-cur-sal	bue-no
Pa-ra-guay	di-fí-cil
la-cul-tu-ra	ba-jan-to-dos
el-ci-ne	ki-ló-me-tro

3. Linking

In spoken Spanish, the different words in a phrase or a sentence are not pronounced as isolated elements but combined together. This is called *linking:*

Pe-pe-co-me-pan	Pepe come pan
To-más-to-ma-le-che	Tomás toma leche
Luis-tie-ne-la-lla-ve	Luis tiene la llave
la-ma-no-de-Ro-ber-to	La mano de Roberto

1. The final consonant of a word is pronounced together with the initial vowel of the following word:

Car-lo-san-da	Carlos anda
u-nán-gel	un ángel
e-lo-to-ño	el otoño
u-no-ses-tu-dio-sin-te-re-san-tes	unos estudios interesantes

2. A diphthong is formed between the final vowel of a word and the initial vowel of the following word. A triphthong is formed when there is a three vowel combination:

suher-ma-na	su hermana
tues-co-pe-ta	tu escopeta
Ro-ber-toy-Luis	Roberto y Luis
ne-go-cioim-por-tan-te	negocio importante
llu-viay-nie-ve	lluvia y nieve
ar-duaem-pre-sa	ardua empresa

3. When the last vowel of a word and the initial vowel of the following word are the same, they are pronounced slightly longer than one vowel:

A-nal-can-za	Ana alcanza	tie-ne-so	tiene eso
lol-vi-do	lo olvido	Ada-tien-de	Ada atiende

The same rule applies when two equal vowels appear within a word:

cr*e*s   cr*ee*s
T*e*-rán   T*e*herán
c*o*r-di-na-ción c*oo*rdinación

4. When the last consonant of a word and the initial consonant of the following word are the same, they are pronounced like one consonant with slightly longer than normal duration:

e-*l*a-do e*l* *l*ado   tie-ne-*s*ed tiene*s* *s*ed
Car-lo-*s*al-ta Carlo*s* *s*alta

4. Intonation

Intonation is the rise and fall of pitch in the delivery of a phrase or a sentence. In most languages intonation is one of the most important devices used to express differences of meaning between otherwise identical phrases or sentences. In general, Spanish pitch tends to change less than English pitch, giving the impression that the language is less emphatic.

As a rule, the intonation for normal statements in Spanish starts in a low tone, raises to a higher one on the first syllable, maintains that stressed tone until the last stressed syllable, and then goes back to the initial low tone, with still another drop at the very end:

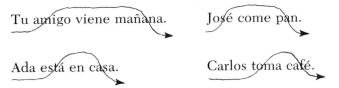

Tu amigo viene mañana. José come pan.

Ada está en casa. Carlos toma café.

5. The alphabet

Letter	Name	Letter	Name	Letter	Name	Letter	Name
a	a	h	hache	ñ	eñe	u	u
b	be	i	i	o	o	v	ve
c	ce	j	jota	p	pe	w	doble ve
ch	che	k	ka	q	cu	x	equis
d	de	l	ele	r	ere	y	i griega
e	e	ll	elle	rr	erre	z	zeta
f	efe	m	eme	s	ese		
g	ge	n	ene	t	te		

6. Syllable formation in Spanish

General rules for dividing words into syllables:

A. Vowels

1. A vowel or a vowel combination can constitute a syllable:

   a-lum-no   a-bue-la   Eu-ro-pa

2. Diphthongs and triphthongs are considered single vowels and can-not be divided:

   bai-le   puen-te   Dia-na   es-tu-diáis   an-ti-guo

3. Two strong vowels do not form a diphthong and are separated into two syllables:

   em-ple-ar   vol-te-ar   lo-a

4. A written accent mark on unstressed **i** or **u** breaks the diphthong, thus the vowels are separated into two syllables:

   trí-o   dí-a   Ma-rí-a

B. Consonants

1. A single consonant forms a syllable with the vowel that follows it:

   po-der   ma-no   mi-nu-to

   NOTE: **ch, ll,** and **rr** are considered single consonants, for example:

   a-ma-ri-llo   co-che   pe-rro

2. Consonant clusters composed of **b, c, d, f, g, p,** or **t** with **l** or **r** are considered single consonants and cannot be separated:

   ha-blar   cla-vo   a-tlán-ti-co   Glo-ria

3. When two consonants appear between two vowels, they are sepa-rated into two syllables:

   al-fa-be-to   cam-pe-ón   me-ter-se   mo-les-tia

   NOTE: When a consonant cluster appears between two vowels, we apply rule 2, and the cluster joins the following vowel, for example:

   so-bre   o-tros   ca-ble   te-lé-gra-fo

4. When three consonants appear between two vowels, only the last one goes with the following vowel:

ins-pec-tor   trans-por-te   trans-for-mar

NOTE: When a consonant cluster appears, the first consonant joins the preceding vowel and the cluster joins the following vowel, for example:

es-cri-bir   ex-tran-je-ro   im-plo-rar   es-tre-cho

7. Accentuation

In Spanish all words are stressed according to specific rules. Words that do not follow the rules must have a written accent mark to indicate the change of stress. The basic rules for accentuation are as follows:

1. Words ending in a vowel, **n,** or **s** are stressed on the next to the last syllable:

hi-jo	**ca**-lle	**me**-sa	fa-**mo**-sos
flo-**re**-cen	**pla**-ya	**ve**-ces	

2. Words ending in a consonant, except **n** or **s,** are stressed on the last syllable:

ma-**yor**	na-**riz**
a-**mor**	re-**loj**
tro-pi-**cal**	co-rre-**dor**

3. All words that do not follow these rules, and also those that are stressed on the second from the last syllable, must have the written accent:

ca-**fé**	sa-**lió**	rin-**cón**	fran-**cés**	sa-**lón**	ma-**má**
án-gel	**lá**-piz	**dé**-bil	a-**zú**-car	**Víc**-tor	
sim-**pá**-tico	**lí**-qui-do	**mú**-si-ca	e-**xá**-me-nes	de-**mó**-cra-ta	

4. Pronouns and adverbs of interrogation and exclamation have a written accent mark to distinguish them from the relative forms:

¿**Qué** comes?   *What are you eating?*
Es el libro que compré.   *It's the book that I bought.*

¿**Quién** está ahí?   *Who is there?*
El hombre a quien vi.   *The man whom I saw.*

¿**Dónde** está?   *Where is he?*
El lugar donde él trabaja.   *The place where he works.*

5. Words that are spelled the same but have a different meaning take a written accent to differentiate one from the other:

el	*the*	él	*he, him*
mi	*my*	mí	*me*
tu	*your*	tú	*you*
te	*you (pronoun)*	té	*tea*
si	*if*	sí	*yes*
mas	*but*	más	*more*

6. The demonstrative adjectives have a written accent when they are used as pronouns:

éste	ésta	éstos	éstas	ése	ésa
ésos	ésas	aquél	aquélla	aquéllos	aquéllas

Prefiero **aquél**. *I prefer that one.*

8. Cognates

When learning a foreign language, being able to recognize cognates is of great value. Let's study some of them:

1. Some exact cognates (only the pronunciation is different):

general	mineral	central	natural
idea	musical	cultural	banana
terrible	horrible	humor	terror

2. Some cognates are almost the same, except for a written accent mark, a final vowel, or a single consonant in the Spanish word:

región	península	México	conversión
persona	arte	importante	potente
comercial	oficial	posible	imposible

3. Most nouns ending in *-tion* in English end in **-ción** in Spanish:

conversación	solución	operación	cooperación

4. English words ending in *-ce* and *-ty* end in **-cia, -cio,** and **-dad** in Spanish:

importancia	competencia	precipicio
universidad	frivolidad	popularidad

5. The English ending *-ous* is often equivalent to the Spanish ending **-oso:**

famoso	amoroso	numeroso	malicioso

6. *S* consonant is often equivalent to **es** consonant in Spanish:

   escuela   estado   estudio   especial

7. Finally, there are less approximate cognates that are still easily recognizable:

millón	norte	millonario	monte
ingeniero	estudiar	artículo	ordenar
deliberadamente	enemigo	mayoría	centro

Appendix B: Verbs

Regular verbs

Model **-ar, -er, -ir** verbs

INFINITIVE		
amar (*to love*)	**comer** (*to eat*)	**vivir** (*to live*)

GERUND		
amando (*loving*)	**comiendo** (*eating*)	**viviendo** (*living*)

PAST PARTICIPLE		
amado (*loved*)	**comido** (*eaten*)	**vivido** (*lived*)

SIMPLE TENSES

Indicative Mood

PRESENT

(*I love*)	(*I eat*)	(*I live*)
am**o**	com**o**	viv**o**
am**as**	com**es**	viv**es**
am**a**	com**e**	viv**e**
am**amos**	com**emos**	viv**imos**
am**áis**[1]	com**éis**	viv**ís**
am**an**	com**en**	viv**en**

IMPERFECT

(*I used to love*)	(*I used to eat*)	(*I used to live*)
am**aba**	com**ía**	viv**ía**
am**abas**	com**ías**	viv**ías**
am**aba**	com**ía**	viv**ía**
am**ábamos**	com**íamos**	viv**íamos**
am**abais**	com**íais**	viv**íais**
am**aban**	com**ían**	viv**ían**

[1] **Vosotros amáis:** The vosotros form of the verb is used primarily in Spain. This form has not been used in this text.

PRETERIT

(*I loved*)	(*I ate*)	(*I lived*)
amé	comí	viví
amaste	comiste	viviste
amó	comió	vivió
amamos	comimos	vivimos
amasteis	comisteis	vivisteis
amaron	comieron	vivieron

FUTURE

(*I will love*)	(*I will eat*)	(*I will live*)
amaré	comeré	viviré
amarás	comerás	vivirás
amará	comerá	vivirá
amaremos	comeremos	viviremos
amaréis	comeréis	viviréis
amarán	comerán	vivirán

CONDITIONAL

(*I would love*)	(*I would eat*)	(*I would live*)
amaría	comería	viviría
amarías	comerías	vivirías
amaría	comería	viviría
amaríamos	comeríamos	viviríamos
amaríais	comeríais	viviríais
amarían	comerían	vivirían

Subjunctive Mood

PRESENT

([*that*] I [*may*] love)	([*that*] I [*may*] eat)	([*that*] I [*may*] live)
ame	coma	viva
ames	comas	vivas
ame	coma	viva
amemos	comamos	vivamos
améis	comáis	viváis
amen	coman	vivan

IMPERFECT

(two forms: **ara, ase**)

([*that*] I [*might*] love)	([*that*] I [*might*] eat)	([*that*] I [*might*] live)
amara -ase	comiera -iese	viviera -iese
amaras -ases	comieras -ieses	vivieras -ieses
amara -ase	comiera -iese	viviera -iese
amáramos -ásemos	comiéramos -iésemos	viviéramos -iésemos
amarais -aseis	comierais -ieseis	vivierais -ieseis
amaran -asen	comieran -iesen	vivieran -iesen

COMMAND FORMS

(*love*)	(*eat*)	(*live*)
ama (tú)	come (tú)	vive (tú)
ame (Ud.)	coma (Ud.)	viva (Ud.)
amemos (nosotros)	comamos (nosotros)	vivamos (nosotros)
amad (vosotros)	comed (vosotros)	vivid (vosotros)
amen (Uds.)	coman (Uds.)	vivan (Uds.)

COMPOUND TENSES

PERFECT INFINITIVE

haber amado	haber comido	haber vivido

PERFECT PARTICIPLE

habiendo amado	habiendo comido	habiendo vivido

Indicative Mood

PRESENT PERFECT

(*I have loved*)	(*I have eaten*)	(*I have lived*)
he amado	he comido	he vivido
has amado	has comido	has vivido
ha amado	ha comido	ha vivido
hemos amado	hemos comido	hemos vivido
habéis amado	habéis comido	habéis vivido
han amado	han comido	han vivido

PLUPERFECT

(*I had loved*)	(*I had eaten*)	(*I had lived*)
había amado	había comido	había vivido
habías amado	habías comido	habías vivido
había amado	había comido	había vivido
habíamos amado	habíamos comido	habíamos vivido
habíais amado	habíais comido	habíais vivido
habían amado	habían comido	habían vivido

FUTURE PERFECT

(*I will have loved*)	(*I will have eaten*)	(*I will have lived*)
habré amado	habré comido	habré vivido
habrás amado	habrás comido	habrás vivido
habrá amado	habrá comido	habrá vivido
habremos amado	habremos comido	habremos vivido
habréis amado	habréis comido	habréis vivido
habrán amado	habrán comido	habrán vivido

CONDITIONAL PERFECT

(*I would have loved*)	(*I would have eaten*)	(*I would have lived*)
habría amado	habría comido	habría vivido
habrías amado	habrías comido	habrías vivido
habría amado	habría comido	habría vivido
habríamos amado	habríamos comido	habríamos vivido
habríais amado	habríais comido	habríais vivido
habrían amado	habrían comido	habrían vivido

Subjunctive Mood

PRESENT PERFECT

([*that*] *I* [*may*] have loved)	([*that*] *I* [*may*] have eaten)	([*that*] *I* [*may*] have lived)
haya amado	haya comido	haya vivido
hayas amado	hayas comido	hayas vivido
haya amado	haya comido	haya vivido
hayamos amado	hayamos comido	hayamos vivido
hayáis amado	hayáis comido	hayáis vivido
hayan amado	hayan comido	hayan vivido

PLUPERFECT

(two forms: **-ra**, **-se**)

([*that*] *I* [*might*] have loved)	([*that*] *I* [*might*] have eaten)	([*that*] *I* [*might*] have lived)
hubiera(-iese) amado	hubiera(-iese) comido	hubiera(-iese) vivido
hubieras(-ieses) amado	hubieras(-ieses) comido	hubieras(-ieses) vivido
hubiera(-iese) amado	hubiera(-iese) comido	hubiera(-iese) vivido
hubiéramos(-iésemos) amado	hubiéramos(-iésemos) comido	hubiéramos(-iésemos) vivido
hubierais(-ieseis) amado	hubierais(-ieseis) comido	hubierais(-ieseis) vivido
hubieran(-iesen) amado	hubieran(-iesen) comido	hubieran(-iesen) vivido

Stem-changing verbs

The **-ar** and **-er** stem-changing verbs

Stem-changing verbs are those that have a change in the root of the verb. Verbs that end in **-ar** and **-er** change the stressed vowel **e** to **ie**, and the stressed **o** to **ue**. These changes occur in all persons, except the first and second persons plural of the present indicative, present subjunctive, and command.

INFINITIVE	PRESENT INDICATIVE	IMPERATIVE	PRESENT SUBJUNCTIVE
perder (*to lose*)	pierdo	—	pierda
	pierdes	pierde	pierdas
	pierde	pierda	pierda
	perdemos	perdamos	perdamos
	perdéis	perded	perdáis
	pierden	pierdan	pierdan
cerrar (*to close*)	cierro	—	cierre
	cierras	cierra	cierres
	cierra	cierre	cierre
	cerramos	cerremos	cerremos
	cerráis	cerrad	cerréis
	cierran	cierren	cierren
contar (*to count, to tell*)	cuento	—	cuente
	cuentas	cuenta	cuentes
	cuenta	cuente	cuente
	contamos	contemos	contemos
	contáis	contad	contéis
	cuentan	cuenten	cuenten
volver (*to return*)	vuelvo	—	vuelva
	vuelves	vuelve	vuelvas
	vuelve	vuelva	vuelva
	volvemos	volvamos	volvamos
	volvéis	volved	volváis
	vuelven	vuelvan	vuelvan

Verbs that follow the same pattern are:

acordarse to remember
acostar(se) to go to bed
almorzar to have lunch
atravesar to go through
cocer to cook
colgar to hang
comenzar to begin
confesar to confess
costar to cost
demostrar to demonstrate, to show
despertar(se) to wake up
discernir to discern
empezar to begin
encender to light, turn on
encontrar to find

entender to understand
llover to rain
mover to move
mostrar to show
negar to deny
nevar to snow
pensar to think, to plan
probar to prove, to taste
recordar to remember
rogar to beg
sentar(se) to sit down
soler to be in the habit of
soñar to dream
tender to stretch, to unfold
torcer to twist

The -ir stem-changing verbs

There are two types of stem-changing verbs that end in -ir: one type changes stressed **e** to **ie** in some tenses and to **i** in others, and stressed **o** to **ue** or **u**; the second type changes stressed **e** to **i** only in all the irregular tenses.

Type I   **ir:**   **e : ie**   or   **i**
                      o : ue   or   **u**

These changes occur as follows:

Present Indicative: all persons except the first and second plural change **e** to **ie** and **o** to **ue**. *Preterit:* third person, singular and plural, changes **e** to **i** and **o** to **u**. *Present Subjunctive:* all persons change **e** to **ie** and **o** to **ue**, except the first and second persons plural which change **e** to **i** and **o** to **u**. *Imperfect Subjunctive:* all persons change **e** to **i** and **o** to **u**. *Imperative:* all persons except the second person plural change **e** to **ie** and **o** to **ue**, and first person plural changes **e** to **i** and **o** to **u**. *Present Participle:* changes **e** to **i** and **o** to **u**.

	Indicative		Imperative	Subjunctive	
INFINITIVE	**PRESENT**	**PRETERIT**		**PRESENT**	**IMPERFECT**
sentir	siento	sentí	—	sienta	sintiera(-iese)
(to feel)	sientes	sentiste	siente	sientas	sintieras
	siente	sintió	sienta	sienta	sintiera
PRESENT	sentimos	sentimos	sintamos	sintamos	sintiéramos
PARTICIPLE	sentís	sentisteis	sentid	sintáis	sintierais
sintiendo	sienten	sintieron	sientan	sientan	sintieran
dormir	duermo	dormí	—	duerma	durmiera(-iese)
(to sleep)	duermes	dormiste	duerme	duermas	durmieras
	duerme	durmió	duerma	duerma	durmiera
PRESENT	dormimos	dormimos	durmamos	durmamos	durmiéramos
PARTICIPLE	dormís	dormisteis	dormid	durmáis	durmierais
durmiendo	duermen	durmieron	duerman	duerman	durmieran

Other verbs that follow the same pattern are:

advertir to warn
arrepentir(se) to repent
consentir to consent, to pamper
convertir(se) to turn into
divertir(se) to amuse (oneself)
herir to wound, to hurt

mentir to lie
morir to die
preferir to prefer
referir to refer
sugerir to suggest

Type II   **-ir: e:i**

The verbs in this second category are irregular in the same tenses as those of the first type. The only difference is that they only have one change: **e:i** in all irregular persons.

	Indicative		Imperative	Subjunctive	
INFINITIVE	PRESENT	PRETERIT		PRESENT	IMPERFECT
pedir	pido	pedí	—	pida	pidiera(-iese)
(*to ask for,*	pides	pediste	pide	pidas	pidieras
request)	pide	pidió	pida	pida	pidiera
PRESENT	pedimos	pedimos	pidamos	pidamos	pidiéramos
PARTICIPLE	pedís	pedisteis	pedid	pidáis	pidierais
pidiendo	piden	pidieron	pidan	pidan	pidieran

Verbs that follow this pattern are:

concebir to conceive
competir to compete
despedir(se) to say goodbye
elegir to choose
impedir to prevent
perseguir to pursue

repetir to repeat
reñir to fight
seguir to follow
servir to serve
vestir(se) to dress

Orthographic-changing verbs

Some verbs undergo a change in the spelling of the stem in some tenses, in order to keep the sound of the final consonant. The most common ones are those with the consonants **g** and **c**. Remember that **g** and **c** in front of **e** or **i** have a soft sound, and in front of **a, o,** or **u** have a hard sound. In order to keep the soft sound in front of **a, o,** and **u,** we change **g** and **c** to **j** and **z,** respectively. And in order to keep the hard sound of **g** and **c** in front of **e** and **i,** we add a **u** to the **g** (**gu**) and change the **c** to **qu**. Following are the most important verbs of this type:

1. Verbs ending in **-gar** change **g** to **gu** before **e** in the first person of the preterit and in all persons of the present subjunctive.

   pagar (*to pay*)
   Preterit: pagué, pagaste, pagó, etc.
   Pres. Subj.: pague, pagues, pague, paguemos, paguéis, paguen

   Verbs with the same change: **colgar, llegar, navegar, negar, regar, rogar, jugar.**

2. Verbs ending in **-ger** and **-gir** change **g** to **j** before **o** and **a** in the first person of the present indicative and in all the persons of the present subjunctive.

proteger (*to protect*)
Pres. Ind.:   protejo, proteges, protege, etc.
Pres. Subj.:   proteja, protejas, proteja, protejamos, protejáis, protejan

Verbs that follow the same pattern: **coger, dirigir, escoger, exigir, recoger, corregir.**

3. Verbs ending in **-guar** change **gu** to **gü** before **e** in the first persons of the preterit and in all persons of the present subjunctive.

averiguar (*to find out*)
Preterit: averigüé, averiguaste, averiguó, etc.
Pres. Subj.:   averigüe, averigües, averigüe, averigüemos, averigüéis, averigüen

The verb **apaciguar** has the same changes.

4. Verbs ending in **-guir** change **gu** to **g** before **o** and **a** in the first person of the present indicative and in all persons of the present subjunctive.

conseguir (*to get*)
Pres. Ind.:   consigo, consigues, consigue, etc.
Pres. Subj.:   consiga, consigas, consiga, consigamos, consigáis, consigan

Verbs with the same change: **distinguir, perseguir, proseguir, seguir.**

5. Verbs ending in **-car** change **c** to **qu** before **e** in the first person of the preterit and in all persons of the present subjunctive.

tocar (*to touch, to play* [*a musical instrument*])
Preterit: toqué, tocaste, tocó, etc.
Pres. Subj.:   toque, toques, toque, toquemos, toquéis, toquen

Verbs with the same pattern: **atacar, buscar, communicar, explicar, indicar, sacar, pescar.**

6. Verbs ending in **-cer** and **-cir** preceded by a consonant change **c** to **z** before **o** and **a** in the first person of the present indicative and in all persons of the present subjunctive.

torcer (*to twist*)
Pres. Ind.:   tuerzo, tuerces, tuerce, etc.
Pres. Subj.:   tuerza, tuerzas, tuerza, torzamos, torzáis, tuerzan

Verbs with the same change: **convencer, esparcir, vencer.**

7. Verbs ending in **-cer** and **-cir** preceded by a vowel change **c** to **zc** before **o** and **a** in the first person of the present indicative and in all persons of the present subjunctive.

conocer (*to know, to be acquainted with*)
Pres. Ind.:   conozco, conoces, conoce, etc.
Pres. Subj.:   conozca, conozcas, conozca, conozcamos, conozcáis, conozcan

Verbs with the same change: **agradecer, aparecer, carecer, establecer, entristecer** (*to sadden*), **lucir, nacer, obedecer, ofrecer, padecer, parecer, pertenecer, relucir, reconocer.**

8. Verbs ending in **-zar** change **z** to **c** before **e** in the first person of the preterit and in all persons of the present subjunctive.

rezar (*to pray*)
Preterit: recé, rezaste, rezó, etc.
Pres. Subj.:   rece, reces, rece, recemos, recéis, recen

Verbs with the same pattern: **alcanzar, almorzar, comenzar, cruzar, empezar, forzar, gozar, abrazar.**

9. Verbs ending in **-eer** change the unstressed **i** to **y** between vowels in the third person singular and plural of the preterit, in all persons of the imperfect subjunctive, and in the present participle.

creer (*to believe*)
Preterit: creí, creíste, creyó, creímos, creísteis, creyeron
Imp. Subj.:   creyera, creyeras, creyera, creyéramos, creyerais, creyeran
Pres. Part.:   creyendo
Past Part.:   creído

Leer and **poseer** follow the same change pattern.

10. Verbs ending in **-uir** change the unstressed **i** to **y** between vowels (except **-quir** which has the silent **u**) in the following tenses and persons:

huir (*to escape, to flee*)
Pres. Part.:   huyendo
Pres. Ind.:   huyo, huyes, huye, huimos, huís, huyen
Preterit: huí, huiste, huyó, huimos, huisteis, huyeron
Imperative: huye, huya, huyamos, huid, huyan
Pres. Subj.:   huya, huyas, huya, huyamos, huyáis, huyan
Imp. Subj.:   huyera(ese), huyeras, huyera, huyéramos, huyerais, huyeran

Verbs with the same change: **atribuir, concluir, constituir, cons-truir, contribuir, destituir, destruir, disminuir, distribuir, excluir, incluir, influir, instruir, restituir, sustituir.**

11. Verbs ending in **-eír** lose one **e** in the third person singular and plural of the preterit, in all persons of the imperfect subjunctive, and in the present participle.

reír (*to laugh*)
Preterit: reí, reíste, rio, reímos, reísteis, rieron
Imp. Subj.:   riera(ese), rieras, riera, rieramos, rierais, rieran
Pres. Part.: riendo

Sonreír and **freír** have the same pattern.

12. Verbs ending in **-iar** add a written accent to the **i,** except in the first and second persons plural of the present indicative and sub-junctive.

fiar(se) (*to trust*)
Pres. Ind.:   fío (me), fías (te), fía (se), fiamos (nos), fiais (os), fían (se)
Pres. Subj.: fíe (me), fíes (te), fíe (se), fiemos (nos), fiéis (os), fien (se)

Other verbs with the same change: **enviar, ampliar, criar, desviar, enfriar, guiar, telegrafiar, vaciar, variar.**

13. Verbs ending in **-uar** (except **-guar**) add a written accent to the **u,** except in the first and second persons plural of the present indica-tive and subjunctive.

actuar (*to act*)
Pres. Ind.:   actúo, actúas, actúa, actuamos, actuáis, actúan
Pres. Subj.: actúe, actúes, actúe, actuemos, actuéis, actúen

Verbs with the same pattern: **continuar, acentuar, efectuar, excep-tuar, graduar, habituar, insinuar, situar.**

14. Verbs ending in **-ñir** remove the **i** of the diphthongs **ie** and **ió** in the third person singular and plural of the preterit and in all per-sons of the imperfect subjunctive. They also change the **e** of stem to **i** in the same persons.

teñir (*to dye*)
Preterit: teñí, teñiste, **tiñó,** teñimos, teñisteis, **tiñeron**
Imp. Subj.:   tiñera(ese), tiñeras, tiñera, tiñéramos, tiñerais, tiñe-ran

Verbs with the same change: **ceñir, constreñir, desteñir, estreñir, reñir.**

Some common irregular verbs

Only those tenses with irregular forms will be given.

acertar (*to guess right*)
Pres. Ind.:   acierto, aciertas, acierta, acertamos, acertáis, aciertan
Pres. Subj.:   acierte, aciertes, acierte, acertemos, acertéis, acierten
Imperative: acierta, acierte, acertemos, acertad, acierten

adquirir (*to acquire*)
Pres. Ind.:   adquiero, adquieres, adquiere, adquirimos, adquirís, adquieren
Pres. Subj.:   adquiera, adquieras, adquiera, adquiramos, adquiráis, adquieran
Imperative: adquiere, adquiera, adquiramos, adquirid, adquieran

andar (*to walk*)
Preterit: anduve, anduviste, anduvo, anduvimos, anduvisteis, anduvieron
Imp. Subj.:   anduviera (anduviese), anduvieras, anduviera, anduviéramos, anduvierais, anduvieran

avergonzarse (*to be ashamed, to be embarrassed*)
Pres. Ind.:   me avergüenzo, te avergüenzas, se avergüenza, nos avergonzamos, os avergonzáis, se avergüenzan
Pres. Subj.:   me avergüence, te avergüences, se avergüence, nos avergoncemos, os avergoncéis, se avergüencen
Imperative: avergüénzate, avergüéncese, avergoncémonos, avergonzaos, avergüéncense

caber (*to fit, to have enough room*)
Pres. Ind.:   quepo, cabes, cabe, cabemos, cabéis, caben
Preterit: cupe, cupiste, cupo cupimos, cupisteis, cupieron
Future: cabré, cabrás, cabrá, cabremos, cabréis, cabrán
Conditional: cabría, cabrías, cabría, cabríamos, cabríais, cabrían
Imperative: cabe, quepa, quepamos, cabed, quepan
Pres. Subj.:   quepa, quepas, quepa, quepamos, quepáis, quepan
Imp. Subj.:   cupiera (cupiese), cupieras, cupiera, cupiéramos, cupierais, cupieran

caer (*to fall*)
Pres. Ind.:   caigo, caes, cae, caemos, caéis, caen
Preterit: caí, caíste, cayó, caímos, caísteis, cayeron
Imperative: cae, caiga, caigamos, caed, caigan
Pres. Subj.:   caiga, caigas, caiga, caigamos, caigáis, caigan
Imp. Subj.:   cayera (cayese), cayeras, cayera, cayéramos, cayerais, cayeran
Past Part.:   caído

cegar (*to blind*)
Pres. Ind.:	ciego, ciegas, ciega, cegamos, cegáis, ciegan
Imperative:	ciega, ciegue, ceguemos, cegad, cieguen
Pres. Subj.:	ciegue, ciegues, ciegue, ceguemos, ceguéis, cieguen

conducir (*to guide, to drive*)
Pres. Ind.:	conduzco, conduces, conduce, conducimos, conducís, conducen
Preterit:	conduje, condujiste, condujo, condujimos, condujisteis, condujeron
Imperative:	conduce, conduzca, conduzcamos, conducid, conduzcan
Pres. Subj.:	conduzca, conduzcas, conduzca, conduzcamos, conduzcáis, conduzcan
Imp. Subj.:	condujera (condujese), condujeras, condujera, condujéramos, condujerais, condujeran

(All verbs ending in **-ducir** follow this pattern)

convenir (*to agree*) See **venir.**

dar (*to give*)
Pres. Ind.:	doy, das, da, damos, dais, dan
Preterit:	di, diste, dio, dimos, disteis, dieron
Imperative:	da, dé, demos, dad, den
Pres. Subj.:	dé, des, dé, demos, deis, den
Imp. Subj.:	diera (diese), dieras, diera, diéramos, dierais, dieran

decir (*to say, to tell*)
Pres. Ind.:	digo, dices, dice, decimos, decís, dicen
Preterit:	dije, dijiste, dijo, dijimos, dijisteis, dijeron
Future:	diré, dirás, dirá, diremos, diréis, dirán
Conditional:	diría, dirías, diría, diríamos, diríais, dirían
Imperative:	di, diga, digamos, decid, digan
Pres. Subj.:	diga, digas, diga, digamos, digáis, digan
Imp. Subj.:	dijera (dijese), dijeras, dijera, dijéramos, dijerais, dijeran
Pres. Part.:	diciendo
Past. Part.:	dicho

detener (*to stop, to hold, to arrest*) See **tener.**

elegir (*to choose*)
Pres. Ind.:	elijo, eliges, elige, elegimos, elegís, eligen
Preterit:	elegí, elegiste, eligió, elegimos, elegisteis, eligieron
Imperative:	elige, elija, elijamos, elegid, elijan
Pres. Subj.:	elija, elijas, elija, elijamos, elijáis, elijan
Imp. Subj.:	eligiera (eligiese), eligieras, eligiera, eligiéramos, eligierais, eligieran

entender (*to understand*)
Pres. Ind.:	entiendo, entiendes, entiende, entendemos, entendéis, entienden
Imperative:	entiende, entienda, entendamos, entended, entiendan
Pres. Subj.:	entienda, entiendas, entienda, entendamos, entendáis, entiendan

entretener (*to entertain, to amuse*) See **tener.**

extender (*to extend, to stretch out*) See **tender.**

errar (*to err, to miss*)
Pres. Ind.:	yerro, yerras, yerra, erramos, erráis, yerran
Imperative:	yerra, yerre, erremos, errad, yerren
Pres. Subj.:	yerre, yerres, yerre, erremos, erréis, yerren

estar (*to be*)
Pres. Ind.:	estoy, estás, está, estamos, estáis, están
Preterit:	estuve, estuviste, estuvo, estuvimos, estuvisteis, estuvieron
Imperative:	está, esté, estemos, estad, estén
Pres. Subj.:	esté, estés, esté, estemos, estéis, estén
Imp. Subj.:	estuviera (estuviese), estuvieras, estuviera, estuviéramos, estuvierais, estuvieran

haber (*to have*)
Pres. Ind.:	he, has, ha, hemos, habéis, han
Preterit:	hube, hubiste, hubo, hubimos, hubisteis, hubieron
Future:	habré, habrás, habrá, habremos, habréis, habrán
Conditional:	habría, habrías, habría, habríamos, habríais, habrían
Imperative:	he, haya, hayamos, habed, hayan
Pres. Subj.:	haya, hayas, haya, hayamos, hayáis, hayan
Imp. Subj.:	hubiera (hubiese), hubieras, hubiera, hubiéramos, hubierais, hubieran

hacer (*to do, to make*)
Pres. Ind.:	hago, haces, hace, hacemos, hacéis, hacen
Preterit:	hice, hiciste, hizo, hicimos, hicisteis, hicieron
Future:	haré, harás, hará, haremos, haréis, harán
Conditional:	haría, harías, haría, haríamos, haríais, harían
Imperative:	haz, haga, hagamos, haced, hagan
Pres. Subj.:	haga, hagas, haga, hagamos, hagáis, hagan
Imp. Subj.:	hiciera (hiciese), hicieras, hiciera, hiciéramos, hicierais, hicieran
Past Part.:	hecho

imponer (*to impose, to deposit*) See **poner.**

introducir (*to introduce, to insert, to gain access*) See **conducir.**

ir (*to go*)
Pres. Ind.:	voy, vas, va, vamos, vais, van
Imp. Ind.:	iba, ibas, iba, íbamos, ibais, iban
Preterit:	fui, fuiste, fue, fuimos, fuisteis, fueron
Imperative:	ve, vaya, vayamos, id, vayan
Pres. Subj.:	vaya, vayas, vaya, vayamos, vayáis, vayan
Imp. Subj.:	fuera (fuese), fueras, fuera, fuéramos, fuerais, fueran

jugar (*to play*)
Pres. Ind.:	juego, juegas, juega, jugamos, jugáis, juegan
Imperative:	juega, juegue, juguemos, jugad, jueguen
Pres. Subj.:	juegue, juegues, juegue, juguemos, juguéis, jueguen

obtener (*to obtain*) See **tener.**

oír (*to hear*)
Pres. Ind.:	oigo, oyes, oye, oímos, oís, oyen
Preterit:	oí, oíste, oyó, oímos, oísteis, oyeron
Imperative:	oye, oiga, oigamos, oid, oigan
Pres. Subj.:	oiga, oigas, oiga, oigamos, oigáis, oigan
Imp. Subj.:	oyera (oyese), oyeras, oyera, oyéramos, oyerais, oyeran
Pres. Part.:	oyendo
Past Part.:	oído

oler (*to smell*)
Pres. Ind.:	huelo, hueles, huele, olemos, oléis, huelen
Imperative:	huele, huela, olamos, oled, huelan
Pres. Subj.:	huela, huelas, huela, olamos, oláis, huelan

poder (*to be able*)
Pres. Ind.:	puedo, puedes, puede, podemos, podéis, pueden
Preterit:	pude, pudiste, pudo, pudimos, pudisteis, pudieron
Future:	podré, podrás, podrá, podremos, podréis, podrán
Conditional:	podría, podrías, podría, podríamos, podríais, podrían
Imperative:	puede, pueda, podamos, poded, puedan
Pres. Subj.:	pueda, puedas, pueda, podamos, podáis, puedan
Imp. Subj.:	pudiera (pudiese), pudieras, pudiera, pudiéramos, pudierais, pudieran
Pres. Part.:	pudiendo

poner (*to place, to put*)
Pres. Ind.:	pongo, pones, pone, ponemos, ponéis, ponen
Preterit:	puse, pusiste, puso, pusimos, pusisteis, pusieron
Future:	pondré, pondrás, pondrá, pondremos, pondréis, pondrán
Conditional:	pondría, pondrías, pondría, pondríamos, pondríais, pondrían
Imperative:	pon, ponga, pongamos, poned, pongan
Pres. Subj.:	ponga, pongas, ponga, pongamos, pongáis, pongan

Imp. Subj.:   pusiera (pusiese), pusieras, pusiera, pusiéramos, pusierais, pusieran
Past Part.:   puesto

querer (*to want, to wish, to like*)
Pres. Ind.:   quiero, quieres, quiere, queremos, queréis, quieren
Preterit: quise, quisiste, quiso, quisimos, quisisteis, quisieron
Future: querré, querrás, querrá, querremos, querréis, querrán
Conditional: querría, querrías, querría, querríamos, querríais, querrían
Imperative: quiere, quiera, queramos, quered, quieran
Pres. Subj.:   quiera, quieras, quiera, queramos, queráis, quieran
Imp. Subj.:   quisiera (quisiese), quisieras, quisiera, quisiéramos, quisierais, quisieran

resolver (*to decide on*)
Pres. Ind.:   resuelvo, resuelves, resuelve, resolvemos, resolvéis, resuelven
Imperative: resuelve, resuelva, resolvamos, resolved, resuelvan
Pres. Subj.:   resuelva, resuelvas, resuelva, resolvamos, resolváis, resuelvan
Past Part.:   resuelto

saber (*to know*)
Pres. Ind.:   sé, sabes, sabe, sabemos, sabéis, saben
Preterit: supe, supiste, supo, supimos, supisteis, supieron
Future: sabré, sabrás, sabrá, sabremos, sabréis, sabrán
Conditional: sabría, sabrías, sabría, sabríamos, sabríais, sabrían
Imperative: sabe, sepa, sepamos, sabed, sepan
Pres. Subj.:   sepa, sepas, sepa, sepamos, sepáis, sepan
Imp. Subj.:   supiera (supiese), supieras, supiera, supiéramos, supierais, supieran

salir (*to leave, to go out*)
Pres. Ind.:   salgo, sales, sale, salimos, salís, salen
Future: saldré, saldrás, saldrá, saldremos, saldréis, saldrán
Conditional: saldría, saldrías, saldría, saldríamos, saldríais, saldrían
Imperative: sal, salga, salgamos, salid, salgan
Pres. Subj.:   salga, salgas, salga, salgamos, salgáis, salgan

ser (*to be*)
Pres. Ind.:   soy, eres, es, somos, sois, son
Imp. Ind.:   era, eras, era, éramos, erais, eran
Preterit: fui, fuiste, fue, fuimos, fuisteis, fueron
Imperative: sé, sea, seamos, sed, sean
Pres. Subj.:   sea, seas, sea, seamos, seáis, sean
Imp. Subj.:   fuera (fuese), fueras, fuera, fuéramos, fuerais, fueran

suponer (*to assume*) See **poner.**

tener (*to have*)
Pres. Ind.:   tengo, tienes, tiene, tenemos, tenéis, tienen
Preterit: tuve, tuviste, tuvo, tuvimos, tuvisteis, tuvieron
Future: tendré, tendrás, tendrá, tendremos, tendréis, tendrán
Conditional: tendría, tendrías, tendría, tendríamos, tendríais, tendrían
Imperative: ten, tenga, tengamos, tened, tengan
Pres. Subj.:   tenga, tengas, tenga, tengamos, tengáis, tengan
Imp. Subj.:   tuviera (tuviese), tuvieras, tuviera, tuviéramos, tuvierais, tuvieran

tender (*to spread out, to hang out*)
Pres. Ind.:   tiendo, tiendes, tiende, tendemos, tendéis, tienden
Imperative: tiende, tienda, tendamos, tended, tiendan
Pres. Subj.:   tienda, tiendas, tienda, tendamos, tendáis, tiendan

traducir (*to translate*)
Pres. Ind.:   traduzco, traduces, traduce, traducimos, traducís, traducen
Preterit: traduje, tradujiste, tradujo, tradujimos, tradujisteis, tradujeron
Imperative: traduce, traduzca, traduzcamos, traducid, traduzcan
Pres. Subj.:   traduzca, traduzcas, traduzca, traduzcamos, traduzcáis, traduzcan
Imp. Subj.:   tradujera (tradujese), tradujeras, tradujera, tradujéramos, tradujerais, tradujeran

traer (*to bring*)
Pres. Ind.:   traigo, traes, trae, traemos, traéis, traen
Preterit: traje, trajiste, trajo, trajimos, trajisteis, trajeron
Imperative: trae, traiga, traigamos, traed, traigan
Pres. Subj.:   traiga, traigas, traiga, traigamos, traigáis, traigan
Imp. Subj.:   trajera (trajese), trajeras, trajera, trajéramos, trajerais, trajeran
Pres. Part.:   trayendo
Past Part.:   traído

valer (*to be worth*)
Pres. Ind.:   valgo, vales, vale, valemos, valéis, valen
Future: valdré, valdrás, valdrá, valdremos, valdréis, valdrán
Conditional: valdría, valdrías, valdría, valdríamos, valdríais, valdrían
Imperative: vale, valga, valgamos, valed, valgan
Pres. Subj.:   valga, valgas, valga, valgamos, valgáis, valgan

venir (*to come*)
Pres. Ind.:   vengo, vienes, viene, venimos, venís, vienen
Preterit: vine, viniste, vino, vinimos, vinisteis, vinieron
Future: vendré, vendrás, vendrá, vendremos, vendréis, vendrán

Conditional:	vendría, vendrías, vendría, vendríamos, vendríais, vendrían
Imperative:	ven, venga, vengamos, venid, vengan
Pres. Subj.:	venga, vengas, venga, vengamos, vengáis, vengan
Imp. Subj.:	viniera (viniese), vinieras, viniera, viniéramos, vinierais, vinieran
Pres. Part.:	viniendo

ver (*to see*)

Pres. Ind.:	veo, ves, ve, vemos, veis, ven
Imp. Ind.:	veía, veías, veía, veíamos, veíais, veían
Preterit:	vi, viste, vio, vimos, visteis, vieron
Imperative:	ve, vea, veamos, ved, vean
Pres. Subj.:	vea, veas, vea, veamos, veáis, vean
Imp. Subj.:	viera (viese), vieras, viera, viéramos, vierais, vieran
Past Part.:	visto

Appendix C:
Glossary of Grammatical Terms

adjective: A word that describes a noun or a pronoun: *tall* girl, *difficult* lesson.

adverb: A word that modifies a verb, an adjective, or another adverb. It answers the questions "How?", "When?", "Where?": She walked *slowly*. She'll be here *tomorrow*. She is *here*.

agree: A term usually applied to adjectives. An adjective is said to show agreement with the noun it modifies when its ending changes in accordance with the gender and number of the noun. In Spanish, a feminine plural noun requires a feminine plural ending in the adjective that describes it (**casas amarillas**) and a masculine singular noun requires a masculine singular ending in the adjective (**libro negro**).

article: See *definite article* and *indefinite article*.

auxiliary verb: A verb that helps in the conjugation of another verb. I *have* finished. He *was* called. She *will* go. He *would* eat.

command form: The form of the verb used to give an order or a direction: *Go! Come back! Turn* to the right!

conjugation: The process by which the forms of the verb are presented in their different moods, persons, and tenses: I *am*, you *are*, he *is*, she *was*, we *were*, etc.

contraction: The combination of two or more words into one: *isn't, don't, can't.*

definite article: A word used before a noun indicating a definite person or thing: *the* woman, *the* money.

demonstrative pronoun or adj.: A word that refers to a definite person or object: *this, that, these, those.*

diphthong: A combination of two vowels forming one syllable. In Spanish, a diphthong is composed of one *strong* vowel (**a, e, o**) and one *weak* vowel (**u, i**) or two weak vowels: **ei, au, ui.**

exclamation: A word used to express emotion: *How* strong! *What* beauty!

gender: A distinction of nouns, pronouns, and adjectives, based on whether they are masculine or feminine.

indefinite article: A word used before a noun that refers to an indefinite person or object: *A* child. *An* apple, *some* students.

infinitive: The form of the verb generally preceded in English by the word *to* and showing no subject or number: *to do, to bring.*

interrogative: A word used in asking a question: *Who? What? Where?*

main clause: A group of words that includes a subject and a verb and by itself has complete meaning: *They saw me. I go now.*

noun: A word that names a per-

285

son, place, thing, etc.: *Ann, London, pencil,* etc.

number: Number refers to singular and plural: *chair, chairs.*

object: Generally a noun or a pronoun that is the receiver of the verb's action. A direct object answers the question "*What?*" or "*Whom?*": We know *her.* Take *it.* An indirect object answers the question "*To whom?*" or "*To what?*": Give *John* the money. Nouns and pronouns can also be objects of prepositions: The letter is *from Rick.* I'm thinking *about you.*

past participle: Past forms of a verb: *gone, worked, written,* etc.

person: The form of the pronoun and of the verb that shows the person referred to: *I* (first person singular), *you* (second person singular), *she* (third person singular), etc.

possessive: A word that denotes ownership or possession: This is *our* house. The book isn't *mine.*

preposition: A word that introduces a noun, pronoun, adverb, infinitive, or present participle and indicates its function in the sentence. They were *with* us. She is *from* Nevada.

pronoun: A word that is used to replace a noun: *she, them, us,* etc. A **subject pronoun** refers to the person or thing spoken of. *They* work. An **object pronoun** receives the action of the verb. They arrested *us* (direct object pronoun). She spoke to *him* (indirect object pronoun). A pronoun can also be the object of a preposition: The children stayed with *us.*

reflexive pronoun: A pronoun that refers back to the subject *myself, yourself, himself, herself, itself, ourselves,* etc.

subject: The person, place, or thing spoken of: *Robert* works. *Our car* is new.

subordinate clause: A clause that has no complete meaning by itself but depends on a main clause: They knew *that I was here.*

tense: The group of forms in a verb that show the time in which the action of the verb takes place: *I go* (present indicative), *I'm going* (present progressive), *I went* (past), *I was going* (past progressive), *I will go* (future), *I would go* (conditional), *I have gone* (present perfect), *I had gone* (past perfect), *that I may go* (present subjunctive), etc.

verb: A word that expresses an action or a state: We *sleep.* The baby *is* sick.

Appendix D:
Careers and Occupations

accountant **contador**
actor **actor**
actress **actriz**
administrator **administrador**
agent **agente**
architect´ **arquitecto**
baker **panadero**
bank officer **empleado bancario**
bank teller **cajero**
banker **banquero**
barber **barbero**
bartender **barman, cantinero**
bill collector **cobrador**
bookkeeper **tenedor de libros**
brickmason (bricklayer) **albañil**
buyer **comprador**
cameraman **camarógrafo**
carpenter **carpintero**
cashier **cajero**
chiropractor **quiropráctico**
clerk **dependiente**
computer operator **computista**
contractor **contratista**
construction worker **obrero de
   la construcción**
constructor **constructor**
cook **cocinero**
copilot **copiloto**
counselor **consejero**
craftsman **artesano**
dancer **bailarín**
decorator **decorador**
dental hygienist **higienista
   dental**
dentist **dentista**
designer **diseñador**
detective **detective**
dietician **especialista en
   dietética**
diplomat **diplomático**
dockworker **obrero portuario**

doctor **doctor**
draftsman **dibujante**
dressmaker **modista**
driver **conductor**
economist **economista**
editor **editor**
electrician **electricista**
engineer **ingeniero**
engineering technician
   ingeniero técnico
farmer **agricultor**
fashion designer **diseñador de
   alta costura, modisto**
fireman **bombero**
fisherman **pescador**
flight attendant **auxiliar de
   vuelo, azafata**
foreman **capataz, encargado**
funeral director **empresario de
   pompas fúnebres**
garbage collector **basurero**
gardener **jardinero**
guard **guardia**
hairdresser **peluquero**
home economist **economista
   doméstico**
housekeeper **ama de llaves**
inspector **inspector**
insurance agent **agente de
   seguros**
interior designer **diseñador de
   interiores**
interpreter **intérprete**
investigator **investigador**
janitor **conserje**
jeweler **joyero**
journalist **periodista**
judge **juez**
lawyer **abogado**
librarian **bibliotecario**
machinist **maquinista**

maid **criada**
mail carrier **cartero**
manager **gerente**
meat cutter **carnicero**
mechanic **mecánico**
midwife **comadrona, partera**
military **militar**
miner **minero**
model **modelo**
musician **músico**
night watchman **sereno, guardián**
nurse **enfermero**
optician **óptico**
optometrist **optometrista**
painter **pintor**
pharmacist **farmacéutico**
photographer **fotógrafo**
physical therapist **terapista físico**
physician **médico**
pilot **piloto, aviador**
plumber **plomero**
policeman **policía**
printer **impresor**
psychologist **psicólogo**
public relations agent **agente de relaciones públicas**
real estate agent **agente de bienes raíces**
receptionist **recepcionista**
reporter **reportero, periodista**
sailor **marinero**
salesman **vendedor**
scientist **científico**
seamstress **costurera, modista**
secretary **secretario**

social worker **trabajador social**
sociologist **sociólogo**
stenographer **estenógrafo**
stewardess **azafata, auxiliar de vuelo**
stockbroker **bolsista**
supervisor **supervisor**
surgeon **cirujano**
systems analyst **analista de sistemas**
tailor **sastre**
taxi driver **chofer de taxi, conductor**
teacher **maestro** (*elem. school*), **profesor** (*high school and college*)
technician **técnico**
telephone operator **telefonista**
therapist **terapista**
television and radio technician **técnico de radio y televisión**
television and radio announcer **locutor**
teller **cajero**
travel agent **agente de viajes**
traveling salesman **viajante de comercio**
truck driver **camionero**
typist **mecanógrafa, dactilógrafa**
undertaker **director de pompas fúnebres**
veterinarian **veterinario**
waiter **mozo, camarero**
waitress **camarera**
watchmaker **relojero**
watchman **sereno, guardián**
worker **obrero**

Appendix E:
Answer Key to Self-Testing Sections

Lesson 1

A. 1. nosotros 2. ellos 3. ustedes 4. ellas 5. nosotras

B. 1. hablo 2. trabajamos 3. estudia 4. necesitas 5. trabajan
6. habla

C. *Interrogative:* 1. ¿Trabaja Elena en Buenos Aires?
2. ¿Hablan Uds. inglés? 3. ¿(Tú) necesitas dinero? 4. ¿Juan y
Amalia estudian español? 5. ¿Trabaja Ud. en Los Ángeles?
Negative: 1. Elena no trabaja en Buenos Aires. 2. Uds. no
hablan inglés. 3. Tú no necesitas dinero. 4. Juan y Amalia no
estudian español. 5. Ud no trabaja en Los Ángeles.

D. 1. quinientos 2. mil 3. quinientos cincuenta 4. doscientos
5. novecientos 6. cuatrocientos cincuenta

Lesson 2

A. 1. cinco libros azules 2. dos señoras norteamericanas 3. un
restaurante grande 4. los estudiantes alemanes 5. un profesor
inteligente

B. 1. las casas verdes 2. los lápices negros 3. los profesores
inteligentes 4. las sillas grandes 5. los libros blancos 6. las
señoritas felices

C. 1. ¿Dónde vive Ud., señora Vera? 2. Ellos beben café. Yo
bebo té. 3. Nosotros leemos las lecciones. 4. Él decide
estudiar inglés. 5. ¿(Tú) entiendes? 6. Uds. comen
temprano. 7. Ella escribe en español. 8. Nosotros abrimos los
libros. 9. Yo aprendo español. 10. Ellos no reciben el dinero.

D. 1. _____ 2. a 3. _____ 4. a 5. a

Lesson 3

A. 1. Nosotros recibimos el dinero de Carlos. 2. Ella lee la
solicitud de la recepcionista. 3. Los estudiantes visitan a la
esposa de Enrique. 4. ¿Tú esperas a la amiga de Teresa?
5. Ud. no necesita el auto de María.

B. 1. tu 2. sus (de ella) 3. nuestro 4. su (de Ud.) 5. mis
6. tus 7. nuestras 8. su (de él)

C. 1. Sí, yo soy alto(a). 2. Sí, soy de California. 3. Sí, somos
felices. 4. Sí, Ud. es el (la) profesor(a). 5. Sí, mi lección de
español es difícil. 6. Sí, ellos son ingenieros.

D. 1. dan / su damos / nuestro das / tu dan / su da / su   2. estoy / mi están / su estamos / nuestra está / su estás / tu están / su
3. vamos / nuestras va / sus vas / tus voy / mis van / sus

E. 1. La mesa es de madera.   2. La señorita López está enferma hoy.   3. Las casas son de mi hija.   4. Los estudiantes son argentinos.   5. El profesor está en el hospital.   6. Yo soy de Puerto Rico.   7. Nosotros estamos bien.   8. María es alta.
9. Gustavo y yo somos casados.   10. Mañana es sábado.
11. ¿Cuál es su profesión?   12. El hijo de la señora Nieto es ingeniero.

Lesson 4

A. 1. Esperamos al supervisor (a la supervisora).   2. Ella visita al señor Linares y a la señora Viera.   3. El dinero es del señor Peña.   4. Él no va a la tienda. Va al mercado.   5. Necesitamos llamar al instructor.

B. 1. No, yo no soy tan alto(a) como el profesor (la profesora).
2. No, el profesor (la profesora) no llega más tarde que los estudiantes.   3. No, yo no soy el (la) estudiante menos inteligente de la clase.   4. No, yo no soy la persona más feliz de la clase.   5. No, yo no soy el (la) peor estudiante.   6. No, nosotros no somos mayores que nuestros amigos.   7. No, Ud. no es el (la) mejor de la clase.   8. No, la casa de mi amigo no es más grande que mi casa.

C. 1. venimos / nuestro vienes /tu vienen / su viene / su viene / su vienen / su   2. tengo / mis tiene / sus tienes / tus tienen / sus

D. 1. Carlos no tiene hambre, pero tiene mucha sed.   2. Ellos tienen mucho cuidado.   3. Mi hija no tiene miedo.   4. Ud. tiene razón, señorita Vera. El(La) instructor(a) tiene prisa.
5. Tengo veintisiete años. ¿Cuántos años tienes tú, Ana?   6. No tengo calor; tengo frío.

Lesson 5

A. (*Possibilities*):   1. Mi clase de español es a las siete.
2. Nosotros comemos a las doce.   3. Yo voy a la universidad a las siete.   4. Yo estudio por la noche.   5. El profesor llega a la clase a las siete menos diez.   6. Son las seis.

B. (*Possibilities*):   1. Nosotros preferimos estudiar francés.   2. No, no quiero ir al cine hoy.   3. La clase de español empieza a las siete.   4. Sí, nosotros entendemos las lecciones.   5. No, nosotros no perdemos mucho dinero en Las Vegas.   6. Cierran la biblioteca a las nueve.   7. Mi programa de televisión favorito comienza a las ocho.   8. Nosotros preferimos viajar en el verano.

C. 1. vamos a comer 2. va a comprar 3. va a empezar 4. vas a visitar 5. va a llegar 6. voy a venir 7. vamos a necesitar 8. Van a ir

D. 1. ¿Cuántos estudiantes hay? 2. No hay dinero. 3. Hay dos vuelos a Lima. 4. Hay una reunión hoy. 5. ¿Cúantas sillas hay?

E. 1. quinto día 2. octavo mes 3. décimo piso 4. primeros estudiantes 5. tercer libro 6. novena casa 7. segunda semana 8. sexta reunión 9. cuarta clase 10. séptimo auto

Lesson 6

A. 1. Hoy es miércoles. 2. Las mujeres quieren igualdad con los hombres. 3. La libertad es importante. 4. Nosotros vamos a visitar la cárcel la semana próxima. 5. Yo no tengo clases los viernes.

B. (*Possibilities*): 1. Yo vuelvo a mi casa a las cinco y media. 2. Cuando nosotros vamos a México, volamos. 3. Sí, nosotros recordamos los verbos irregulares. 4. Yo duermo ocho horas. 5. No, nosotros no podemos ir a la iglesia hoy.

C. 1. Ellos recuerdan algo. 2. Hay alguien en la escuela. 3. Yo quiero volar también. 4. Recibimos algunos regalos. 5. Siempre tiene éxito.

D. 1. Para tener éxito, hay que trabajar. 2. Ud. tiene que volver la semana próxima, señor Vega. 3. Ella tiene que trabajar mañana. 4. Hay que comenzar temprano. 5. ¿Tenemos que empezar a los ocho?

E. 1. ¿Puede venir conmigo? 2. ¿Va a trabajar con ellos? 3. El piano es para ti, Anita. 4. El regalo no es para mí. Es para ella. 5. No, Paco, no puedo ir contigo.

Lesson 7

A. (*Possibilities*): 1. Nosotros servimos sopa. 2. Yo pido Coca-Cola para beber. 3. No, yo no digo mi edad. 4. Sí, yo sigo en la universidad. 5. Sí, nosotros siempre pedimos postre.

B. 1. conduzco 2. salgo 3. pongo 4. traduzco 5. conozco 6. quepo 7. hago 8. veo 9. sé 10. traigo

C. 1. Yo conozco a su hijo. 2. Él no sabe francés. 3. ¿Sabe usted nadar, señorita Vera? 4. ¿Conoce usted al instructor? 5. ¿Conocen los estudiantes las novelas de Cervantes?

D. (*Possibilities*): 1. En Estados Unidos se habla inglés. 2. Se dice *a menudo*. 3. La biblioteca se cierra a las diez. 4. Mi apellido se escribe ese-eme-i-te-hache 5. Las tiendas se abren a las diez.

E. 1. Yo las conozco. 2. Uds. van a comprarlo. 3. Nosotros no queremos verte. 4. Ella la sirve. 5. ¿Ud. no me conoce? 6. Él los escribe. 7. Carlos va a visitarnos. 8. Nosotros no lo vemos.

Lesson 8

A. 1. Necesito estas revistas y aquéllas. 2. ¿Quiere usted este cuaderno o ése? 3. Yo prefiero estos periódicos, no aquéllos. 4. Papá, ¿quieres comprar esta corbata o ésa? 5. No quiero comer en este restaurante. Prefiero aquél. 6. Yo no entiendo eso.

B. 1. está estudiando 2. está comiendo 3. estamos leyendo 4. estás diciendo 5. estoy tomando

C. 1. Me va a comprar los pasajes. 2. Le doy las revistas. 3. Nos habla en español. 4. Les voy a decir la verdad. 5. Les pregunto la dirección de la oficina. 6. Le estamos escribiendo a nuestro padre. 7. Le escribo los lunes. 8. Le doy la información al presidente. 9. Te hablo en inglés. 10. No me compran nada.

D. 1. ¿El dinero? Se lo doy mañana, señor Peña. 2. Yo sé que necesitas un diccionario, Anita, pero no puedo prestártelo. 3. Necesito mi abrigo. ¿Puede traérmelo, señorita López? 4. ¿Las plumas? Ella nos las trae. 5. Cuando yo necesito zapatos nuevos, mi mamá me los compra.

E. 1. Voy a preguntarle dónde vive. 2. Yo siempre le pido dinero a mi esposo. 3. Ella siempre pregunta cómo está usted, señora Nieto. 4. Me van a pedir los libros de química. 5. Quiero preguntarle cuántos años tiene (él).

Lesson 9

A. 1. No, no son mías. 2. No, no son de ella. 3. No, no es mío. 4. No, no es nuestra. 5. No, no es de ellos. 6. No, no son míos. 7. No, no es nuestro. 8. No, no es de ustedes.

B. 1. Yo me levanto a las siete, me baño, me visto y salgo a las siete y media. 2. ¿A qué hora se despiertan los niños? 3. Ella no quiere sentarse. 4. Ud. siempre se preocupa por su hijo, señora Cruz. 5. ¿Te acuerdas de tus maestros, Carlitos? 6. Siempre se están quejando. 7. Primero ella acuesta a los niños, y entonces (luego) ella se acuesta. 8. ¿Quiere probarse este abrigo, señorita? 9. ¿Dónde van a poner el dinero, señoras? 10. Los estudiantes siempre se duermen en esta clase.

C. 1. Abra 2. Hablen 3. Traiga 4. Vengan 5. Cierre
6. Doblen 7. Siga 8. Den 9. Estén 10. Sean 11. Vaya
12. Vuelva 13. Sirva 14. Pongan 15. Escriban

D. 1. Dígales la verdad, señor Mena. 2. ¿El postre? No me lo
traiga ahora, señorita Ruiz. 3. No se lo diga a mi secretaria, por
favor. 4. Traigan las sillas, señores. Tráiganlas a la terraza.
5. No se levante, señora Miño. 6. ¿El té? Tráigaselo a las
cuatro de la tarde, señor Vargas.

Lesson 10

A. 1. Ayer ella entró en la cafetería y comió una ensalada.
2. Ayer María le escribió a su suegra. 3. El viernes pasado ella
me prestó su bicicleta. 4. El año pasado ellos fueron los
mejores estudiantes. 5. El sábado pasado ellos te esperaron
cerca del cine. 6. El verano pasado mi dentista fue a Buenos
Aires. 7. Ayer por la mañana le di el impermeable. 8. El
lunes pasado nosotros decidimos comprar la bicicleta.
9. Anoche le pregunté la hora. 10. Anoche tú no pagaste la
cuenta. 11. El jueves pasado fuimos los primeros. 12. Ayer
me dieron muchos problemas. 13. Anoche mi suegro no bebió
café. 14. Ayer yo no fui al laboratorio. 15. La semana pasada
te dimos el suéter.

B. 1. El ladrón entró por la ventana. 2. Ella pasó por mi casa.
3. No vino por la lluvia. 4. Hay vuelos para México los
sábados. 5. Vamos por avión. 6. El límite de velocidad es
cincuenta y cinco millas por hora. 7. Necesito la lección de
economía para mañana. 8. ¿Para quién es el paraguas?
9. Necesito el dinero para pagar la cuenta. 10. Ella pagó
doscientos dólares por ese vestido.

C. 1. Hace mucho viento hoy. 2. Hace mucho frío, y también
nieva (está nevando). 3. Hace mucho calor en Cuba. 4. ¿Qué
tiempo hace hoy? 5. ¿Hace sol o está nublado? 6. No hay
vuelos a causa de la niebla.

Lesson 11

A. 1. (a) ¿Cuánto tiempo hace que trabajan en Lima? (b) ¿Cuánto
tiempo llevan trabajando en Lima? 2. (a) Hace cinco años que
trabajamos en Lima. (b) Llevamos cinco años trabajando en
Lima. 3. (a) ¿Cuánto tiempo hace que esperan? (b) ¿Cuánto
tiempo llevan esperando? 4. (a) Hace tres horas que esperan.
(b) Llevan tres horas esperando. 5. (a) ¿Cuánto tiempo hace
que estudia español? (b) ¿Cuánto tiempo lleva estudiando
español? 6. (a) Hace dos años que ella estudia español. (b) Ella
lleva dos años estudiando español.

B. 1. Ayer María estuvo muy ocupada. 2. Anoche no pudieron venir. 3. La semana pasada puse el dinero en el banco. 4. El domingo pasado no hiciste nada. 5. Ayer ella vino con Juan. 6. La semana pasada no quisimos venir a clase. 7. Anoche yo no dije nada. 8. Ayer trajimos la máquina de escribir. 9. Anoche yo conduje mi coche. 10. Ayer ellos tradujeron las lecciones.

C. 1. ¿De quién es ese paraguas? 2. ¿De quiénes son esos revólveres? 3. ¿De quién son estos zapatos? 4. ¿De quién es este dinero? 5. ¿De quién es aquella silla?

D. 1. Vivíamos en Alaska. 2. Hablaba inglés. 3. Veía a mi abuela. 4. Depositábamos el dinero en el Banco de América. 5. Se acostaban a las nueve. 6. Iba a su trabajo. 7. Compraba café. 8. Gastábamos nuestro dinero en libros.

Lesson 12

A. 1. estábamos comiendo 2. estaban haciendo 3. estaba escribiendo 4. estaba hablando 5. estabas pensando 6. estaba leyendo 7. estaban estudiando 8. estaba trabajando

B. 1. Nos acostamos a las once anoche. 2. Ella estaba muy ocupada cuando la vi. 3. Íbamos a Buenos Aires. 4. Eran las diez y media cuando llamé a mi cuñada. 5. Ella dijo que quería leer.

C. 1. conocía/conocí 2. sabíamos/supimos 3. podía 4. pudieron 5. quiso (pudo) 6. quería/supe

D. 1. Nosotros llegamos al aeropuerto a las seis y media. 2. Mi cuñada está en casa. 3. Ellos están en la esquina de Unión y Figueroa. 4. El accidente fue a las doce. 5. Yo estuve en la estación de policía ayer.

Lesson 13

A. 1. Ayer él sintió mucho dolor. 2. Anoche Marta no durmió bien. 3. Ayer no le pedí nada. 4. La semana pasada ella te mintió. 5. El sábado pasado ellos sirvieron los refrescos. 6. Ayer no lo repetí. 7. Anoche ella siguió estudiando. 8. El lunes pasado tú no conseguiste nada.

B. 1. Sí, acabo de encontrarlo. 2. Sí, acabo de tomársela. 3. Sí, acaban de comprarlos. 4. Sí, acabamos de medirla. 5. Sí, acabo de bañarme. 6. Sí, acaban de llegar.

C. 1. me gustan 2. le hace falta 3. le duele 4. nos hace falta 5. Le gusta 6. Me hacen falta 7. Me duele 8. le (te) gusta

D. 1. ¿Qué es la libertad? 2. ¿Cuál es su (tu) dirección? 3. ¿Qué es un termómetro? 4. ¿Cuál es su (tu) número de teléfono? 5. ¿Cuáles son sus ideas acerca de esto?

Lesson 14

A. 1. (a) Hace tres meses que nosotros llegamos a California. (b) Nosotros llegamos a California hace tres meses. 2. (a) Hace dos horas que el niño tomó un poco de leche. (b) El niño tomó un poco de leche hace dos horas. 3. (a) Hace dos días que ellos terminaron el trabajo. (b) Ellos terminaron el trabajo hace dos días. 4. (a) Hace veinte años que ella lo vio. (b) Ella lo vio hace veinte años. 5. (a) Hace quince días que tú viniste a esta ciudad. (b) Tú viniste a esta ciudad hace quince días.

B. 2. recibido 3. volver 4. usado 5. escrito 6. ir 7. aprendido 8. abrir 9. cubierto 10. comido 11. ver 12. hecho 13. sido 14. decir 15. cerrado 16. morir 17. romper 18. dormido 19. estado 20. poner

C. 1. El artículo está escrito. 2. Él tiene una pierna rota. 3. La puerta está abierta. 4. ¿Están cerrados los libros? 5. El trabajo está terminado.

D. 1. he venido 2. Han terminado 3. hemos hablado 4. han dicho 5. has escrito 6. hemos hecho/hemos tenido 7. ha abierto 8. ha puesto 9. se han casado 10. me he roto

E. 1. Yo ya había traído las sábanas. 2. Nosotros le habíamos escrito sobre nuestros experimentos con plantas tropicales. 3. Ellos habían roto los lápices. 4. Él ya había visto al administrador. 5. ¿Había cubierto usted las mesas, señorita Peña?

Lesson 15

A. 1. Hacía diez horas que yo no comía. 2. Hacía media hora que lo esperábamos. 3. Hacía dos meses que yo estudiaba español. 4. Hacía dos horas que la paciente no bebía. 5. Hacía quince años que nosotros trabajábamos para el gobierno.

B. 1. El tema de la conferencia será la civilización y la cultura de Europa. 2. Los análisis estarán listos la semana que viene. 3. (Yo) enseñaré el español. 4. Para esa fecha estaremos en Chile. 5. Le diremos que sí. 6. No haré nada el domingo. 7. Sabremos el resultado pronto. 8. El mecánico arreglará el coche. 9. Mis sobrinos podrán venir. 10. Pondré el dinero en el banco. 11. Los niños volverán de México el sábado. 12. Vendré a la reunión con la señorita Vargas. 13. Tendremos que estudiar para el examen. 14. Le daré las cartas mañana sin falta. 15. Saldremos con Raúl y Mario.

C. 1. iríamos 2. venderían 3. habría 4. serviría 5. trabajarías 6. pondría 7. preferirían 8. seguirían 9. Te levantarías 10. nos quejaríamos

D. 1. No llegaremos a la universidad a tiempo.   2. ¿Llevaste a tu perro al veterinario, María?   3. Después viajaremos en avión.   4. Ella está en el hospital. Está mejorando.   5. ¿De qué están hablando ellos?

Lesson 16

A. 1. aconsejemos   2. lave   3. escriban   4. vivas   5. diga   6. cierre   7. vengan   8. se levante   9. pida   10. hagan   11. traiga   12. recomiende   13. movamos   14. vaya   15. se afeite   16. durmamos   17. dé   18. sepan (conozcan)   19. salga   20. tengas

B. 1. Ella quiere que yo traiga los paquetes.   2. Prefiero que vayamos a la oficina de correos.   3. ¿A qué hora quiere que esté allí mañana, señor Acevedo?   4. Pídale que la ayude, señora Portillo.   5. Dígales que no tengan miedo.   6. Que lo haga tu novio.   7. Que pasen (entren).   8. Él quiere que yo sea su novia.   9. ¿Necesita que le den el dinero hoy, señor Ortiz?   10. No quiero que hagas nada, Juancito.

C. 1. ¡Ah, sí! Es altísimo.   2. ¡Ah, sí! Estamos ocupadísimas.   3. ¡Ah, sí! Son lentísimos.   4. ¡Ah, sí! Es buenísima.   5. ¡Ah, sí! Es dificilísima.   6. ¡Ah, sí! Es bellísima.   7. ¡Ah, sí! Es facilísima.   8. ¡Ah, sí! Estoy ocupadísimo.

Lesson 17

A. 1. Espero que puedas cortarte el pelo esta tarde, Robertito.   2. Me alegro de que su mamá se sienta mejor, Sr. Gómez.   3. Temo que no podamos reunirnos hasta el lunes, señorita Herrero.   4. Nos alegramos de estar aquí hoy.   5. Ella espera salir mañana por la mañana.   6. Espero que pueda venir a la reunión, señor Peña.   7. Tememos no poder terminar el trabajo esta noche.   8. Siento que esté tan enferma, señora Treviño.

B. 1. tengan   2. estudiar   3. escribir   4. terminaremos   5. esté   6. hacer   7. llegan   8. firmar

C. 1. felizmente   2. especialmente   3. rápidamente   4. fácilmente   5. lenta y cuidadosamente

Lesson 18

A. 1. el café ya está frío.   2. Pedro vaya con nosotros.   3. María esté muy enferma.   4. una casa que quede cerca del centro   5. sabe escribir a máquina.   6. quieran hacer traducciones.   7. él se levanta a las cuatro de la mañana.   8. tiene seis cuartos.

B. 1. Ven acá, por favor.   2. Habla con la maestra.   3. Dime tu dirección.   4. Lávate la cara.   5. Ponte el abrigo.   6. Tráenos agua caliente.   7. Termina el trabajo.   8. Hazme el favor. 9. Apaga la luz.   10. Ve a tu habitación.   11. Sal temprano. 12. Quédate afuera.   13. Ten paciencia.   14. Sé buena. 15. Cena con nosotros.

C. 1. No se lo digas (a él).   2. No salgas ahora.   3. No te levantes.   4. No hagas las traducciones.   5. No bebas la limonada.   6. No lo rompas.   7. No les hables.   8. No vayas al centro.   9. ¿Ese vestido? ¡No te lo pongas!   10. No hagas eso.

D. 1. arbolito   2. hermanita/Teresita   3. vestidito/hijita 4. Juancito   5. cochecito

Lesson 19

A. 1. Le hablaré tan pronto como vea a mi abogado(a). 2. Quédese aquí en caso de que él llame, señorita González. 3. Él me escribió en cuanto llegó.   4. Vamos a esperar hasta que él venga.   5. No puedo ir sin que lo sepan mis padres. 6. Compraremos el coche cuando tengamos el dinero.

B. 1. haya visto   2. hayan hecho   3. hayas aprendido   4. hayan firmado   5. haya arreglado   6. hayamos archivado   7. haya vuelto   8. se haya acostado

C. 1. Ellos sienten que ustedes hayan estado enfermos.   2. Rosa no cree que yo lo haya hecho.   3. Nosotros tememos que él haya muerto.   4. No es verdad que nosotros hayamos escrito esa carta.   5. Ojalá que papá haya podido venir.

Lesson 20

A. 1. asistiéramos   2. dejaras   3. se lavaran   4. recogiera 5. pudiera   6. trajera   7. devolvieran   8. tuviera

B. 1. Le pedí que viniera en seguida.   2. Me alegro de que pudieras terminarlo anoche.   3. No creí que ella lo hiciera. 4. No es verdad que mi hermano estuviera preso el año pasado.   5. Temíamos que ella no supiera escribir a máquina. 6. Dudo que la conferencia fuera el sábado pasado.

C. (*Possibilities*):   1. tuviera dinero   2. tenemos tiempo 3. estuviera enfermo   4. no llueve   5. pudieran   6. lo vemos 7. tuviera sueño   8. tenemos hambre

Vocabulary

Spanish — English

A

a at, to, in
¿a dónde? where (to)?
a casa home
a la derecha to the right
a la izquierda to the left
a menos que unless
a menudo often
¿a quién? to whom?
a tiempo on time
a veces sometimes
abogado(a) (*m.f.*) lawyer
abrigo (*m.*) coat
abril April
abrir to open
abuela grandmother
abuelo grandfather
abuelos grandparents
acabar to finish
acabar de to have just
accidente (*m.*) accident
acerca de about
aconsejar to advise
acordarse (o > ue) (de) to remember
acostar(se) (o > ue) to put to bed, to go to bed
adentro inside
adiós good-bye
administrador(a) (*m.f.*) administrator
aeropuerto (*m.*) airport
afeitar(se) to shave (oneself)
afuera outside
agosto August
agua (*f.*) water
ahora now
ahorrar to save (i.e., *money*)
alcohólico(a) alcoholic
alegrarse (de) to be glad
alemán (*m.*) German (*language*)
algo something
alguien someone, somebody
alguno(a) any, some
alquilar to rent
alto(a) tall

allá over there
allí there
amigo(a) (*m.f.*) friend
análisis (*m.*) test
anoche last night
antes (de) before
antes de que before
año (*m.*) year
apagar to turn off
apellido (*m.*) surname; **— de soltera** maiden name
aprender to learn
aquel(los), aquella(s) (*adj.*) that, those (*distant*)
aquél(los), aquélla(s) (pron.) that (one), those (*distant*)
aquello (*neuter pron.*) that
aquí here
árbol (*m.*) tree
archivar to file
archivo (*m.*) file
argentino(a) (*m.f.*) Argentinian
artículo (*m.*) article
arreglar to fix, to repair
arroz (*m.*) rice; **— con pollo** chicken and rice
asamblea (*f.*) assembly
asistir to attend
aspirina (*f.*) aspirin
atención (*f.*) attention
auto (*m.*) auto, automobile
autobús (*m.*) autobus, bus
automóvil (*m.*) automobile, auto
autopista (*f.*) freeway
avenida (*f.*) avenue
avión (*m.*) plane
ayer yesterday
ayudante (*m.f.*) assistant
ayudar to help
azul blue

B

banana (*f.*) banana
banco (*m.*) bank
bañar(se) to bathe

barbero (*m.*) barber
beber to drink
bello(a) pretty
biblioteca (*f.*) library
bicicleta (*f.*) bicycle
bien well, fine
blanco(a) white
blusa (*f.*) blouse
bonito(a) pretty
botella (*f.*) bottle
brazo (*m.*) arm
buenas noches good evening, good night
buenas tardes good afternoon
bueno(a) good, kind, nice
buenos días good morning, good day
buscar to look for

C

caber to fit
cabeza (*f.*) head
caer(se) to fall
café (*m.*) coffee
cafetería (*f.*) cafeteria
caliente hot
calle (*f.*) street
cama (*f.*) bed
caminar to walk
camisa (*f.*) shirt
cansado(a) tired
cara (*f.*) face
cárcel (*f.*) jail
carne (*f.*) meat
carpeta (*f.*) folder
carro (*m.*) car
carta (*f.*) letter
casa (*f.*) house
casado(a) married
casarse (con) to get married
casi nunca hardly ever
cenar to have supper, to dine
centro (*m.*) downtown (area)
cerca (de) near, next to
cerrar (e:ie) to close
cine (*m.*) movie theater
ciudad (*f.*) city
civilización (*f.*) civilization
clase (*f.*) class, kind, type

cliente (*m.f.*) customer, client
clima (*m.*) climate
coctel (*m.*) cocktail
coche (*m.*) car
comenzar (e:ie) to begin
comer to eat
comida (*f.*) dinner, meal
¿cómo? how?
¿cómo es? what is (it, she, he) like?
comprar to buy
comprender to understand
con with
¿con quién? with whom?
con tal que provided that
concierto (*m.*) concert
conducir to drive, to conduct
conferencia (*f.*) lecture
conocer to know, to be acquainted with
conseguir (e > i) to obtain, to get
consulado (*m.*) consulate
contador(a) (*m.f.*) accountant
contrato (*m.*) contract
conviene it is advisable
copia (*f.*) copy
corbata (*f.*) tie
correo (*m.*) post office
cortar to cut
creer to believe
cuaderno (*m.*) notebook
¿cuál? which?, what?
¿cuándo? when?
¿cuánto(a)? how much?
¿— tiempo? how long?
¿cuántos(as)? how many?
cuarto (*m.*) room
cuarto(a) fourth
cubrir to cover
cuenta (*f.*) bill, account
cuidadoso(a) careful
cultura (*f.*) culture

CH

cheque (*m.*) check
chequear to check
chica girl
chico boy
chico(a) (*adj.*) little, small
chocar to collide, to run into

D

dar   to give
de   of, from, about, within
¿de dónde?   from where?
de nada   you're welcome
¿de quién?   whose?
de vez en cuando   once in a while
deber   must, should
decidir   to decide
décimo(a)   tenth
decir (e > i)   to say, to tell
dejar   to leave (behind)
dentista (*m.f.*)   dentist
depositar   to deposit
desear   to wish, to want
despedirse (e > i)   to say goodby
despertar(se) (e > ie)   to wake up
después   afterwards, later
desvestir(se) (e > i)   to get undressed
devolver (o > ue)   to return
día (*m.*)   day
diccionario (*m.*)   dictionary
diciembre   December
difícil   difficult, unlikely
dinero (*m.*)   money
dirección (*f.*)   address
director(a) (*m.f.*)   director
divorciado(a)   divorced
doblar   to turn
doctor(a) (*m.f.*)   doctor
documento (*m.*)   document
dólar (*m.*)   dollar
doler (o > ue)   to hurt, to ache
dolor (*m.*)   pain
domicilio (*m.*)   address
domingo   Sunday
¿dónde?   where?
dormir(se) (o > ue)   to sleep, to fall asleep
dormitorio (*m.*)   bedroom
dudar   to doubt

E

economía (*f.*)   economics
echar al correo   to mail
edad (*f.*)   age
edificio (*m.*)   building
él   he
elegir (e > i)   to choose

ella   she
ellas (*f.*)   they
ellos (*m.*)   they
embajador(a)   ambassador
empezar (e > ie)   to begin
empleado(a) (*m.f.*)   employee
empleo (*m.*)   job
en   in, at, on
en casa   at home
en caso de que   in case
en cuanto   as soon as
en seguida   right away
encontrar (o > ue)   to find
enero   January
enfermero(a) (*m.f.*)   nurse
enfermo(a)   sick
ensalada (*f.*)   salad
enseñar   to teach
entender (e > ie)   to understand
entrar (en)   to enter, to come in
escribir   to write; — **a máquina**   to type
escritorio (*m.*)   desk
escuela (*f.*)   school
ese(os), esa(as) (*adj.*)   that, those (*nearby*)
ése(os), ésa(as) (*pron.*)   that (one), those (*nearby*)
eso (*neuter pron.*)   that
español(a)   Spanish
español (*m.*)   Spanish (*language*)
especial   special
esperar   to wait, to hope, to wait for
esposa   wife
esposo   husband
esquina (*f.*)   corner
esta noche   tonight
estación (*f.*)   season
estación (*f.*)   station; — **de servicio** (*f.*)   service station
estado civil   marital status
Estados Unidos (*m.*)   United States
estar   to be; — **listo(a)**   to be ready; — **preso(a)**   to be in jail
este(os), esta(as) (*adj.*)   this, these
éste(os), ésta(as) (*pron.*)   this (one), these, the latter
esto (*neuter pron.*)   this
estómago (*m.*)   stomach
estudiante (*m.f.*)   student

estudiar   to study
examen (*m.*)   exam
experimento (*m.*)   experiment

F

fácil   easy
familia (*f.*)   family
fantástico(a)   fantastic
favor (*m.*)   favor
favorito(a)   favorite
febrero   February
fecha (*f.*)   date; — **de nacimiento**
    date of birth
feliz   happy
femenino(a)   feminine
fichero (*m.*)   file
fiesta (*f.*)   party
fin (*m.*)   end
firmar   to sign
físico(a)   physical
francés (*m.*)   French (*language*)
francés(esa) (*m.f.*)   French
frío(a)   cold

G

gasolinera (*f.*)   service station
gastar   to spend (*money*)
generalmente   generally
generoso(a)   generous
geografía (*f.*)   geography
gerente (*m.f.*)   manager
gobierno (*m.*)   government
gracias   thanks
grande   big, large
guapo(a)   handsome
gustar   to please, to be pleasing, to
    like

H

haber   to have (*aux.*)
habitación (*f.*)   room
hablar   to speak
hacer   to do, to make; — **calor**   to
    be hot; — **falta**   to need; —
    frío   to be cold; — **sol**   to be
    sunny; — **viento**   to be windy
hasta (que)   until

hasta luego   I'll see you later
hasta mañana   see you tomorrow
hay que . . .   one must . . .
hermana   sister
hermano   brother
hija   daughter
hijo   son
historia (*f.*)   history
hombre   man
hora (*f.*)   hour
horrible   horrible
hospital (*m.*)   hospital
hotel (*m.*)   hotel
hoy   today

I

idea (*f.*)   idea
idioma (*m.*)   language
iglesia (*f.*)   church
impaciente   impatient
impermeable (*m.*)   raincoat
importante   important
inflación (*f.*)   inflation
información (*f.*)   information
informe (*m.*)   report
ingeniero (*m.*)   engineer
inglés (*m.*)   English (*language*)
inspector(a) (*m.f.*)   inspector
instructor(a) (*m.f.*)   instructor
instrumento (*m.*)   instrument
inteligente   intelligent
invierno (*m.*)   winter
ir   to go
ir de vacaciones   to go on vacation
irse   to leave, to go away
italiano(a)   Italian

J

jabón (*m.*)   soap
jamás   never
jefe(a) (*m.f.*)   boss, chief
jueves   Thursday
jugar   to play (*a game*)
julio   July
junio   June
junta (*f.*)   meeting
juntos(as)   together

L

la (*pl.* **las**)   the (*f.*)
la (*dir. obj. pron.*)   her, it (*f.*), you (*formal f.*)
laboratorio (*m.*)   laboratory
ladrón(ona) (*m.f.*)   thief
lápiz (*m.*)   pencil
las (*dir. obj. pron.*)   them (*f.*), you (*formal f.*)
lavar(se)   to wash (oneself)
le (*ind. obj. pron.*)   to him, her, it, you (*formal m.f.*)
lección (*f.*)   lesson
leche (*f.*)   milk
leer   to read
lengua (*f.*)   language
leer   to read
lento(a)   slow
les (*ind. obj. pron.*)   to them, you (*formal, pl. m.f.*)
levantar(se)   to lift, to raise, to get up
libertad (*f.*)   liberty
libro (*m.*)   book
licencia (*f.*)   license
— para conducir   driver's license
límite (*m.*)   limit
limonada (*f.*)   lemonade
lo (*dir. obj. pron.*)   him, it, (*m.*), you (*formal m.*)
lo siento   I'm sorry
los (*dir. obj. pron.*)   them, you (*m. pl.*)
lugar (*m.*)   place
lunes   Monday
luz (*f.*)   light

LL

llamar   to call
llegar   to arrive
llevar   to take, to carry
llover (**o > ue**)   to rain
lluvia (*f.*)   rain

M

madera (*f.*)   wood
madre   mother
maestro(a)   teacher

mal   badly
maleta (*f.*)   suitcase
malo(a)   bad
mamá   mom
mano (*f.*)   hand
mañana (*f.*)   morning
mañana   tomorrow
máquina de escribir (*f.*)   typewriter
marido   husband
martes   Tuesday
marzo   March
más   more, most
matar   to kill
matemáticas (*f.*)   mathematics
matrícula (*f.*)   registration
mayo   May
mayor   older, oldest
me (*obj. pron.*)   me, to me, (to) myself
mecánico (*m.f.*)   mechanic
media hora   half an hour
medianoche (*f.*)   midnight
medicina (*f.*)   medicine
médico (*m.f.*)   medical doctor
medir (**e > i**)   to measure, to be . . . tall
mejor   better, best
mejorar   to improve
menor   younger, youngest
menos   less, least, fewer
mentir (**e > ie**)   to lie
mercado (*m.*)   market
mes (*m.*)   month
mesa (*f.*)   table
metal (*m.*)   metal
mi (*adj.*)   my
mí (*obj. of prep.*)   me
miércoles   Wednesday
milla (*f.*)   mile
millón (*m.*)   million
mineral (*m.*)   mineral
mío(a) (*adj.*)   my, of mine
mío(a) (*pron.*)   mine
modelo (*m.*)   model
momento (*m.*)   moment
morir (**o > ue**)   to die
mover (**o > ue**)   to move
muchacha   girl, young woman
muchacho   boy, young man
muchas gracias   thank you very much

muchas veces   many times
mucho(a, os, as)   much (many); very
mucho (*adv.*)   (very) much, a great deal, a lot
mucho gusto   how do you do, much pleasure
mudarse   to move
muebles (*m.*)   furniture
muela (*f.*)   tooth, molar
mujer (*f.*)   woman
museo (*m.*)   museum
muy   very

N

nacimiento (*m.*)   birth
nacionalidad (*f.*)   nationality
nada   nothing
nadar   to swim
nadie   nobody, no one
necesitar   to need
negocios (*m.*)   business
negro(a)   black
nevar (e > ie)   to snow
ni   neither, nor
niebla (*f.*)   fog
ninguno(a)   no, none, not any
niña   girl, child
niño   boy, child
no   no, not
noche (*f.*)   evening, night
nombre (*m.*)   name
norteamericano(a)   North American
nos (*obj. pron.*)   us, to us, (to) ourselves
nosotros(as)   we, us
novela (*f.*)   novel
noveno(a)   ninth
novia   girl friend, bride
novio   boy friend, groom
noviembre   November
nublado   cloudy
nuestro(s), nuestra(s) (*adj.*)   our
nuestro(s), nuestra(s) (*pron.*)   ours
número (*m.*)   number
nunca   never

O

o   or, either
octavo(a)   eight

octubre   October
ocupación (*f.*)   occupation
ocupado(a)   busy
oficina (*f.*)   office
oficina de correos (*f.*)   post office
ómnibus (*m.*)   omnibus
otoño (*m.*)   fall
otra vez   again
otro(a)   other, another

P

paciencia (*f.*)   patience
paciente (*m.f.*)   patient
padre   father
padres (*m.*)   parents
pagar   to pay
pantalones (*m.*)   trousers
papá   dad
paquete (*m.*)   package
para   to, for, by, in order
para que   in order that
paraguas (*m.*)   umbrella
pariente (*m.f.*)   relative
parque (*m.*)   park
pasado(a)   last
pasaje (*m.*)   ticket
pasajero(a) (*m.f.*)   passenger
pasaporte (*m.*)   passport
pasar   to go by, to pass, to spend (*time*), to come in
pedir (e > i)   to ask for, to request, to order
pelo (*m.*)   hair
pensar (e > ie)   to think
peor   worse, worst
pequeño(a)   small, little (size)
perder (e > ie)   to lose
perfume (*m.*)   perfume
periódico (*m.*)   newspaper
pero   but
perseguir (e > i)   persecute
personal (*m.*)   personnel
perro (*m.*)   dog
pescado (*m.*)   fish
piano (*m.*)   piano
pierna (*f.*)   leg
piso (*m.*)   floor, story
planta (*f.*)   plant
plástico(a)   plastic
playa (*f.*)   beach

plomero (*m.*) plumber
pluma (*f.*) pen
poco(a) little (*quantity*)
pocos(as) few
poder (o > ue) to be able to
policía (*f.*) police (*organization*)
policía (*m.f.*) policeman, policewoman
pollo (*m.*) chicken
poner(se) to put, to put on
por around, along, by, for, through
por favor please
¿por qué? why?
porque because
posible possible
postre (*m.*) dessert
precio (*m.*) price
preferir (e > ie) to prefer
preguntar to ask (a question)
preocupar(se) to worry
presidente(a) (*m.f.*) president
prestar to lend
primavera (*f.*) spring
primero(a) (*m.f.*) first
primo(a) (*m.f.*) cousin
probar(se) (o > ue) to try, to taste,
to try on
problema (*m.*) problem
profesión (*f.*) profession
profesor(a) (*m.f.*) professor
programa (*m.*) program
pronto soon
próximo(a) next
puerta (*f.*) door
pues well, then
puesto (*m.*) position, job

Q

¿qué? what?
que viene next
quedar(se) to be located, to stay, to
remain
quejarse to complain
querer (e > ie) to want, to wish
querido(a) dear
¿quién? who?, whom?
química (*f.*) chemistry
quinto(a) fifth
quitar to take away
quitarse to take off

R

radio (*f.*) radio
rápido(a) fast
recepcionista (*m.f.*) receptionist
recibir to receive
reciente recent
recoger to pick up
recomendar (e > ie) to recommend
recordar (o > ue) to remember
refresco (*m.*) soda
refrigerador (*m.*) refrigerator
regalo (*m.*) present, gift
repetir (e:i) to repeat
restaurante (*m.*) restaurant
resultado (*m.*) result
reunión (*f.*) meeting
revisar to check
revista (*f.*) magazine
revólver (*m.*) revolver
rojo(a) red
romper to break

S

sábado Saturday
sábana (*f.*) sheet
saber to know, to know how
sacar to take out; — **copia** to
photocopy
salir to go out, to leave
se (*reflex.*) (to) himself, herself,
etc.
secretario(a) (*m.f.*) secretary
seguido often
seguir (e > i) to follow, to continue; — **derecho** to continue
straight ahead
segundo(a) second
seguro(a) sure, certain
seguro social (*m.*) social security
semana (*f.*) week
sentar(se) (e > ie) to sit, to sit
down
sentir (e > ie) to regret
sentir(se) (e > ie) to feel
señor (*abr.* **Sr.**) Mister, sir, gentle-
man
señora (*abr.* **Sra.**) Mrs., Madam,
lady
señorita (*abr.* **Srta.**) Miss, young
lady

separado(a) separated
septiembre September
séptimo(a) seventh
ser to be
servir (e > i) to serve
sexo (*m.*) sex
sexto(a) sixth
sí yes
siempre always
silla (*f.*) chair
sin falta without fail
sistema (*m.*) system
sobre about
sobrevivir to survive
sobrina niece
sobrino nephew
sofá (*m.*) sofa
solamente only
solicitud (*f.*) application
solo only
solo(a) alone
soltero(a) single
sopa (*f.*) soup
su his, her, its, your (*formal*), their
suegra mother-in-law
suegro father-in-law
suéter (*m.*) sweater
sugerir (e > ie) to suggest
suicidarse to commit suicide
sumamente extremely
supervisor(a) (*m.f.*) supervisor
suyo(s), suya(s) (*pron.*) yours (*formal*) his, hers, theirs

T

talonario de cheques (*m.*) checkbook
también also, too
tampoco neither
tan so
— pronto como as soon as
tarde (*f.*) afternoon
tarde late
tarea (*f.*) homework
te (*pron.*) you (*fam.*), to you, (to) yourself
té (*m.*) tea
teatro (*m.*) theater
teléfono (*m.*) telephone

telegrama (*m.*) telegram
televisión (*f.*) television
tema (*m.*) theme
temer to fear
temperatura (*f.*) temperature
tener to have
tener . . . años to be . . . years old; **— calor** to be warm; **— frío** to be cold; **— hambre** to be hungry; **— miedo** to be afraid; **— prisa** to be in a hurry; **— razón** to be right; **— sed** to be thirsty; **— sueño** to be sleepy
tener éxito to succeed
tener que to have to
tercero(a) third
terminar to finish
termómetro (*m.*) thermometer
terraza (*f.*) terrace
testamento (*m.*) testament, will
tía aunt
tiempo (*m.*) time
tienda (*f.*) store
tintorería (*f.*) cleaner
tío uncle
toalla (*f.*) towel
todavía yet
todo(a) all, every
todos(as) everybody, all
tomar to take, to drink
trabajar to work
trabajo (*m.*) work, job
traducción (*f.*) translation
traducir to translate
traer to bring
traje (*m.*) suit
tropical tropical
tu your (*inf.*)
tú you (*inf.*)
tuyo(s), tuya(s) (*adj.*) your (*inf.*) of yours
tuyo(s), tuya(s) (*pron.*) yours (*inf. sing.*)

U

un poco de some, a little
universidad (*f.*) university
usar to use, to wear

usted (*abr.* **Ud.**)   you (*form.*)
ustedes (*abr.* **Uds.**)   you (*pl.*)

V

vacaciones (*f.*)   vacation
valer   to be worth
vecino(a) (*m.f.*)   neighbor
velocidad (*f.*)   speed
vender   to sell
venir   to come
ventana (*f.*)   window
ver   to see
verano (*m.*)   summer
verdad (*f.*)   truth
verde   green
vestido (*m.*)   dress
vestir(se) (**e** > **i**)   to dress, to get
   dressed
veterinario(a) (*m.f.*)   veterinary
vez (*f.*)   time

viajar   to travel
viajero(a) (*m.f.*)   traveller
vidrio (*m.*)   glass
viernes   Friday
visitar   to visit
viuda   widow
viudo   widower
vivir   to live
volar (**o** > **ue**)   to fly
volver (**o** > **ue**)   to come (go) back
vuelo (*m.*)   flight

Y

y   and
yo   I

Z

zapato (*m.*)   shoe

English — Spanish

A

a un(a)
about de, acerca de, sobre
accident accidente (*m.*)
account cuenta (*f.*)
accountant contador(a) (*m.f.*)
ache doler (o > ue)
address domicilio (*m.*)
administrator administrador(a) (*m.f.*)
advise aconsejar
afternoon tarde (*f.*)
afterwards después
again otra vez
age edad (*f.*)
airport aeropuerto (*m.*)
alcoholic alcohólico(a) (*m.f.*)
all todos(as)
alone solo(a)
also también
always siempre
ambassador embajador(a) (*m.f.*)
and y
any alguno(a); cualquier(a)
anyone alguien
application solicitud (*f.*)
April abril
Argentinian argentino(a)
arm brazo (*m.*)
another otro(a)
around alrededor (de), por
arrange arreglar
arrive llegar
article artículo (*m.*)
as soon as en cuanto, tan pronto como
ask (*a question*) preguntar
ask (*for*) pedir (e > i)
aspirin aspirina (*f.*)
assembly asamblea (*f.*)
assistant ayudante (*m.f.*)
at en; a
at home en casa
attend asistir (a)
attention atención (*f.*)
August agosto
aunt tía

auto; automobile auto (*m.*); automóvil (*m.*); coche (*m.*), carro (*m.*)
autobus autobús (*m.*)
avenue avenida (*f.*)

B

bad(ly) malo(a) (*adj.*); mal (*adv.*)
banana banana (*f.*)
bank banco (*m.*)
barber barbero(a) (*m.f.*)
bathe bañarse
be ser, estar; — **able** poder (o > ue); — **acquainted with** conocer; — **advisable** convenir (e > ie); — **glad** alegrarse (de); — **ready** estar listo(a); — **cold** (*weather*) hacer frío; — **hot** (*weather*) hacer calor; — **windy** hacer viento; — **sunny** hacer sol; — **cold** tener frío; — **thirsty** tener sed; — **hungry** tener hambre; — **hot** tener calor; — **sleepy** tener sueño; — **in a hurry** tener prisa; — **afraid** tener miedo; — **right** tener razón; — . . . **years old** tener (cumplir) . . . años
beach playa (*f.*)
because porque
bed cama (*f.*)
bedroom dormitorio (*m.*)
before antes de
begin comenzar (e > ie); empezar (e > ie)
believe creer
best (el, la) mejor
better mejor
bicycle bicicleta (*f.*)
big grande
bigger más grande
bill cuenta (*f.*)
birth nacimiento (*m.*)
black negro(a)
blouse blusa (*f.*)
blue azul
book libro (*m.*)

boss   jefe(a) (*m.f.*)
bottle   botella (*f.*)
boy   niño, chico, muchacho
boy friend   novio
break   romper
bring   traer
brother   hermano
building   edificio (*m.*)
bus   autobús (*m.*)
business   negocios (*m.*)
busy   ocupado(a)
but   pero
buy   comprar
by   por; para

complain   quejarse (de)
concentration   concentración (*f.*)
concert   concierto (*m.*)
conduct   conducir
consulate   consulado (*m.*)
continue   seguir (e > i); — straight
  ahead   seguir derecho
contract   contrato (*m.*)
copy   copia (*f.*)
corner   esquina (*f.*)
cousin   primo(a) (*m.f.*)
cover   cubrir
culture   cultura (*f.*)
customer   cliente (*m.f.*)
cut   cortar

C

cafeteria   cafetería (*f.*)
call   llamar
car   carro (*m.*); coche (*m.*)
careful   cuidadoso(a)
certain   seguro(a)
chair   silla (*f.*)
check   cheque (*m.*)
check   revisar, chequear (verb)
checkbook   talonario de cheques
  (*m.*)
chemistry   química (*f.*)
chicken   pollo (*m.*)
chicken and rice   arroz con pollo
chief   jefe(a) (*m.f.*)
child   niño(a) (*m.f.*)
choose   elegir (e > i)
church   iglesia (*f.*)
citizenship   nacionalidad (*f.*)
city   ciudad (*f.*)
civilization   civilización (*f.*)
class   clase (*f.*)
cleaner   tintorería (*f.*)
climate   clima (*m.*)
close   cerrar (e > ie)
cloudy   nublado(a)
coat   abrigo (*m.*)
cocktail   coctel (*m.*)
coffee   café (*m.*)
collide   chocar
come   venir; — back   volver (o >
  ue); — in   entrar
commit suicide   suicidarse

D

dad   papá
date   fecha (*f.*)
daughter   hija
day   día (*m.*)
dear   querido(a)
December   diciembre
decide   decidir
dentist   dentista (*m.f.*)
deposit   depositar
desk   escritorio (*m.*)
dessert   postre (*m.*)
dictionary   diccionario (*m.*)
die   morir (o > ue)
difficult   difícil
dine   cenar
dinner   cena (*f.*)
director   director(a) (*m.f.*)
divorced   divorciado(a)
do   hacer
doctor   doctor(a) (*m.f.*)
document   documento (*m.*)
dog   perro (*m.*)
dollar   dólar (*m.*)
door   puerta (*f.*)
downtown (*area*)   centro (*m.*)
dress   vestido (*m.*)
dress (*oneself*)   vestir(se) (e > i)
drink   tomar; beber
drive   conducir
driver's license   licencia para
  conducir

E

early temprano
easy fácil
eat comer
economics economía (f.)
eighth octavo(a)
either . . . or o . . . o
employee empleado(a) (m.f.)
end terminar
engineer ingeniero(a) (m.f.)
English (language) inglés (m.)
end fin (m.)
enter entrar
envelope sobre (m.)
evening noche (f.)
every todo(a, os, as)
exam examen (m.)
experiment experimento (m.)

F

face cara (f.)
fall otoño (m.)
fall caerse (verb)
fall asleep dormirse (o > ue)
fantastic fantástico(a)
fast rápido(a)
father padre
father-in-law suegro
favor favor (m.)
favorite favorito(a)
fear temer
February febrero
feel sentir(se) (e > ie)
feminine femenino(a)
few pocos(as)
fewer menos
file archivo (m.); fichero (m.)
file archivar (verb)
fifth quinto(a)
find encontrar (o > ue)
fine bien
finish terminar
first primero(a)
fish pescado (m.)
fit caber
fix arreglar
flight vuelo (m.)
floor (story) piso (m.)
fly volar (o > ue)

fog niebla (f.)
folder carpeta (f.)
follow seguir (e > i)
for por; para
for whom? ¿para quién?
fourth cuarto(a)
freeway autopista (f.)
French (language) francés (m.)
French (adj.) francés(esa)
Friday viernes
friend amigo(a)
furniture (pieces of) muebles (m.)

G

generally generalmente
generous generoso(a)
geography geografía (f.)
German (language) alemán (m.)
get obtener; conseguir (e > i); — dressed vestirse (e > i); — undressed desvestirse (e > i); — up levantarse; — married casarse (con)
gift regalo (m.)
girl niña, chica, muchacha
girl friend novia
give dar
glass vidrio (m.)
go ir; —to bed acostarse (o:ue); —away irse; —by pasar; —on vacation irse de vacaciones; —out salir
good bueno(a)
good afternoon buenas tardes
good-bye adiós
good day buenos días
good evening buenas noches
good morning buenos días
good night buenas noches
government gobierno (m.)
grandfather abuelo
grandmother abuela
grandparents abuelos
green verde

H

hair pelo (m.)
half medio(a)

hand mano (*f.*)
handsome guapo(a)
happy feliz
hardly ever casi nunca
have haber; tener; **—a good time** divertirse (e : ie); **—just** acabar de; **— supper** cenar; **— to** tener que
he él
head cabeza (*f.*)
her su(s) (*adj.*); la (*dir. obj.*); le (*ind. obj.*)
here aquí
hers suyo(a, suyos, as) (el, la, los, las) de ella
herself se
help ayudar
him lo (*dir. obj.*); le (*ind. obj.*)
himself se
his suyo(a, suyos, as) (el, la, los, las) de él
his su(s) (*adj.*)
history historia (*f.*)
home casa; a casa
homework tarea (*f.*)
hope esperar
horrible horrible
hospital hospital (*m.*)
hot caliente
hotel hotel (*m.*)
house casa (*f.*)
hour hora (*f.*)
how? ¿cómo?
how do you do mucho gusto
how long? ¿cuánto tiempo?
how many? ¿cuántos(as)?
how much? ¿cuánto(a)?
hurt doler (o > ue)
husband esposo, marido

I

I yo
idea idea (*f.*)
impatient impaciente
important importante
improve mejorar
in en
information información (*f.*)
inflation inflación (*f.*)

inside adentro
inspector inspector(a) (*m.f.*)
instructor instructor(a) (*m.f.*)
instrument instrumento (*m.*)
intelligent inteligente
it lo (*m.*); la (*f.*)
Italian italiano(a)
its su(s) (*adj.*)
itself se

J

jail cárcel (*f.*)
January enero
job empleo (*m.*); puesto (*m.*)
July julio
June junio

K

kill matar
kind clase (*f.*)
kind bueno(a) (*adj.*)
know conocer; saber

L

laboratory laboratorio (*m.*)
language idioma (*m.*); lengua (*f.*)
large grande
last pasado(a)
last night anoche
late tarde
later después
lawyer abogado(a)
learn aprender
least menos
leave irse; dejar, salir
lecture conferencia (*f.*)
leg pierna (*f.*)
lemonade limonada (*f.*)
lend prestar
less menos
lesson lección (*f.*)
letter carta (*f.*)
liberty libertad (*f.*)
library biblioteca (*f.*)
license licencia (*f.*)
lie mentir (e > ie)
lift levantar

light   luz (*f.*)
like   gustar
limit   límite (*m.*)
little   chico(a), pequeño(a) (*size*);
   poco(a) (*quantity*)
live   vivir
look for   buscar
lose   perder (e > ie)

M

magazine   revista (*f.*)
maiden name   apellido de soltera
   (*m.*)
mail   echar al correo
make   hacer
man   hombre
manager   gerente (*m.f.*)
many   muchos(as)
March   marzo
marital status   estado civil (*m.*)
market   mercado (*m.*)
married   casado(a)
masculine   masculino(a) (*m.f.*)
mathematics   matemáticas (*f.*)
May   mayo
me   me (*dir. and indir. obj.*)
meal   comida (*f.*)
measure   medir (e > i)
meat   carne (*f.*)
mechanic   mecánico (*m.f.*)
medical doctor   médico (*m.f.*)
medicine   medicina (*f.*)
meeting   reunión (*f.*), junta (*f.*)
metal   metal (*m.*)
midnight   medianoche (*f.*)
mile   milla (*f.*)
million   millón (*m.*)
milk   leche (*f.*)
mine   mío(a), míos(as) (*pron.*)
mineral   mineral (*m.*)
Miss, young lady   señorita
model   modelo (*m.*)
mom   mamá
moment   momento (*m.*)
Monday   lunes
money   dinero (*m.*)
month   mes (*m.*)
more   más
morning   mañana (*f.*)

most   más
move   mover (o > ue), mudarse
movie (*theater*)   cine (*m.*)
mother   madre
mother-in-law   suegra
Mr.   señor
Mrs.   señora
much   mucho(a) (*adj.*);
   mucho (*adv.*)
museum   museo (*m.*)
must   deber
my   mi(s) (*adj.*)
myself   me

N

name   nombre (*m.*)
nationality   nacionalidad (*f.*)
near   cerca de
need   necesitar; hacerle falta a uno
neighbor   vecino(a) (*m.f.*)
neither   tampoco
neither . . . nor   ni . . . ni
nephew   sobrino
never   nunca; jamás
newspaper   periódico (*m.*)
next   próximo(a), que viene
next to   cerca de
nice   bueno(a)
niece   sobrina
night   noche (*f.*)
ninth   noveno(a)
no   no
no one   nadie
nobody   nadie
none   ningún, ninguno(a)
North American   norteamericano(a)
not any   ningún, ninguno(a)
notebook   cuaderno (*m.*)
nothing   nada
novel   novela (*f.*)
November   noviembre
now   ahora
number   número (*m.*)
nurse   enfermero(a) (*m.f.*)

O

obtain   conseguir (e > i)
occupation   ocupación (*f.*)

October   octubre
of   de
office   oficina (*f.*)
often   a menudo, seguido
older   mayor
oldest   (el, la) mayor
omnibus   ómnibus (*m.*)
on   en
on time   a tiempo
once in a while   de vez en cuando
only   sólo, solamente
open   abrir
or   o
order   pedir (e > i)
other   otro(a)
our   nuestro(a), nuestros(as) (*adj.*)
ours   nuestro(a), nuestros(as)
   (*pron.*)
ourselves   nos
outside   afuera
over there   allá

P

package   paquete (*m.*)
pain   dolor (*m.*)
pants   pantalón; pantalones (*m.*)
parents   padres (*m.*)
park   parque (*m.*)
party   fiesta (*f.*)
pass   pasar
passport   pasaporte (*m.*)
passenger   pasajero(a) (*m.f.*)
passport   pasaporte (*m.*)
patience   paciencia (*f.*)
patient   paciente (*m.f.*)
pay   pagar
pen   pluma (*f.*)
pencil   lápiz (*m.*)
per   por
perfume   perfume (*m.*)
persecute   perseguir (e > i)
personnel   personal (*m.*)
photocopy   sacar copia
physical   físico(a)
piano   piano (*m.*)
pick up   recoger
place   lugar (*m.*)
place   poner (*verb*)
plane   avión (*m.*)

plant   planta (*f.*)
plastic   plástico(a)
play (*a game*)   jugar
please   por favor
plumber   plomero(a) (*m.f.*)
police (*organization*)   policía (*f.*)
policeman   policía (*m.*)
policewoman   policía (*f.*)
position   puesto (*m.*)
possible   posible
post office   oficina de correos (*f.*)
prefer   preferir (e > ie)
present   regalo (*m.*)
president   presidente(a) (*m.f.*)
pretty   bello(a); bonito(a)
price   precio (*m.*)
problem   problema (*m.*)
program   programa (*m.*)
profession   profesión (*f.*)
professor   profesor(a) (*m.f.*)
put (on)   poner; ponerse; — to bed
   acostar (o > ue)

R

radio   radio (*f.*)
rain   llover (o > ue)
rain   lluvia (*f.*)
raincoat   impermeable (*m.*)
raise   levantar
read   leer
receive   recibir
recent   reciente
receptionist   recepcionista (*m.f.*)
recommend   recomendar (e > ie)
red   rojo(a)
refrigerator   refrigerador (*m.*)
registration   matrícula (*f.*)
regret   sentir (e > ie)
relative   pariente (*m.f.*)
remain   quedarse
remember   acordarse (de) (o > ue);
   recordar (o > ue)
rent   alquilar
repair   arreglar
repeat   repetir (e : i)
report   informe (*m.*)
request   pedir (e > i)
restaurant   restaurante (*m.*)
result   resultado (*m.*)

S

revolver   revólver (*m.*)
rice   arroz (*m.*)
right away   en seguida
room   cuarto (*m.*), habitación (*f.*)
run into   chocar

salad   ensalada (*f.*)
Saturday   sábado
save (*money*)   ahorrar
say   decir (e : i) —**good-bye** despedirse (e : i)
school   escuela (*f.*)
season   estación (*f.*)
second   segundo(a)
secretary   secretario(a) (*m.f.*)
see   ver
sell   vender
separated   separado(a)
September   septiembre
serve   servir (e > i)
service station   estación de servicio, gasolinera (*f.*)
seventh   séptimo(a)
sex   sexo (*m.*)
shave   afeitarse
she   ella
sheet   sábana (*f.*)
shirt   camisa (*f.*)
shoe   zapato (*m.*)
should   deber
sick   enfermo(a)
sign   firmar
single   soltero(a)
sister   hermana
sit down   sentar(se) (e : ie)
sixth   sexto(a)
sleep   dormir (o > ue)
slow   lento(a)
small   pequeño(a)
smaller   más pequeño (a)
snow   nevar (e > ie)
so   tan
soap   jabón (*m.*)
social security   seguro social (*m.*)
soda   refresco (*m.*)
sofa   sofá (*m.*)
some   algún, alguno(a), algunos(as)
someone   alguien

something   algo
sometimes   a veces
son   hijo
soon   pronto
sorry   lo siento
soup   sopa (*f.*)
Spanish (*language*)   español (*m.*)
Spanish (*nationality*)   español(a)
speak   hablar
special   especial
speed   velocidad (*f.*)
spend (*time*) pasar; — (*money*) gastar
spring   primavera (*f.*)
station   estación (*f.*)
stay   quedarse
stomach   estómago (*m.*)
store   tienda (*f.*)
street   calle (*f.*)
student   estudiante (*m.f.*)
study   estudiar
succeed   tener éxito
suggest   sugerir (e > ie)
suit   traje (*m.*)
suitcase   maleta (*f.*)
summer   verano (*m.*)
Sunday   domingo
supervisor   supervisor(a) (*m.f.*)
sure   seguro(a)
surname   apellido (*m.*)
survive   sobrevivir
sweater   suéter (*m.*)
swim   nadar
system   sistema (*m.*)

T

table   mesa (*f.*)
take   tomar; llevar; — **away** quitar; — **off** quitarse; — **out** sacar
tall   alto(a)
talk   hablar
taste   probar (o > ue)
tea   té (*m.*)
teacher (*elementary school*)   maestro(a)
telegram   telegrama (*m.*)
telephone   teléfono (*m.*)
television   televisión (*f.*)

tell decir (e > i)
temperature temperatura (f.)
tenth décimo(a)
terrace terraza (f.)
test análisis (m.)
testament testamento (m.)
thanks gracias
that (adj.) (near person addressed) ese, esa(os, as); (distant) aquel, aquella(os, as); (pron.) ése, ésa(os, as), aquél, aquélla(os, as); (neuter) eso, aquello; (relative pron.) que, quien
theater teatro (m.)
their su(s) (adj.)
theirs suyo(a), suyos(as) (el, la, los, las), de ellos, de ellas
them los, las (dir. obj.); les (ind. obj.)
theme tema (m.)
themselves se
there allí
thermometer termómetro (m.)
these (adj.) estos(as); (pron.) éstos(as)
they ellos; ellas
thief ladrón(ona) (m.f.)
think pensar (e > ie)
third tercero(a)
this (adj.) este, esta; (pron.) éste, ésta; (neuter) esto
those (adj.) (near person addressed) esos, esas; (distant) aquellos, aquellas; (pron.) ésos(as), aquéllos(as)
Thursday jueves
ticket pasaje (m.)
tie corbata (f.)
time hora (f.); tiempo (m.f.); vez (f.)
tired cansado(a)
to para; a
today hoy
together juntos(as)
tomorrow mañana
tonight esta noche
too también
tooth diente (m.); muela (f.)
towel toalla (f.)

translate traducir
translation traducción (f.)
travel viajar
traveller viajero(a) (m.f.)
tree árbol (m.)
tropical tropical
trousers pantalones (m.)
truth verdad (f.)
try; try on probar(se) (o > ue)
Tuesday martes
turn doblar
turn off apagar
twenty veinte
type clase (f.); tipo (m.)
type escribir a máquina
typewriter máquina de escribir (f.)

U

umbrella paraguas (m.)
uncle tío (m.)
understand comprender; entender (e > ie)
United States Estados Unidos
university universidad (f.)
unless a menos que
unlikely difícil
until hasta, hasta que
us nos (dir. and ind. obj.)
use usar

V

vacation vacaciones (f.)
very muy
veterinary veterinario(a)
visit visitar

W

wait esperar
wake up despertar(se) (e : ie)
walk caminar
want querer (e > ie)
wash (oneself) lavar(se)
water agua (f.)
we nosotros(as)
Wednesday miércoles
week semana (f.)
well bien, pues

what? ¿qué?; ¿cuál?
when? ¿cuándo?
where? ¿dónde?
where (to) a dónde
which? ¿cuál?
white blanco(a)
who? ¿quién?; ¿quiénes?
whom? ¿quién?; ¿a quién?
whose? ¿de quién?
why ¿por qué?
widow viuda
widower viudo
wife esposa
window ventana (*f.*)
winter invierno (*m.*)
wish desear
with con
within dentro (de)
without sin
without fail sin falta
woman mujer
wood madera (*f.*)
work trabajo (*m.*)
work trabajar (*verb*)
worry preocupar(se)
worse peor

worst peor
write escribir

Y

year año (*m.*)
yes sí
yesterday ayer
yet todavía
you (*fam. sing.*) tú; (*dir. and indir. obj.*) te
you (*polite*) (*subj. pron.*) usted (Ud.), ustedes (Uds.); (*dir. obj.*) le, la, los, las; (*indir. obj.*) les, se
younger menor
youngest menor
your (*adj.*) (*fam.*) tu(s); (*formal*) su(s), de Ud., de Uds.
yours (*pron.*) (*fam.*) (el) tuyo, (la) tuya, (los) tuyos, (las) tuyas; (*formal*) (el) suyo, (la) suya, (los) suyos, (las) suyas; (el, la, los, las) de Ud., de Uds.
yourself (*fam.*) te; (*formal*) se
yourselves se

Index